WITHDRAWN

D1116786

WILDFIRE
and AMERICANS

WILDFIRE
and AMERICANS

HOW TO SAVE LIVES, PROPERTY, AND YOUR TAX DOLLARS

Roger G. Kennedy

HILL AND WANG

A DIVISION OF FARRAR, STRAUS AND GIROUX

NEW YORK

Hill and Wang
A division of Farrar, Straus and Giroux
19 Union Square West, New York 10003

Distributed in Canada by Douglas & McIntyre Ltd.
Printed in the United States of America
First edition, 2006

Library of Congress Cataloging-in-Publication Data
Kennedy, Roger G.
    Wildfire and Americans : how to save lives, property, and your tax
dollars / by Roger G. Kennedy.
        p.   cm.
    Includes index.
    ISBN-13: 978-0-8090-6581-3 (hardcover : alk. paper)
    ISBN-10: 0-8090-6581-9 (hardcover : alk. paper)
    1. Urbanization—United States.   2. Wildfires—United States.
3. Cold War.   I. Title.

HT123.K45 2006
307.76′0973—dc22

                                                    2005025914

Designed by Cassandra J. Pappas

www.fsgbooks.com

10 9 8 7 6 5 4 3 2 1

Frontispiece: A memorial to a firefighter who died trying to save a
settlement at South Canyon, Colorado, in 1994. (Photograph by Casey
A. Cass/*Glenwood Post*)

For Frances and Ruth

There are two loves, the one of which is holy, the other unholy; one social, the other selfish; one takes heed of the commonweal because of the heavenly society, the other reduces even the commonweal to its own ends because of a proud lust of domination; the one is subject to God; the other sets itself up as a rival to God.

—SAINT AUGUSTINE

Contents

Maps   xi

PART ONE PEOPLE IN FLAME ZONES

  1. The Plan of the Work   3

  2. "The Lab" and "The Lab" Extended   17

PART TWO THE POLITICS OF COLD WAR MIGRATION

  3. From Danger into Danger   27

  4. Unforeseen Consequences   39

  5. Truman, Eisenhower, and the Road Gang   59

PART THREE AT THE END OF THE LINE

  6. Managing Wildfire   79

  7. Scapegoating as Distraction in 2000   88

  8. Scapegoating and False Remedies   105

PART FOUR LEARNING FROM THE HISTORY OF FIRE

  9. The Mentors: Marsh, Gallatin, Olmsted,
      and Thoreau   119

10. Carl Schurz, Fire, and the Wisconsin Example   138

11. Migration, Fire, Erosion, and
John Wesley Powell   151

12. Smoke, Dust, and the Land   159

13. Urbanism, Dispersion Theory, Migration,
and Fire Danger   179

PART FIVE   WHEREAS . . . AND THEREFORE . . .

14. Longer and Larger Precedents   195

15. Toward a Healthy Forests and
Communities Corps   214

16. Toward a National Flame Zone Atlas   223

17. Managing Both Sides of the Interface   235

18. The Legacies of Stewart Chase and
Gilbert White   248

19. Sun Daggers, Grace, Limits, and Theology   261

Appendix: Jonathan Edwards and
Imperial Connecticut   279

Notes   283

Acknowledgments   311

Index   315

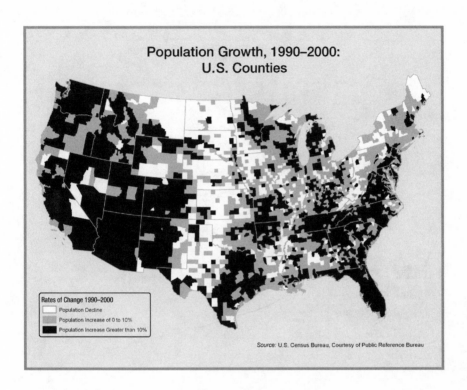

Population Growth, 1990–2000:
U.S. Counties

Rates of Change 1990–2000

☐ Population Decline
▨ Population Increase of 0 to 10%
■ Population Increase Greater than 10%

Source: U.S. Census Bureau, Courtesy of Public Reference Bureau

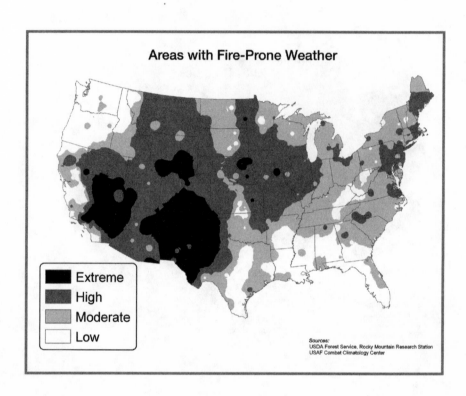

Areas with Fire-Prone Weather

Extreme
High
Moderate
Low

Sources:
USDA Forest Service, Rocky Mountain Research Station
USAF Combat Climatology Center

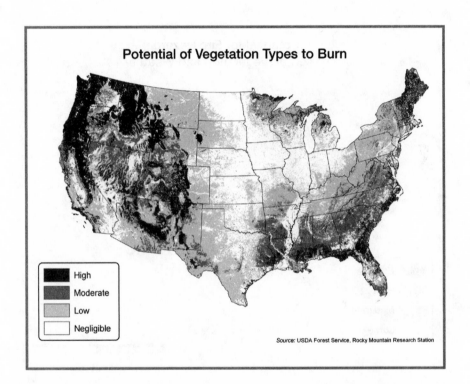

Potential of Vegetation Types to Burn

High
Moderate
Low
Negligible

Source: USDA Forest Service, Rocky Mountain Research Station

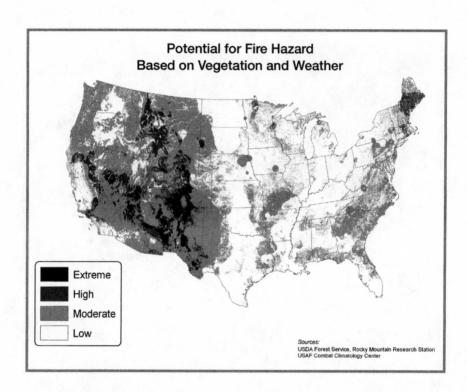

**Potential for Fire Hazard
Based on Vegetation and Weather**

Extreme
High
Moderate
Low

Sources:
USDA Forest Service, Rocky Mountain Research Station
USAF Combat Climatology Center

People in Flame Zones

1. THE PLAN OF THE WORK

Los Alamos is a bomb factory set in a firetrap. It was put there by scientists adept at physics and chemistry but not universally wise. They could make nuclear weapons, and they could teach others how to deliver those weapons to their targets. They were not, however, good at everything their country asked of them, or at solving every problem about which some of them felt impelled to offer advice. Few of them, for example, were trained in the biological sciences or the dynamics of wildfire. Nevertheless, on their recommendation, landscapes were shaped and entirely new cities situated at Los Alamos, New Mexico; Oak Ridge, Tennessee; and Hanford, Washington. Wildfire was not a problem addressed by their founding fathers.

Los Alamos lies on the Pajarito Plateau of New Mexico, above the Rio Grande Gorge. Eroded ochre slopes decline to the river on the south and east. To the north and west, "the Lab" backs onto steep forested mountainsides managed by the National Park Service and the United States Forest Service. It seems safe, and so it is, from a political or military threat. Not since the "Pueblo Revolt" of the seventeenth century has there been a military action against a central government in the region, and there was little resistance when the Hispanic villages of New Mexico were conquered by the United States Cavalry in the 1840s, and thereafter formally ceded by treaty. The scientists who

founded Los Alamos did not worry about domestic insurrection anyway; they had other things on their minds—espionage and the range
of missiles that might be launched from warships.

However, Los Alamos is not safe. Further consultation with the
people of the pueblos, or with the fire managers of Bandelier National
Monument or of the Forest Service would have yielded the information that the plateau had been burned by wildfire about every ten
years on average since people first came there. The climate is dry.
The woods are filled with trees oozing pitch that is a sort of gummy
turpentine, awaiting the lightning that strikes the mesa hundreds of
times each summer. Still in living memory is the large fire on Forest
Service land that burned its way down to Los Alamos Canyon in 1954;
the La Mesa Fire of 1977 broke out on Forest Service land amid the
slash left by a lumbering operation, and though it spread into Los
Alamos, it, too, was treated as a fluke. During the early 1990s, the
Dome Fire reduced to charred sticks and cinders more than sixteen
thousand acres in the National Forest seven miles from Los Alamos.
"Had not the wind shifted on the Dome Fire, it would have entered
upper Frijoles and probably Los Alamos. That wind shift saved the
town."[1]

Still, no serious effort was made to reduce the danger of wildfire in
Los Alamos. Only a few fuel breaks were built and some trees
thinned, until the laboratory administration of the mid-1990s began
to step up the work and actually transferred funds to help the Forest
Service with the reduction of fire load—fallen limbs, brush, and
small, highly inflammable trees. This help was necessary. Congress,
while always ready to put up more concrete bunkers, administration
buildings, block-long laboratories, mysterious tubes and towers, and
mile after mile of metal fencing, showed little interest in providing
protection to the people of the laboratory or town against natural
hazards the founders of the laboratory had failed to notice. Ribbon-
cutting was more pictorial than brush-cutting. Science stopped at the
laboratory door.

Nonetheless, some of the administrators living on the property did begin to take action in the 1990s, and because of their late, uncelebrated efforts, it is likely that the Cerro Grande Fire in 2000 was less destructive than it might have been. Inside the town, life went on. Park Service and Forest Service employees, knowing the dangers at hand, went house to house to warn the inhabitants of the urgent need to remove the fire load in their yards. By that time, however, those inhabitants were accustomed to a garrisonlike situation in which it seemed reasonable to assume that if there were perils they would have been warned of them by their superiors. Only a few, heeding the warnings that came to them from outsiders, adopted measures that have subsequently become called "fire-wise principles."

Next to the laboratory, after the 1977 fire, the National Park Service had begun cutting out brush and small trees by a series of small, deliberate controlled burns. Much of the Bandelier National Monument was covered by such burns or by the big recurring natural burns. On Sunday, May 7, 2000, one of the last of these controlled or "prescriptive" fires was set. Then came a series of misfortunes, and a hundred-foot wave of scarlet fire rushed toward Los Alamos, disregarding fencing or NO TRESPASSING signs. All through several nights, a ferocious blaze illuminated those proud concrete bunkers, administration buildings, block-long laboratories, tubes, and towers.

By the evening of the tenth, five hundred firefighters were at risk. When the winds were not too powerful, and there was daylight to penetrate the smoke, seven helicopters and five air tankers were in use. By the time the fire burned itself out, eighteen thousand acres had burned, including 235 houses in Los Alamos. Thousands of people had been evacuated.

Those who had located the laboratory and town at Los Alamos had been thinking politically, not environmentally. They were worried about human systems, not natural systems. It was characteristic of a kind of nature-blindness that afflicted national policies at the time, not only in placing defense installations but also in channeling migration and altering urban life across the entire nation. During the Cold War decades, success in developing atomic bombs gave science, even nature-blind science, great prestige. Experts in urban destruction were assumed to be experts in urban safety. Though for a time capable of perceiving only one set of dangers—those likely to come from political enemies—they provided arguments useful to people whose motives were not primarily patriotic but pecuniary. A dispersion-industrial complex exploited arguments to disperse targets in order to secure government financing. This led to the location of many millions of people in places dangerous for other reasons. Much unintended harm was done to the health of American cities and of the American countryside.

The story of urban dispersion in the United States has been told from many perspectives, and in a large literature well worth reading. I do not attempt to do more in these pages than give emphasis to some sets of events that I believe to have been insufficiently apprehended. I do so not for the purpose of finding fault—indeed, I would not have written this book at all if I were not offended by fault-finding as a distraction from correction. It is correction that I seek, encouraged by the conviction that much of what is lamentable in these pages is also remediable. The weakening of the old industrial cities of America was done on purpose. Populations were relocated purposefully into places imperiled by natural forces such as fire. Cities were gutted and their inhabitants displaced by the deliberate use of federal subsidies and governmental planning.

But deliberate actions can often be deliberately reversed. Not always, of course, for there are irreversible consequences. Yet because there was nothing mysterious in the devices used to weaken old ways of life among humans in cities and among other living creatures in remote valleys and watersheds, there need be nothing mysterious in the ways in which desirable and surviving conditions can be strengthened.

Citizens can rise up in a taxpayers' revolt to stop subsidizing a land rush into fire danger. To assist them, some facts must be fished out of some crannies and locked files and pasted onto placards. The most compelling of those facts have to do with how and why the subsidies developed—and how they work today.

I hope to help in that process. It seems to me that I should begin with a candid statement of the direction from which my effort to convince is offered: I was an Eisenhower Republican, precinct chairman, ward chairman, district chairman, winner of a congressional primary election, and loser of the general election (to Eugene McCarthy). I was assistant successively to three cabinet officers in the Eisenhower Administration, and served on presidential commissions or special assistancies for Presidents Nixon, Reagan, Carter, and Bush the First, before being appointed by the Secretary of the Smithsonian Institution to be the first director of the National Museum of American History, and then by President Clinton to be director of the National Park Service, an office I occupied from 1993 through 1997.

As a reporter for NBC and as the producer or presenter of documentaries based in Washington for PBS, the BBC, and the Discovery Channel, I have had the opportunity to observe how the federal government works. I have written eleven books about American history and many prefaces, and edited the twelve-volume *Guide to Historic America* for the Smithsonian Institution and also a reissue of a WPA guide. I've been trying to understand government for a long time.

I cannot pretend that this book arose from cool, detached, scholarly inquisitiveness. It didn't. It arose from outrage. In May 2000, I witnessed an orgy of scapegoating and misinformation after the great fire on the Pajarito Plateau burst into flame in what has come to be known as the Cerro Grande Fire, from Bandelier National Monument into Los Alamos National Laboratory. That was three years after I retired as director of the Park Service, but I knew enough about the scientific fire management at Bandelier during the previous decade to respect those who had done the work, and to be disquieted by the rush to pin responsibility on them for the devastation caused by the fire. I was living nearby and watched the fire move across the western horizon. As the press reported that a "blame game" was under way, there was a stench of injustice in the air along with the smoke.

In other settings in military and civilian life, I have had some experience with searches for scapegoats that distracted attention from systemic needs. In the aftermath of the Cerro Grande Fire I felt—though did not then have enough of the facts to be certain—that the problem was unlikely to lie where politicians and the press were pointing: "criminal negligence" on the part of Park Service employees. As I learned more, it became clear that the scapegoats were being lied about. They were being singled out because important people did not want the grievous flaws in the nation's system of settlement and interaction with natural systems fully disclosed. There were then, and are still today, powerful persons who are not enthusiastic about such discussion, despite the increasing dangers of the fire-prone landscape of the nation and the increasing number of people exposed to those dangers.

Much of the impulse to satisfy a public outcry with hasty dismissals has been orchestrated to avoid discussion of the root causes of these disasters. This book was written to stimulate that discussion and to bring into it recognition of the profitable businesses that thrive on a culture that subsidizes settlement beyond safe limits, putting settlers and those who must rescue them at risk. I have written it because I hope to have some part in rousing a taxpayer revolt that is also a moral revolt against circumstances imperiling people and, also, our fragile habitat, this precious earth.

TELLER AND DISPERSION

If Edward Teller was "the Father of the H-Bomb," Albert Einstein could be said with equal justice to have been its grandfather. At Teller's urging, Einstein sent a letter to President Franklin Roosevelt urging development of atomic weapons; no letter from Teller, then known to only a few scientists, would have been sufficient to launch the undertaking that sent J. Robert Oppenheimer to find a proper site upon which to build a laboratory before he had passed his fortieth birthday. Soon after Oppenheimer selected a boys' camp he had attended as the location of "the Lab," Teller was on the scene. Their subsequent achievement was proclaimed by Roosevelt's successor, Harry S. Truman, to be "the greatest achievement of organized science in history." Many at the time believed that their nuclear weapons had secured Allied victory over Japan. Crowned with laurels, encomiated in purple prose by the press, asked their advice on a multitude of matters domestic and foreign, most nuclear scientists were content to speak to what they knew and understood, with enormously beneficial results.

A few, most conspicuously Teller, answered any question asked with the confidence of men of narrow education who have known only success. Teller himself became very influential—he gave briefings to a sequence of presidents from Roosevelt through Reagan, and sometimes to the entire cabinet. He was presented a medal by President Kennedy in 1962, and by 1987 he was telling audiences, "I have experience that our president [it was Ronald Reagan at the time] is a very good listener." By then he was so frequent a visitor to the White House that he did not need to ask the location of the washrooms on the ground floor.[2]

Teller and his immediate circle had strong views about which cities should decline and which should arise, and spoke of such matters with the self-assurance of those who had had not just one great success, the atomic bomb, but a second—the hydrogen bomb. They could even claim a third—city building. They and their military partners were the first Americans since 1776 to have made a city—from plan to the steeple of the town hall—and they had done it three times: at Los Alamos; at "Uranium City," Oak Ridge, in Tennessee; and at "Plutonium City," Hanford, in Washington State. Before the arrival on the scene of the atomic scientists, with their military partners, the term "new town" had long meant only greenbelt suburbs, not freestanding cities. The Highland Parks and Oak Parks were supporting players, not protagonists; moons, not planets. Kohler was to Sheboygan what Mariemont was to Cincinnati and what Reston and Columbia would be to Washington—handsome but collateral. Los Alamos grew to have more than twelve thousand people, Oak Ridge nearly thirty thousand, and Raymond, Washington, of which the Hanford works is a part, nearly forty thousand.[3]

"The Lab" at Los Alamos was itself the nucleus of the shiny new technopolis that grew around it, as hierarchic sociologically as any garrison town or warship. Equally straightforward in design, intention, and governance were the other two towns brought into quick life by the ironically named Manhattan Project. Manhattan was a long time a-building, an organic growth, like an animal. The atomic towns were necessary but unnatural, as artificial as prosthetic limbs or mechanical livers. They had no past, no traditions, no subcultures of size, no layered continuities, and no complexities like those of New York City. Manhattan might be guided or cajoled, but it could never be governed as Oak Ridge or Hanford or Los Alamos could be governed.

Those appointed to manage these humming hives of science were protected from internal dissent, while basking in the world's wonder, the darlings of an American culture notoriously sentimental about technology. For years, Teller seemed credible on any subject he chose to discuss, though he had no training in the messiness of democratic institutions or in the complexities and ambiguities that are typically the truths discovered through an education in the humanities. No wonder it went to his head. Consider, please, Teller's environmental and sociological recommendations for Alaska: he was said by the later chairman of the Atomic Energy Commission, James Schlesinger, to have difficulty discerning "environmental aesthetics," an understatement akin to calling a nuclear explosion "unpleasant." Teller was wont to refer to his hubris as merely a desire "to remedy nature's oversights." One such remedy was Project Chariot, a plan to make a harbor in Alaska by moving aside seventy million cubic yards of permafrost by programmed nuclear explosions. He tried that out on George Rogers, educated at Harvard but resident in Alaska, who later reported their breakfast conversation this way: "I said well, the Native people, they depend on the sea mammals and the caribous. He said well, they're going to have to change their way of life. I said what are

they going to do? Well, he said, when we have the harbor we can create coal mines in the Arctic, and they can become coal miners."[4]

Teller's phenomenal memory, quickness of synthesis, confident
narrowness of vision, and crabbed moral sense were observed by colleagues as soon as he arrived at Los Alamos. After he left "the Lab,"
he displayed those qualities not only in his advocacy of his Arctic harbor but also in urging the dispersion of the cities of the "lower forty-
eight." He was believed to have proposed damming the Straits of
Gibraltar to irrigate the Sahara—though losing Venice in the process.
That tale may be apocryphal, but he did convince several U.S. administrations to subsidize his planning process for a bomb-blasted path-
way for a new canal across Central America and another to replace
that across the Suez. No wonder it required the threat of revolt by biologists and Alaska natives to withstand his sustained effort to use
nuclear explosions to build a new harbor on the Arctic shore. At the
flood tide of his own enthusiasm, he said to a press conference in Anchorage in June 1959: "If your mountain is not in the right place, just
drop us a card."[5]

Teller did not succeed in moving mountains, but he did succeed in
moving a lot of people. No one needed to drop him a card to spur him
to do so.

THE DISPERSION LOBBY

The dispersion that Teller and his colleagues advocated was not accomplished by them alone. It was compatible with some centrifugal
impulses in the American tradition—though I think these impulses
are overestimated in most writing on the subject. It was also good
business. Great corporate interests were delighted to find justification
in the arguments offered by the atomic scientists for a strategy of
breaking up the old cities, spreading them out, and building new
ones, a process in which a great deal of money could be made. This
dispersion-industrial complex had come from small beginnings and

had been growing in influence. But after the prestige of the atomic scientists and the patriotism they could rally were brought to the cause, a great deal more gasoline, cement, automobiles, asphalt, steel, and real estate were sold. The nation was transformed: to the satisfaction of some, to the profit of some, and with dangerous consequences at the fringes of dispersed settlement.

By the 1980s and 1990s, the dispersion-industrial complex was fully operational, its messages flooding the airwaves and its lobbying richly rewarded at budget hearings. The course of history may not be changed by successful lobbying and governmental subsidies, but the magnitude of a historical surge can be. So it was with the pace and volume of migration out of the old industrial cities. There are centrifugal propensities present in all cities, worldwide, and there is a tradition of westering among European Americans entering North America from the eastern seaboard. But the opposites to these statements are also true. There are centripetal propensities in the countryside worldwide, and powerful traditions in the United States, as in Europe and Asia, of country people going to the city when they can. Furthermore, all European Americans did not enter North America from the east, and the ancestors of all Americans did not come from Europe. Clustering, gathering, nucleating, and centering traditions were and are also potent in our history.

Bearing these countervailing impulses in mind, I believe that the continental migrations of the last half of the twentieth century were artificially enlarged and prolonged. Cold War policies played into industrial and commercial objectives, and the taxpayers paid for it. The patriotic, industrial, and commercial sponsors of those subsidies did not include in their planning a due regard for the consequences of their actions. In my view, it is high time for these subsidies to be reexamined by the taxpayers, and for frugality to be encouraged by decency. Those who care about the personal safety of their fellow citizens may also care both about their checkbooks and about the degradation of the earth. There is a great deal more to this story than cheap land and personal preference. Among other things, this book will offer some answers to the question "How come the land out there seemed so cheap?"

Changing things will not be easy. The inertia of vested and deeply invested programs and bureaucracies is often sustained long after their initial justifications have faded from memory. That has been the way of agricultural subsidies for crops in surplus, and of tariff protection for ancient arthritic corporations sustained as if they were infant industries. In Washington, the reform-minded learn soon enough that there is a subterranean landscape excavated and bored to accommodate lobbyists' back channels from K Street to Capitol Hill. Along its catacombs of ancient alliances, affinities, conveniences, and habits await doorkeepers, gatekeepers, and guides, holding torches aloft with one hand while keeping the other palm-up for tips. However anachronistic or pernicious an old way of doing business as usual may become, however distant memories of how it all started may be, it will be reinforced from the chambers of that subterranean city until finally something happens to send the rats scurrying back to their lair. Thus it has been with the Cold War dispersion strategies. Now, that "something" is approaching.

At this juncture, it may be useful to the reader to have available in one place some of the key numbers confirming the general themes of this work: that thousands of people are moving unwarned into firetraps every day; indeed, they are being encouraged to settle there by taxpayer subsidies—among them direct loans to developers—federally insured mortgages, roads, and insurance rates kept artificially low by state regulators. The devastating hurricanes of 2005, Katrina and Rita, reinforced the similarities of the circumstances of Americans now at risk of catastrophic wildfire to those now settling, and resettling, into flood zones, encouraged by federal flood insurance. In both instances, individual choices are being made in fields of force determined by huge amounts of taxpayers' money, inducing settlement in dangerous places. And lives are being unnecessarily lost.

Seven of the nine most fire-endangered states are also among those gaining most population. Since 1950, nearly half the nation's population growth has occurred in these fire-prone seven. In the same period, wildfires have doubled in frequency and in the size of the areas burned each year, both in total acreage across the country—eight million acres in several recent years—and in the average size of the areas burned each year. Nevada, the most fire-prone of all states, was also the most rapidly growing in population. Furthermore, within each fire-prone state, the most fire-prone communities were among the fastest growing: in New Mexico, the counties containing Santa Fe and Albuquerque grew from 38,000 to 136,000 and 146,000 to 581,000; the most fire-endangered city on the Colorado Front Range, Boulder, grew from 48,000 to 278,000 people.

The billions in federal mortgage insurance and highway subsidies spent to underwrite this growth have been in effect transfer payments from the citizens of older cities being stripped of population to the new, widespread, fire-endangered cities of the West where that uprooted population is settling. On the receiving end of these subsidized population transfers, in the last three years the annual costs of firefighting and restoration after wildfire have run over $2 billion a year. As more and more people settle in firetraps, there are also more and more wildfires, and the fires that occur are twice as big, on average, and much more costly than they were a mere two decades ago.

California is among the most fire-prone of states. When it burns—or floods—it does so expensively, largely because it has encouraged people to come and live in dangerous places without adequate warning about both fire and floods. Of the costliest fires in the nation's history, twenty-two of thirty-eight have been in California. In 1991, the Oakland/Berkeley Tunnel Fire alone cost twenty-five lives, 3,400 buildings, and $2 billion. That seemed big until 1993, when the total cost of wildfires in California exceeded $2.1 billion—and yet the people kept following the subsidies into fire and flood zones.

The two problems of fire and flood have much in common, and policy toward each is in urgent need of reform. Though the focus of this book is on fire, in the aftermath of Hurricane Katrina we can at least allude to the failures of policy and practice that preceded and followed that human tragedy. And events in New Orleans are fair warning—fire and flood are two apocalyptic forces that are at once opposite in chemistry and similar in their disastrous effects upon people. Therefore we must ask: What might happen in Boulder or Santa Fe if the present trend toward greater and more damaging wildfires continues? What if there is a fiery Katrina on the flanks of the Rockies?

In the winter of 2004–2005, fifty-eight thousand houses were under construction in one California county in areas flooded as recently as 1997. In the five counties of Colorado that suffered most from recent fires, there was at the same time a construction boom of houses set in the most dangerous portions of those counties. Over the din of hammers and saws, voices are heard calling for federal fire insurance, which would be another taxpayer inducement for people to assume undue risk—in this case fire—as federal flood insurance already induces them to accept undue risk of flood. The taxpayers pick up the financial cost and the people flooded or incinerated pay the cost in death and destruction; half of federally insured flood insurance covers properties already flooded once; one in four has had four or more claims, or claims exceeding twice their initial value; one Houston house that cost $114,000 has claimed $806,000 in federal flood insurance; one Canton, Mississippi, house valued at $49,000 has claimed $161,000. The American taxpayer is paying these bills. Even without federal fire insurance, that taxpayer is on the hook for the subsidies that draw people into danger and also for the $2 billion a year that goes into rescuing them and putting them back into danger again. And the highest prices of all are being paid by the courageous flood fighters and firefighters. Too often they pay with their lives when things go wrong.

The conditions for catastrophe are accumulating. Nature has long been the loser in the environmentally heedless dispersion of urban America, and nature is nursing its wrath. As the climate warms, wildfire will increase, while at the same time more and more people are being subsidized by the government to move where wildfire will strike. Soon enough, disaster will become catastrophe. These pages urge that things be done to slow the pace at which that catastrophe is being made more likely and more terrible. The best way to stop doing dumb things is to recognize how dumb they were and are. Dumb and wrong.

That is the first of many value judgments in these pages. Though I have been admonished by social scientists to be resolutely secular and statistical, a values-based discourse seems to me natural when recommending changes in behavior. In my view, a civil war is being fought between humans in North America and the rest of creation. There are good, prudent, fiscally sound reasons for ceasing that war, yet the primary case made in this book is a religious and ethical one.

That is why Jonathan Edwards will have the last word. Edwards stands as the polar opposite of Edward Teller, though both learned from fire. The eighteenth-century theologian was the first American to state an environmental philosophy recognizing that all human pretensions have natural limits. He had observed fire firsthand, as a tool for agriculture. Teller, the twentieth-century scientist, had observed its effects on a vaster scale. Heedless and hubristic, he had rejoiced in what he saw. In retrospect, I suggest that Teller represents a technocratic, dominance-seeking epoch in human history that has done its best and, we may hope, its worst. Edwards, I believe, holds out to humankind a humbler yet grander future than any that might be achieved by narrowly technical means.

2. "THE LAB" AND "THE LAB" EXTENDED

Los Alamos is a city, a laboratory, and a citadel of applied science. Long after the war that gave it life was concluded, the people of the town continued to defer to the appointed successors to its founders. It is still like a garrison town in its deferential ways, and many who live and work there have assumed that because geniuses planned the place, it must be safe from wildfire. It is not. Nor are many other places, though some of the same geniuses influenced our government to urge settlement in them.

Over the Cold War years, American cities were treated as targets under threat of fire bombings and nuclear attacks like those suffered in Europe and Japan during the Second World War. Consequently, the citizens of these cities were both pressed and pulled to disperse. Little attention was given to the fire danger into which these dispersed populations were being directed. Out of the bomb-imperiled cities fled the millions, encouraged by governmental subsidies that channeled their household decisions. The end of many of their journeys brought them into fire-imperiled landscapes. The cities they left languished, while the fringes of settlement into which they moved became more dangerous with each new arrival. When those dangers flamed into disaster, their conscientious fellow citizens could not leave the inhabitants to perish in the flames. They were rescued, and the nation developed a firefighting culture that endangered the lives of the young people sent to rescue the subsidized emigrants.

More and more people make the problem worse every day by settling into those zones, assured by their own governments—federal, state, and local—that they are doing what they should be doing. That assurance comes from the presence of new roads, sewers, and power lines built into fire-prone landscapes, and from federally insured mortgages issued without any warnings attached or any geographic limits set on their availability. Further tax subsidies come in the form of deductions from income taxes for interest paid on such mortgages— again, with no consideration of the incentive such deductions provide to building and living in fire danger. It is as if that flow of funds were as socially desirable as deductible charitable giving. The full range of devices initially recommended by the atomic scientists to disperse urban populations during the Cold War is still in full force and growing—as is the fire danger at the destinations to which these populations have dispersed. And all the while, global warming is making wildfire more likely. The "tinder," as city people often call what foresters call "fire load," is dry and hot, and getting drier and hotter.

LOS ALAMOS WRIT LARGE

The people of Los Alamos did not bring nature's retribution upon themselves; they were placed in a situation in which it became inevitable. That occurred as a part of a dispersion strategy not limited to bomb factories, a strategy still directing expenditures long after Cold War imperatives set it in motion. If Los Alamos were the only instance of a subsidized rupturing of nature's limits, this would be a much shorter book. But the vulnerability of Los Alamos is merely the most conspicuous instance of a much larger situation. The problem is not fire. Fire has its rights and its function. The problem is people in the wrong places. The fire is where it has been for thousands of years. By encroaching upon it, the newcomers have created an urgent moral dilemma: they are there now, and they are in trouble. That is a second implacable truth. Nature has its rights and will insist upon them. But as fellow citizens of those whom public policy has placed in peril of fire, we have an obligation to go to their rescue. Everything possible should be done to make them less vulnerable to the fires that will befall them.

As a society, however, we must cease making the problem worse by encouraging more people to settle where they cannot be protected and where nature cannot be protected from them. We should stop subsidizing and encouraging people to join the land rush into fire danger, a danger increasing with global warming. Deliberate, planned, expensive programs encouraging migration into flame zones are still going forward as national policy in the United States. The flanks of the forested mountains, the chaparral-cluttered hillsides, and the brushy grasslands at the receiving end of subsidized migrations are Los Alamos writ large.

The general theme of the story before us is migration from relatively safe places into relatively dangerous ones. I have chosen to put the focus on fire danger to keep things as simple as possible, though much of what will be laid out in the ensuing pages is germane to migration into flood danger and hurricane danger as well. Wildfire is a big enough problem on its own, however. In the last half century, about one-fifth of the American people have moved into flame zones, insufficiently aware of the perils awaiting them and inadvertently testing the limits of nature's tolerance. The exact number could be established only by bringing the definition of that term down to area-by-area studies, at a level of definition no larger than a zip code, and preferably down to an address, providing coded gradations of inflammability of vegetation, in combination with weather, including lightning frequency, humidity, distribution of rainfall, and temperature. That can be done, and is being done, commercially, for some areas already. The nation should demand that national fire policy be based upon that sort of precision now. When more people are in the wrong places and those places become even more dangerous, wildfire can bring true catastrophe. As things stand, no public body possesses the kind of information required to act with humane intelligence in a situation that insufficient intelligence and bad policy created.

One reason we live in such ignorance is that the problem has seemed so far to be a local or regional one and the evolution of much of the United States into a post-urban condition has not yet been fully apprehended. Most migrants into forested areas came from the North and East during a period in which they could recall conditions in which the categories "town" and "country" still had meaning, and in which fire was domesticated in both. Before the Second World War, eastern cities were grounded in industry and the eastern countryside was farmed. There were smokestack cities and there were grain fields and dairy farms. Factories, tenements, and John Sloan were set next to barns, grain elevators, and Grant Wood.

Most Americans lived either in the city or in the country, and in city and country, fire was in its place. On the farm, it was in the fireplace around which the family gathered. In town, fire was in turbines, furnaces, engines, and barbeques, helping people to cook, stay warm, make steel, drive pistons—to feel both cozy and controlling. These were not the emotions aroused by two great sets of interregional migrations of the twentieth century, and concurrently, by the dispersal of the old core-and-spokes cities. The industrial cities of the Midwest and the farmsteads and villages of the Great Plains were emptied out. Like water flowing uphill out of a basin, population flowed uphill out of the American heartland and into the mountain states of the West and Southeast, and oozed around the Rockies and Appalachians into Florida, Georgia, California, New Mexico, Arizona, and Nevada.

Some of this occurred before the Second World War, in Depression-era movements out of the North and Midwest and toward the Sunbelt. However, it was not until the Cold War era that tens of millions of people broke away from their fireplaces and their fire-tamed places, and migrated into forests, grasslands, and chaparral-covered slopes, where fire often goes wild. As the forested fringes of the mountains filled and the core cities were evacuated, the population of many counties in the Great Plains declined to the densities of the early 1890s, when the historian Frederick Jackson Turner proclaimed the ending of the frontier and the smokestack industrial centers became the Rust Belt.

From a fire manager's perspective, these migrations evacuated old cities equipped with fire departments and depopulated fire-safe corn and wheat belts. Population shifted from safe states to dangerous ones, southward and westward into places where nature presents perils greater than any fire department can manage. Shown below is the relative rating of seven states in population growth for the decades from 1950 through 2000 according to the United States Census; juxtaposed are their ratings of exposure to fire danger as compiled by the National Fire Center. The states receiving the most people are in general the states most exposed to wildfire. The bar chart's background photograph is a testament to the problem: the smoke plume shows a wildfire blowing up even as a bulldozer works to prepare ground for more building.

Update these rankings to the end of 2004, and the ten fastest-growing of the fifty states show half the nation's population growth.

Colorado drops a little below the first ten, but Nevada's population continues to increase more rapidly than that of any other state for the eighteenth consecutive year. In both cases that growth has occurred in the states' most fire-prone counties.

Population-exporting states, on average wetter and freer from fire than importing states, showed small increases in population over the fifty years from 1950 through 2000; though a lot of people left home, those remaining did have babies. Iowans increased only from 2,621,000 to 2,954,000. The citizens of Massachusetts grew in number from 4,690,000 to 6,616,000; Alabama's from 3,062,000 to 4,530,000; Kansas's from 1,925,000 to 2,688,000; and Nebraska's from 1,305,000 to 1,711,000. In the same period, inflammable Nevada's population grew from 160,000 to 2,334,000; Arizona's from 750,000 to 5,743,000; Utah's from 689,000 to 2,389,000; Colorado's from 1,325,000 to 4,601,000; Idaho's from 588,000 to 1,393,000; New Mexico's from 681,000 to 1,900,000; and Wyoming's from 290,000 to 507,000.

Within each of these rapidly growing states, the hottest spots for population growth almost precisely correlate with the worst fire danger. Along the Rocky Mountain front this is easy to understand— topographically these elevated areas rise stepwise from the depopulating Great Plains to the mountains, which are "risers," physically, demographically, and socially. In Montana, New Mexico, and Colorado, this has meant moving from safe counties to dangerous counties. Counties gaining population were more endangered by fire than counties losing population. For example, fire-prone Santa Fe and Bernalillo counties in New Mexico have grown from 38,000 to 136,000 and 146,000 to 581,000, respectively, while the most fire-endangered city on the Colorado Front Range, Boulder, has grown from 48,000 to 278,000 people.

WHAT IT MEANS TO BE FIRE-PRONE

As people from eastern farms and cities arrive in the western flame zones, they have to learn what it means to live amid dangerously inflammable woodlands. They have not come from places where they had to be wary that the shrubbery would become hostile, or where the woods were perilous because they were in fact woody. In Iowa or Massachusetts, shrubbery is not thought to be fire load, nor are trees perceived as candidates for "towering infernos," though global climate change may well alter these cheerful perceptions.[1]

Sylvan amenities become fire load when they are continuously exposed to heat, desiccation, and wind. That is not yet the case in New England, or in the Piedmont, though it may become so. The citizens of Amherst and Atlanta have been able to think of wildfire as rare, spotty, and easily extinguished. During the long, relatively cool and moist epoch in which we have so far lived, Iowans, too, have been able to think of wildfire as a western problem, not theirs. They have come to expect that nearly all grass and brushfires can be put out by householders with hand pumps. It has been front-page local news when wailing and clanging fire trucks must be summoned. Though wildfire has not been "just a western problem," for the past six decades it has seemed so. For one or two more, as the climates of the East and Midwest become warmer and drier, it may still seem so. As things are at the moment, most true flame zones will be in the dry, hot, and windy West, where there is ample stuff to burn and to spread a fire. The East has not yet noticed how much of it is also covered with fire load.

Yet even now, there is great variability in wildfire danger in all regions of the country. A lightning strike upon the Malpais lava beds of New Mexico is not as dangerous as one hitting the tangled woody growth on the slopes of the Santa Fe River watershed; lava beds are hot, dry, and subject to hot and dry wind, but lava does not grow much wood. Nor are the materials for big fires present on the great sand dunes of Colorado; lightning is dangerous there only to people and other living things taking its immediate electric shock.

Woody material alone does not excite the appetite of a fire; fire load, the food of fire, must be dry and warm. The drenched rain forest on the wet coast of the island of Maui is not, therefore, a flame zone—

its orchid and tree fern have not had to become fire-accustomed species like ponderosa pine and chaparral.

The suburbs of Los Angeles, Tucson, Reno, Denver, Boulder, Santa Fe, and Albuquerque are all exposed to wildfire, each zip code and each address to a differing degree. None, however, is so barren or so damp as to be safe from wildfire. When people move into places like these, nature will respond. Fire will come upon them. Some flames will be easily ignited, and some easily put out. There is no mystery in all this. The only mystery is why it has taken so long for an intelligent democratic society to act upon what is known. As climate change makes wildfire more dangerous every day, more and more people are settling in flame zones. A system of subsidies, set in place with insufficient understanding of their consequences, continues to make matters worse, as settlers, firefighters, and the men and women asked to rescue both settlers and firefighters go into harm's way. At the very least, the nation can require consumer protection through admonitory information about where the flame zones are, and how dangerous they are. Probabilities of fire should be known to the public, ranked—as are probabilities of flood—as zones where wildfire can be expected once every five years on average, every ten years on average, every hundred years on average, and so on. That would be a good beginning. Then can come a good, healthy taxpayer revolt against subsidizing migration into the worst of these flame zones.

PART TWO

The Politics of
Cold War Migration

3. FROM DANGER INTO DANGER

Abraham Lincoln once told an audience of farmers that "a great amount of locomotion is spared by thorough cultivation." Some of these potential voters might have scowled; others might have grinned at his wry reference to the habit of "moving on" instead of manuring, leaving the depleted and ravaged land behind. The grins would have come from those who needed no exhortation to practice sustainable farming, among whom were hay farmers who kept cattle as much for fertilizer as for milk and meat. In that Bible-reading generation it was not unusual for preachers and even politicians to cite the words of the prophet Ezekiel in chapter 34, verses 18 and 19:

> Seemeth it a small thing unto you to have eaten up the good pasture, but ye must tread down with your feet the residue of your pastures? and to have drunk of the deep [clear] waters, but ye must foul the residue with your feet? And as for my flock, they eat that which ye have trodden with your feet; and they drink that which ye have fouled with your feet.

Ezekiel was chiding herdsmen; Lincoln was drawing a distinction between practitioners of good husbandry and bad. Today, when only 2 percent of the American population is still engaged in full-time professional farming, the message needs a little translation: the "fouling" of the water and the "residue" of the countryside most conspicuous among our contemporaries does not come from cattle or an unwillingness to cultivate the farm, but from a migratory "locomotion" that has left the cities uncultivated, much of the countryside no longer productive, and many of the people themselves imperiled.

The most visible consequence of subsidized migration into danger was the evacuation of cities after the Second World War, and the ensuing land rush into dangerous places. Migration came as a result of policies seeking to induce both abandonment and dispersion. Cold War dispersion was a triumph of patriotism twisted awry by commercial interests. For fifty years, these interests swayed appropriations committee after appropriations committee, so stealthily that few members of Congress noticed how the lobbyists' tailoring was improving. As sartorial improvement became manifest in Washington, the condition of the land got worse, and more and more people were placed in peril. Thruway construction, urban destruction, allocation of government contracts, systematic denial of mortgages in cities, and their easy availability in suburban developments changed migration and settlement patterns radically.

The iron filings did not form their new patterns on their own. There were magnets under the table. They can be discerned in every comprehensive study of twentieth-century migration. Recently, a group of scholars at the University of Wisconsin concluded that "governmental subsidies and infrastructural improvements in the metropolitan fringe have historically facilitated this decentralization, as have racial fears, traffic congestion, and rising property values."[1]

These forces did not proceed independently. One might think of "racial fears" as disassociated from irritation caused by traffic congestion, but there were clever people who saw a connection. Insufficient attention has been given to the deliberate playing to these emotions by those having a commercial or political interest in driving people toward the exurbs. That would be a subject worthy of a book of its own. However, that is not the book before you—one thing at a time.

In the ensuing chapters, "the Negro problem" is glimpsed only as one of several Cold War justifications for gutting the older cities. (There is ample literature examining the degree to which suburbanization was truly "white flight." I do not intend to amplify that discussion, because it is not a subject to which I can add anything useful to future policy.) Traffic congestion was also a propellant outward, though some people predicted rightly that what seemed to be a core-city problem would become a post-urban problem. Now, indeed, wherever there are paved streets there are frustrated drivers, and where there are pavements and stoplights the exhaust fumes hang heavy in the air— a difficulty not remedied by wider roads inviting more cars to bring more tailpipes emitting more exhaust. Since the 1920s, highway engineers have been warning their clients that roads suck up cars— "supply creates demand."

Property values are not set in the heavens. They too rise with demand, which may be expected to increase when customers are delivered to the sellers on federally subsidized roads, carrying money provided by federally subsidized mortgage payments, and assured of cheap power because the federal government has built for them dams and a power-distribution grid. These "externalities" have powerfully elevated property values—drawing populations away from the old cities. Racial fear and an aversion to traffic jams may explain some of that movement, but more of it can be understood as the consequence of intelligent responses to subsidies. The deliberate manipulation of market forces for patriotic purposes during the Cold War contributed substantially to the dispersion of old cities and the movement of masses of people from the Northeast and Midwest southward and westward. In the process, measures intended to reduce the density of target cities pressed public funds into the palms of those with products to sell along the way and property to sell at the end of the line. There was nothing disreputable or covert in this, though at the time the consequences to the people of the old cities, and the people at the dangerous extremities of all this migration, were not taken seriously enough. Now, finally, they should be.

MEMORIES OF FIRE

Memories of wartime experience often linger long into postwar periods, shaping behavior long after circumstances have changed. John C. Calhoun, Secretary of War in the years after the War of 1812, wrote that the humiliations suffered during that conflict, especially the burning of the nation's Capitol by the British and the hasty evacuation of the White House by President James Madison, subsequently fueled what we might today call "militant nationalism." Without further argument, the nation taxed itself willingly to build its merchant marine, its protective naval forces, and its internal communications, including its turnpike systems. The disgraces of "the late war" were "too recent to require details, and the impression too deep to be forgotten."[2]

After the Second World War, horrifying successes in warfare, rather than humiliating failures, sustained policies long after they ceased to be good ideas. Dangerous lessons for peacetime were drawn from wartime experience. Policies whose usefulness had passed and had then become stale encrusted and befouled contemporary needs.

For those of us who returned from the Second World War bearing personal recollections of firebombed cities, recent history provided propulsion for our ideas about what we wanted to prevent—and to escape if we could. With these scenes engraved in our memories, we came back to a country in which there was much grief, but no physical destruction. Friends were missing, and many families were bereft of fathers, mothers, sisters, brothers, daughters, and sons. The place itself, however, was not much different from what it had been in 1940, except that mobilization had meant more industrial production. This production had ended economic depression, and for the first time in their lives a lot of people had money to spend on sprucing things up.

Unlike the Europeans, who were living amid ruins, the generation of Americans who survived the war did not do much sprucing up of the cities where they lived. Instead, from 1945 until the mid-1970s, it seemed that everyone was moving out to the "country." So many did so that after a while it was no longer "country." From the point of view of those who thought of the old cities primarily as potential targets for Soviet airborne bombs, this was a great success. Not only had American urban targets been dispersed but, contrary to the assertions of the dispersion theorists and their advocates, this had to be accomplished against the American grain.

I am aware that that statement is itself against the grain of doctrine now entrenched in some academic circles—dispersion theory—aware enough to write two later chapters to offer my detailed reasons for taking this contrary view. I believe that simple economics explain much more of the great postwar migrations than does the hypothesis that those migrations were foreordained by a migratory madness. I do not believe that Americans are so repelled by one another and so drawn to extremes that they will disperse whenever and wherever they can. No doubt some are neurotically bent upon self-destruction and will seek out dangerous places to die spectacular deaths. But not many. Those seeking urban dispersion for patriotic purposes—however mistaken— could not have counted upon any universal and ineluctable American disposition to move outward from cities into the countryside. Instead, the general tendency of movement in America over the preceding two hundred years had been out of the country and into the city. It was only within that general nucleating movement that, within each metropolis, there were suburbanizing swirls outward.

I do not argue that in the postwar decades every move outward from central cities was induced by purposeful dispersion policies. Many people needed little urging to think of cities as dangerous. No one who had served in the Second World War, or observed it, could have been unimpressed by the destruction of cities caused by firebombing; we were willing to do many things to prevent that happening to our country. Specialists in warfare drew more specific lessons; General Eisenhower, for example, was especially impressed by the Germans' use of autobahn networks to move troops and refugees, and dispersing targets "to reduce vulnerability to bombing" was on the agenda of the National Security Council from 1947 onward.[3] As the British and Americans had come to dominate the airspace over German cities, they sought "victory through airpower," which translated into obliterating whatever enemy productive capacity lay within reach of their aircraft. Bombs were dropped not only for their explosive impact but, increasingly, for their capacity to start fires; as a consequence, civilian losses from fire became greater than battlefield casualties. It was, however, also becoming manifest that the Germans were able to disperse and thus sustain their industrial production. For example, their ball-bearing production scarcely paused as the Allies carpet bombed the small target area in Schweinfurth where the older plants had been located; production had been shifted into the suburbs.

Both carpet bombing and nuclear attacks were efficient uses of fire to kill and to shatter the physical structure of a city and civilian morale. Yet even if an enemy were conscientious enough to seek to spare civilians from such an attack, the early technology for delivering nuclear weapons was so imprecise that it would have been difficult to do so. The bombs dropped on Japan were wonders of explosive science, but the targeting was vague.

From 1946 onward, the older industrial cities of the United States were deliberately dispersed lest they be bombed as Dresden and Nagasaki had been. Their people were induced by immense subsidies to find themselves homes as far away from industrial sites as possible— and thus some of them wound up in danger of another kind of fire. As memories of Coventry and Dresden faded, and the Cold War thawed, commerce reappeared as the driving force in shaping the evolution of transportation and, with transportation, urban life. Dispersion had been a patriotic strategy. Now it became good business. Sellers of gasoline, fast food, tourist accommodations, and automobiles formed alliances of convenience and complicity with producers of cement, steel, and asphalt. Vast sums were spent on making the joys of the "open" road glamorous even after traffic jams began closing them down. Real estate pages portrayed idylls of "open" space that was rapidly being filled. To this day, television depicts Jeep Cherokees on canyon rims and cheery families picnicking from the tailgates of SUVs. The message, not so subtly implied, was and is: no highways, no escape to tailgated nature. The good life became the subsidized life.

Memories of smoking urban rubble during the Second World War no doubt caused many people to abandon the city. Those memories faded over time, but meanwhile great fortunes were made from urban dispersion by selling concrete, asphalt, gasoline, developmental land, fast food, and, of course, new construction. There remained a national interest in the rapid transfer of troops and matériel across a continent of highways, though that interest was less and less significant when compared with the aggregate of private interests that paid for the advertising of suburban wonderlands. The weather helped: the unusually salubrious 1950s in the usually arid West started things out handsomely. Thereafter, a trillion dollars in pro-dispersion public spending tilted a multitude of personal computations, as mere hankerings hardened into decisions to make the move. Americans went where their government made it cheaper to live.

After the firebombing of Dresden during World War II. Fire from the skies was feared even before the atomic bombs were dropped.
(Library of Congress)

That government failed to inform them that at the extremes of their migration it was also riskier. At those extremes it was cheaper *only* because the costs of protecting the settlers from wildfire and rescuing them from it had not been made part of the price of the land they had bought. The subsidies inherent in settling and rescuing and resettling flame zones were left unaccounted. Fortunes were made dispersing the old industrial cities. An enthusiasm of planners was transmuted by the plausibility of Cold War science into the business of the dispersion-industrial complex.

Nothing in the current situation was inevitable, nor is any part of it beyond redemption. Bringing the nation's civil and natural systems back to health by bringing them into better harmony with one another will require action grounded in confidence in what an informed public can do in a democracy. Too much discussion of the present state of things lacks that confidence and, instead, treats the worsening circumstances of the moment as if they were inevitable. That is not the point of view presented here. The history of Cold War dispersion does not support a fatalistic acquiescence to a continued land rush into fire danger, because it demonstrates that much of that land rush was propelled by deliberate policy. Not all of it, of course. There were other factors at work, including individual preferences augmented by skillful advertising and persuasion. Racial fears did play a part, and so did deference to certain city-planning traditions. In later chapters all these factors will receive some discussion, but because the full story of the origins and workings of Cold War dispersion policy has only lately emerged, that story will be told first.

FIRE FROM THE SKIES

The story of the postwar American city begins with three military lessons learned during the Second World War.

The first was that cities full of civilians were targets of modern war.

The second was that bombers using primitive radar and staying high enough to escape antiaircraft batteries could not direct bombs precisely;

even if the strategy of air war did not ordain attacks against civilians, the tactics of delivery did. As a result, carpet bombing distributed fire across entire cities. Obliterating specific "hard" targets could be accomplished only by promiscuously obliterating everything around them.

The third was that large paved highways connecting cities could be used to distribute quickly a lot of troops and equipment, even when the cities themselves were bombed into smoking rubble.

These lessons were integrated into the defense and urban policies formulated during the Eisenhower Administration, through the creation of "firebreaks" in cities. The bulldozing of highways through urban centers rather than around them was, however, an idea of atomic-scientists-turned-planners, not of the president.

Cities and civilians had been targets during Europe's religious wars of the seventeenth century, but until the First World War, the military classes retained enough chivalry to profess a disinclination to kill civilians. The Hague Convention enshrining that principle was signed by all the great nations in 1910. The millions of civilian casualties during the First World War were perceived by many to have been unfortunate victims of a conflict still fought by uniformed armies against uniformed armies. The Russian Revolution changed part of that, but it was not until the 1930s that the Germans, Italians, and Japanese developed the practice of deliberately herding civilians by aerial attack to distract and impede defending armies. The Luftwaffe attack on Guernica in Spain, recalled by Picasso, and assaults upon Nanking and Addis Ababa were rehearsals for carnage among civilians in cities to break their will to resist. In September 1939, the Luftwaffe sent four hundred bombers to reduce much of Warsaw to rubble, though the city offered no resistance—six days of *Schrechlichkeit,* Hitler's term for frightfulness to induce terror. Rotterdam was also bombed after it surrendered in May 1940, and Belgrade in 1941, while the Luftwaffe went to work on Coventry and London as well.

The Hague Convention became a casualty of the Battle of Britain after Winston Churchill heeded the advice offered by his scientific adviser, Lord Cherwell:

In 1938 over 22 million Germans lived in 58 towns of over 100,000 inhabitants. If even half our bombs were dropped on . . . these 58
towns the great majority of these inhabitants (about one third of the
German population) would be turned out of house and home. Investigation seems to show that having one's home demolished is most
damaging to morale. . . . There seems little doubt that this would
break the spirit of the people.[4]

By the end of the European war, the British and Americans had destroyed three and a half million German houses, sending seven million
people into the streets. More people died in five nights in Hamburg in
the summer of 1943 than in London and Coventry over the course of
the entire war. Frustrated in the West, the Germans spent their last fu-
ries upon the Poles, who rose against them in 1944. Eighteen thousand
armed insurgents and more than 150,000 civilians were killed in Warsaw in accordance with Heinrich Himmler's recommendation to Hitler
that the Polish nation be exterminated or enslaved to clear the way for
a renewed German drive to the east. The Russians, eager to eliminate
the possibility of Polish resistance to their own westward drive, stood
by on the outskirts of Warsaw while the Germans did their worst.
Then, resuming their advance, the Russians herded German civilian
refugees into vulnerable masses. The streets of Dresden were full of
refugees and slave workers from Eastern Europe on February 13, 1945,
when 773 British bombers and 527 American bombers began their systematic destruction of the city and everyone within it. The orders to the
British Air Force were to repeat firebombing until it could "cause confusion in the evacuation from the east" and "hamper the movements of
troops from the west." Toward these ends, four thousand tons of bombs
were dropped, destroying six out of every seven houses in the central
city, seventy-two schools, twenty-two hospitals, nineteen churches,
five theaters, fifty banks and insurance companies, thirty-one department stores, thirty-one large hotels, and sixty-two administration
buildings. As had been the case with Hamburg, so many unregistered
slave laborers and refugees were present that exact casualty figures are

unknown, but there are estimates exceeding those of civilian loss of life at Hiroshima and Nagasaki.[5]

As the German war reached its climax, the Cold War began. Warfare against civilians in cities was now the norm. The bombing of Dresden was officially intended to demonstrate to "the Russians when they arrive, what Bomber Command can do." The Russians were to be similarly instructed by the two mushroom clouds that bloomed over Hiroshima and Nagasaki. After August 1949, the world became aware that the Russians had no need for such instruction, for the Soviets had been developing their own nuclear weapons. Suddenly, the threat of nuclear attack filled the nightmares of many Americans of my generation.[6]

But we had our faith in science. It had brought a speedier end to the war. As a nation we were already inclined to revere science and scientists. We did not pay much attention to those who insisted, even then, that scientists should be accorded deference only commensurate with their training in, and understanding of, the subjects about which we asked their opinions. Many nuclear scientists confined themselves

Mushroom cloud over Hiroshima: the indelible image of urban destruction. The firebombing of European cities and the nuclear bombs that devastated Hiroshima and Nagasaki in Japan were lessons heeded by the U.S. government in dispersing American industrial cities. (Library of Congress)

Another kind of danger: a sign posted at the entrance of the Three
Rivers community, on the boundary of the Deschutes National Forest
in Oregon, warning residents of another period of extreme wildfire
danger. (USDA; photograph by Bob Nichols)

to those subjects, and provided much sound advice, heeded because
their public spirit, their intellectual qualities, and their self-restraint had
justified deference. There was a time, however, when a few—Edward
Teller was chief among them—permitted themselves to become useful
instruments of economic interests, which led them into providing advice that, when heeded, served the welfare neither of their fellow citizens nor of the physical world of which they thought themselves
masters. Insufficiently wary of the company they kept, and too little
aware of the limits of their understanding, they were used, and did
much harm.

4. UNFORESEEN CONSEQUENCES

In 1942, the thirty-six-year-old physicist J. Robert Oppenheimer was appointed to lead the "Manhattan Project," which sought to develop nuclear weapons. His Manhattan Project could not be carried forward in Manhattan, or any other large city, because a nuclear weapons factory required an isolated techno-city of its own. Oppenheimer chose Los Alamos despite its being rejected a year earlier for other top-secret war work because it lacked adequate water. Whether or not it was also acknowledged to be fire-prone is unclear. In any case, Oppenheimer was undeterred. The site of his former boys' camp and school, Los Alamos—Spanish for "the willows"—lay atop a mesa, an idyllic place on which to learn to ride a horse or build "the Gadget." The bomb designed and built in the artificial town that grew up around "the Lab" became the ultimate anti-urban and anti-civilian weapon.

Oppenheimer and his associates were under intense pressure; the Germans were at work on a nuclear bomb of their own and the rockets to deliver it. And the Russians, it was feared, might not be far behind. The German nuclear team in an underground bunker were slow, perhaps purposely slow, and their bomb was still not ready when the war came to an end. On April 25, 1945, the Allies flew their last bombing mission against a city, Pilsen, containing the Skoda armament works. On that day, the American and Soviet forces came in sight of each other on the shores of the Elbe River. On May 2, German forces in Italy ceased firing, and five days later, at 2:41 a.m., General Alfred Jodl signed an unconditional surrender of Germany's remaining armies, to take effect at 11:00 a.m. on the eighth—VE-day.

At Los Alamos, at 9:00 a.m. on April 10, 1945, and again on the eleventh at 10:00 a.m., the Target Committee of the Manhattan Project met in Oppenheimer's office. The three military men attending both meetings, and the dozen or so scientists, determined that the Japanese city of Hiroshima was the best target for the first nuclear bomb. It was "an important army depot and port of embarkation in the middle of an urban industrial area. It is a good radar target and it is such a size that a large part of the city could be extensively damaged. There are adjacent hills which are likely to produce a focusing effect which would considerably increase the blast damage." It was further agreed "that for the initial use of the weapon any small and strictly military objective should be located in a much larger area subject to blast damage in order to avoid undue risks of the weapon being lost due to bad placing of the bomb." A "lost" bomb would be one that produced an insufficiently dramatic effect. The purpose was to end the war by breaking Japan's will to fight, not just to destroy buildings or kill people.[1]

The first nuclear weapon was tested at 5:45 a.m. on July 16, at the Trinity Site, within White Sands Proving Grounds, where the effects, though distant, could be observed by the workers of Los Alamos and their families. The people of distant El Paso thought that they had heard an "ammunition explosion," which indeed they had. On August 6, 1945, the center of Hiroshima was destroyed by the second nuclear bomb, which killed between 100,000 and 150,000 people. President Harry Truman threatened the Japanese with "a rain of ruin from the air, the like of which has never been seen on this earth."[2]

Science was wonderful, but technology was far from perfect. On August 9, the third atomic bomb in the nation's arsenal was set aboard a B-29 on Tinian Island. Delays due to a faulty fuel pump caused the bomber to start late, and then "into a horizon pierced by lightning." The city of Kokura was the preferred target of a group to which Nagasaki had been added to replace Kyoto. To ensure that the effects of the bomb would not be "lost" in the political sense, a camera plane was expected to photograph them. And to improve the odds that the bomb would not be lost geographically, an instrument plane was expected to make certain it reached its assigned target. Faulty communications, however, kept the camera and instrument plane from the rendezvous.[3]

Another flaw in the planning emerged. The pilot of the bomber had been told to expect clear skies, but he arrived to find Kokura hidden beneath the smoke of an earlier incendiary attack. He made three passes over the city without finding an opening in the clouds, and then, with barely enough reserve fuel to make it to a friendly airfield, he headed south toward the secondary target, Nagasaki. Confined within a bowl of mountains, the city was indeed a "good incendiary target." On that day, however, the bowl was lidded by a white cloud. Knowing that his fuel was low, and that he would therefore "have to jettison the bomb before landing . . . at the last moment, glimpsing a tiny bit of city through a cloud hole below," the bombardier released the weapon. It "missed its aiming point by over a mile . . . searing Pentecostal fire over the Catholic neighborhoods of Uragami . . . and the largest cathedral in Asia." Japan surrendered unconditionally on August 15, 1945.[4]

THE DE-NUCLEATION OF THE AMERICAN CITY

Sixty years later, it is still possible to recover the feelings of horror, awe, and a strange—perhaps perverse—sort of pride. Those of us in training to use torpedo boats in the Sea of Japan were grateful, though when we actually landed in Japan after the peace and saw what had been done, we felt a rush of other, stronger emotions. We came home ready to do anything necessary to make it less likely that any American city would look like Nagasaki or Hiroshima. We were affirmed in that determination by publications such as a book issued by the National Fire Protection Association containing many horrifying images of charred bodies, and maps with captions such as "United States cities corresponding approximately to destroyed cities of Germany and Japan." The association recommended that while fireproofing buildings was desirable, "more important" would be "spacing them properly . . . to reduce the number of people as well as buildings which are subject to destruction in single attacks." This would require "radical changes in a city or its industries . . . [by] planning boards . . . [that] become something more than the advisory committees most of them now are."[5]

That all made sense at the time, though nobody could be sure how radical those changes ought to be. For advice on that, the nation turned to experts. If indeed an "overriding lesson of the air war is that fire destruction is a major problem," how radical should the "spacing" be? How might "planning boards" not just advise that spacing, but acquire authority to provide incentives to secure it? Nearly sixty years later, we can observe how those general precepts worked their way into the policies and programs that actually led to the dispersion of American cities during the Cold War.

How much of the gutting out of the American industrial centers, and how much westward and southward migration, was due to such policies and programs, and who were the agents propelling them? A useful lead came in 1988 from the historian Elaine Tyler May, in a reference in her *Homeward Bound* to a 1951 issue of the *Bulletin of the Atomic Scientists* as being devoted to "defense through decentralization." Within that issue was a further reference, to an article written for the *Bulletin* on April 16, 1946, by E. Teller, L. R. Klein, and J. Marshak, on the desirability of dispersing cities to make essential industries less vulnerable to atomic attack.[6]

As manager of the endowment of the Ford Foundation in the 1970s, I had made frequent use of the capital market models developed by Lawrence R. Klein of the Wharton School at the University of Pennsylvania. This monumental work of his was one of the contributions to economics that brought him the Nobel Prize in 1980. One morning I thought, "Well, it's a while since 1946, and I'm still going. Maybe Dr. Klein is, too." So I called the Wharton School and asked if Professor Klein was still alive, still functional, and likely to return a telephone call. They said yes three times, so I left a message for him. That afternoon, the telephone rang. "Roger, this is Larry." I was surprised, pleased, and baffled. There was a chuckle. "You don't remember? The Holiday Inn in Plains, Georgia. We worked on Jimmy Carter's economics program." Then, only then, did I remember—but that is a tale for another book.

After this re-introduction, Klein confirmed earlier accounts of memoranda and working papers shared among economists and atomic scientists about the desirability of dispersing American cities to spread out potential targets of Soviet nuclear attacks. A week less than a year after the last firebombing of the war in Europe, on April 16, 1946, one of the primary authors of those memoranda, Edward Teller, and two economists, Jacob Marshak and Klein, published an article in the *Bulletin of the Atomic Scientists* entitled "Dispersal of Cities and Industries," in which the lessons of Schweinfurth, Hiroshima, and Nagasaki were applied to American domestic policy.[7]

"In atomic war," they wrote, "congested cities would become deathtraps. . . . Dispersal of cities may mean the difference between extermination of one third of our population and the death of only a few million people." With that conviction foremost in their minds, the authors were willing to sacrifice many of the continuities of human experience and practice that were embedded in the life of the city as an ancient and continuous organism. It has not been for nothing that the words "civic" and "civilian" and "civilized" come from the same root. Yet in the perilous circumstances of the world as they saw it, Teller, Marshak, and Klein expressed a patriotic duty to warn the nation that cities were too dangerous in their traditional forms; each was a "tempting target." Civilians must be induced to seek greater safety by abandoning their homes and factories and moving out. It was some consolation that "a considerable part of the protection provided by complete dispersal can . . . be obtained even if people live in clusters, provided these are properly spaced." Lest anyone visualize such "clusters" as villages in the old, dense, around-the-green style, the three made it clear that "proper spacing" would produce "continuous ribbons" or "a mesh of squares." These "linear" cities would be "safer than round clusters," and much less tempting targets than the hub-and-spokes cities of the past. A "good compromise" would be to disperse "about 600 people and 160 houses per linear mile along a communications artery."[8]

The determining pattern would be "our transportation system." Cities laid along widely spaced highways would produce a brave new world—a corridopolis, freshly built, and therefore uniformly nice. "The new dwellings should be built . . . to conform to minimum standards and thus slums are eliminated." Of course that might mean some adjustments; affinities and loyalties would have to be ruptured, and some communities that had lived together for decades would no doubt fracture and collapse: "In order to live in ribbon cities we shall have to abandon many of the habits which the people of our big cities have acquired in the course of a century."[9]

The people so released could live along the fast lane—literally: "Life will depend upon fast transportation . . . in the age of the automobile." The best example would be Teller's favorite existing city, "decentralized . . . modern Los Angeles." Aside from the necessity to learn new habits, to forfeit old ones, and to accept the highway as the defining tool for urban life, some individual preferences would have to yield to a collective: "A master plan of network cities and communications will have to be adopted." To achieve that end, economic pressures would be needed to homogenize otherwise lumpy idiosyncrasies in order to induce "the free and automatic flow of labor and enterprise which will follow the relocated key industries along the main communications arteries. . . . The shorter the time, the less we can rely upon the free movement of labor and the free planning of private enterprise." Perfection could not be expected without a little abrogation of such luxuries. "We cannot do this without government regulations, just as restrictive, or more restrictive than those of the recent war years."[10]

Thus were set forth the elements of Cold War dispersion policy:

- breaking up cities in the interest of both national security and "slum clearance";

- creation of ribbon cities along superhighways;

- provision of federal subsidies to standardized exurban housing;

- channeling of market forces to secure non-market objectives through the manipulation of the "free and automatic flow" of labor and business;

- disparagement of traditions, or "habits," of traditional communities;

- federal intrusion in local economies through "regulation"— and subsidies—to achieve regional plans; and

- emulation of Los Angeles—an urban cluster without a core— as the model city.

THE LAUREATES

Two of the authors of the policy, Teller and Marshak, were major figures. The third, Klein, was still a fledgling, but on his way toward his Nobel Prize. Soon after my talk with Klein, I had a risotto lunch in Cambridge, Massachusetts, with Carl Kaysen, the eminent economist, adviser to the Ford Foundation, and for some decades now at MIT. Kaysen informed me that during one summer, fifty-four years earlier, he and James Tobin (later himself a Nobel laureate), then graduate students at Harvard, were directed by Paul Samuelson (another laureate) to work on further dispersion memoranda as elements in "Project Charles." Its lineaments are still shrouded in classified documents presumably remaining in the archives of Teller's Livermore Laboratory, but its general purpose was the same as his work with Marshak and Klein.[11]

This was the age of projects: the Manhattan Project, Teller's Project Chariot, Project Charles, and others. There is an archive in the Eisenhower Library deposited there by the widow of Virgil L. Couch, in August 1991. The library tells us that Couch earned the title of "Mr. Civil Defense" as head of the Industry Office and director of the industrial civil defense program for the Federal Civil Defense Administration (1951–1958) and its successor agencies until 1972. As such, he guided Project Charles at Harvard and MIT, under the umbrella of Project East River, which added to the roster professors at Cornell, Columbia, the University of Pennsylvania, Yale, Johns Hopkins, and the University of Rochester. All these were coordinated with the National Security Resources Board, and developed programs now published in twelve volumes—though exceedingly hard to find. It is interesting to note that the intended outcome was not only to disperse populations at large, but also to be sure that "key men" were distributed where they could not all be efficiently bombed.[12]

If there ever was a "key man" in that period it was Gordon Gray, heir to a tobacco fortune, president of the University of North Carolina, lawyer, media magnate, Secretary of the Army, Special Assistant to the President of the United States, and Director, Psychological Strategy Board of the Central Intelligence Agency. Gray's most distasteful task, perhaps, was presiding as chairman of the Personnel Security Board of the Atomic Energy Commission, which, nudged along by Teller, removed the security clearance for Oppenheimer. Gray agreed as well with Teller's views of how American cities should be reconfigured. While serving as a civilian official of the U.S. Air Force, Gray "was responsible for long-range research and development planning in such areas as tactical air warfare (Project Vista), civil defense (Project East River), and air defense (Project Charles)."[13]

Those of us who have discussed these proceedings with people who participated in them, or who had minor roles in the politics of the 1950s, are often prompted by students of a new century to extend the discourse into the unanticipated consequences of these many projects, and to explain why so little thought was given at the time to the limits of planning, or to any competing imperatives of nature. Where were the Environmental Impact Statements? The answer is: in the same womb of history in which awaited greater interracial justice.

The requirements of national defense were deeply considered. Thought was given to how dispersion might conflict with traditional habits, loyalties, communities, and values, but only to the extent that it might be necessary to countervail or evade them. The domineering spirit of progressivism persisted, with its faith in experts. Though the name on Gray's final seat of power was "Chairman, Psychological Strategy Board," the word "psychology" was used synonymously with "persuasion" or, some might say, "propaganda." It did not connote consideration of human nature except as a problem. This was not Gray's choice. But just as the constraints of natural systems were not on the table, neither were the constraints of tradition, or of social cohesion.

The "conquest of the atom"—an astonishing phrase in common use—seemed to impart special "expertness" to physicists and chemists, though not to biologists, and certainly not to mere "essay-writing" historians and social psychologists. How could those worrying about nuclear weapons—or rejoicing in them—have space in their heads for biology, history, or—dare it be said in this context—religion? There were no clergy present, either. Perhaps the evidence of the first decade of the twenty-first century suggests that this was just as well, but Jonathan Edwards would have had some useful things to add to the discussion.

TECHNOLOGY TRIUMPHS

The foregoing is not intended to imply that no other considerations were used in the "psychological" arguments for dispersion. The National Municipal League and the Stanford Research Institute produced statements about clearing "blighted areas" and "congestion." At the 1951 convention of the American Institute of Architects, the colleagues of Victor Gruen who were beginning to design bigger and bigger shopping centers extolled the patriotic utility of such "big boxes" as evacuation centers. Within the previous year, President Truman had ordered the director of the Office of Defense Mobilization to commence encouraging suburban construction with "certificates of necessity," which later were used to provide income tax–free profits to shopping center developers after a brief period in which those incentives were restricted to defense plants. No wonder Tracy Augur of the American Institute of Planners assured the readers of the *Bulletin of the Atomic Scientists* that "dispersal is good business."[14]

The nation was assured that nothing radical was going forward—only "sound direction to trends already discernable." That is still said; "Relax and enjoy it" is the implied message. However, the Commission on Intergovernmental Relations, quoting Project East River, told those privy to its proceedings that matters could not be left there. Neither unsubsidized business-as-usual, nor "slum clearance," nor "trends," nor local preference would be enough to overwhelm the existing preferences and loyalties of many Americans. "No community or local community or local committee can carry out what is essentially a major responsibility of the Federal government." The latter must define "the program" and move things ahead.[15]

Federal initiative was necessary because tax dollars in large quantities would have to be spent to achieve results for which even atomic energy—as threat and as promise—would not be sufficient. No, not even after atomic energy was added to the power of the internal combustion engine—which had gotten all this started. In 1913, its advent as a political force was proclaimed at the departure from Indianapolis, Indiana, of a caravan led by Carl Fisher, the swashbuckling founder of the Prest-O-Lite headlight company. Following Fisher's limousine, "the first Chryslers, Packards, and Model Ts clattered down Route 40." Behind the chauffeurs of those splendid machines reposed "executives from the automobile, tire, and cement industries." Not yet were there limousines in the parade for the asphalt, gasoline, and fast-food magnates, the developers of shopping centers and industrial parks. But they would come ere long.[16]

Carl Fisher and his co-founders of the Lincoln Highway Association "foreshadowed the later relationship between the car industry and highway construction" that "seeded a thriving roadside culture . . . a venue for innovative ways to market gas, food and lodging." It did much more, of course. It "seeded" the growth of a culture that eviscerated the old cities and dispersed their inhabitants into a post-urban landscape that was neither rural nor urban. Some of that seeding would have happened, no doubt, had there been no Second World War, no atomic bombs, no *Bulletin of the Atomic Scientists*, and no congressional and administrative deference to advisers urging the dispersion of the American city as a patriotic necessity.[17]

THE LEGACIES OF EDWARD TELLER

Though the minds of Samuelson, Tobin, Klein, and Kaysen were among the ablest ever set to think about urban planning, none of these great figures stayed with the subject after their Cold War work was done, and none of them had Teller's aspirations to shape cities. Teller, the "father of the hydrogen bomb," was a Hungarian émigré of ferocious ambition, who came to meetings with a black-browed intensity, bearing a nimbus of nuclear wisdom. He loved power and, until he died at ninety-five, used it with the in-fighting skills of a Mafia don.

In 1946, Teller was already famous, leaping from branch to branch amid the upper elevations of an evolving scientific-academic-governmental jungle. From his arrival at Los Alamos in 1942, he had advocated the development of tritium, a heavy isotope of hydrogen that can vastly accelerate the rate at which the explosive process proceeds. Very early on, he evidenced a conviction that American cities should be redistributed to make them more secure from whatever weapons his counterparts in the Soviet Union might be able to develop, and he never wavered from the belief that he was the man who knew how it should be done.[18]

Teller displayed little interest in cities as political organisms or carriers of culture, nor did he evidence concern for the dangerous outcomes of dispersion beyond prudent limits. Indeed, he never seems to have been conscious of the setting in which he did his work at Los Alamos. It is probable that he was too intent upon making fire in a laboratory to pay much attention to smoke on the horizon. Besides, he was fully occupied in a Tong war against Oppenheimer, who was developing worries about further use of nuclear weapons against civilians and about their environmental effects. Teller was unworried, and also ambitious for his own laboratory. The account of his career on the Web site of the Academy of Achievement provides a delicately phrased version of the events of the following two decades: "Teller . . . lobbied Congress and the armed services vigorously for the establishment of a second laboratory for thermonuclear research. The Atomic Energy Commission responded by establishing the Lawrence Livermore Laboratory in northern California. Teller served in succession as consultant, associate director and finally director of the Livermore lab." He was emerging from Oppenheimer's shadow, but when Teller's rival "was accused of disloyalty on the basis of some past associations" and many of his colleagues rallied to his defense, "Teller made no accusations himself, but when Oppenheimer's security clearance was revoked, many of his friends blamed Teller."

Many indeed returned to academic pursuits, as Teller moved into the opportunity that had opened, with phenomenal success, employing his extraordinarily focused power of persuasion to advocate both a "super" development program for a hydrogen weapon and urban dispersal. In his pursuit of the latter objective as a "geographical engineer," he sought out Marshak, director of the Cowles Commission for Research in Economics, for which Klein was a researcher.

The commission had been founded by a Colorado investor to do stock market research. After being moved to the University of Chicago, it turned its attention first to the economics of wartime mobilization, and after 1945 to the economic implications of atomic energy and also—concurrently and not at first in relationship—to transportation economics. Klein reports that soon after the detonation of the nuclear weapons at Hiroshima and Nagasaki, Teller appeared in Marshak's office to ask him to join him in espousing the dispersion of American cities. Marshak turned to Klein to work out the costs.[19]

How, they asked Teller, might his newly engineered America look on a map? At an Italian restaurant on the South Side of Chicago, Teller pointed at the interlaced red-and-white ribbons of the tablecloth. "That's how!" he said. The ensuing article spoke of "cities . . . in more or less continuous ribbons from east to west and . . . crossed by another network of parallel ribbons from north to south . . . a mesh of squares."[20]

City planners have generally been trained in sociology, political science, architecture, or all three. The most famous of them was Daniel Burnham, architect of the Columbian Exposition of 1893, and author of the famous injunction to his profession: "Make no little plans." Teller's were bigger than the biggest. His Orion Project, to give one example, on which was expended a million dollars of the taxpayers' money, called for a rocket taller than Burnham's highest skyscraper, to be propelled by successive nuclear blasts and capable of tugging a city the size of Chicago into space. The Orion staff spent an afternoon in the 1950s computing the aggregate weight of Chicago and how much nuclear energy it would take to get it aloft.[21]

As early as his conversation with Marshak and Klein, Teller was engaged in what he called "a new and important discipline: Geographical engineering. We will change the earth's surface to suit us." The marvel, perhaps, is that he remained an adviser to presidents for nearly a half century thereafter. Though he accomplished nothing so bold as the Orion Project with all his power and persuasion, Chicago did lose mass and weight along with population. In some measure, that was because Edward Teller was so convincing.[22]

THE BULLETIN

Under the editorial direction of Eugene Rabinowitch, the *Bulletin of the Atomic Scientists* became for a time the journal of urban dispersion, not because that was Teller's idea but because the editors were moved by a passionate sense of the horrors of nuclear war. "Dispersal is the only measure which could make an atomic 'super Pearl Harbor' impossible," wrote Rabinowitch. Gutting out the core cities and beginning a vast highway-building program were important as well. "Radical alterations of many existing buildings, creation of broad fire lanes and wide new radial and circular thoroughfares . . . [could diminish] . . . the danger of 'fire storms.'" The nation should bend its will and expend its treasure to construct "new, dispersed communities" and break up the nation's "present concentration of attractive targets."[23]

The cause was also taken up in two articles in the *Bulletin* in 1948 and in a third in 1950. A full issue, with a range of articles by many authors, appeared in September 1951, to celebrate President Truman's appointment of a National Security Resources Board (NSRB). Truman ordered the Office of Defense Mobilization to act upon his conviction—possibly arising from direct conversations with Teller—that because "our continued existence as a free nation depend[s] largely upon our industrial capacity . . . [and because the] core of this capacity . . . lies in a relatively few densely built up centers," these centers must be broken up. Truman further directed the NSRB "to establish general standards with respect to dispersal, which shall be followed in the granting of certificates of necessity, in the allocation of critical materials for construction purposes, and in the making of emergency loans."[24]

Fiscal devices designed in the Cold War years were still being applied at considerable expense in the year 2006. In 1951, dissatisfied with the pace of "spontaneous dispersal," or "planless flight," two Detroit city planners, Donald and Astrid Monson, advocated large federal subsidies to accelerate "breaking up the central mass of a large city." Because the automobile rendered "the distance from the center of town . . . relatively unimportant," the government should initiate "a program of planned dispersal . . . speeding up construction of broad express highways through our large cities." Dense old cities should "receive no additional defense work in order . . . [to] induce workers to transfer to less hazardous areas." The Monsons were able to offer a more detailed prescription for tax-subsidized urban dispersal than had Teller, Marshak, and Klein six years earlier.[25]

- FHA mortgage and GI insurance would be granted only to housing built in accordance with the plan [of dispersal].

- FHA public housing would be built only in accordance with the plan, [with priority to those] displaced from slum or other central city areas being cleared.

- Federal slum clearance loans and grants would be given only . . . [when] fitted into the dispersal plan—i.e., . . . reduced the density of an overcrowded area.

- RFC and other government loans would be made only to industries locating in areas designated by the plan.

- Defense contracts, materials, allocations, tax concessions and other inducements would be given to firms locating new plants . . . with special encouragement [to relocate] to firms now located in areas within the central city designated for clearance.

- Federal aid for highway construction and other public works would be granted only for projects essential in carrying out the dispersal plan and would be stepped up in order to speed the rate of their completion.

- Other aids to cities would be conditional on their implementing the dispersal plan by amending and enforcing zoning regulations, refusing building permits for new construction . . . etc.

- Land . . . within the central city . . . cleared . . . and not rebuilt, such as strips bordering on expressways . . . can serve as separation strips buffering off one community from another.

• Such slum areas are not to be rebuilt. . . . [They] will form . . . firebreaks. . . . Slum clearance should be speeded up . . . breaking up the central mass of the city . . . as rapidly . . . as possible.[26]

How might a "slum" be defined? What exactly was meant by "clearance," and by "buffering"? An indication of the loads borne by those words in the 1950s and 1960s was provided in the next essay in the special issue of the *Bulletin*. Its author was Alderman Robert E. Merriam of Chicago, later Deputy Director, U.S. Bureau of Budget, and Eisenhower's Deputy Assistant to the President for Interdepartmental Affairs. Referring to "the Negro problem," Merriam implied an argument for breaking up the cities that did not arise specifically from Cold War strategy. In the 1950s and 1960s, northern cities were becoming, in his terms, increasingly problematical, as they received large in-migrations from the Cotton Belt. Merriam, a scholarly fellow who wrote books on how government ought to be conducted and by whom, quoted Tocqueville as stating that cities containing many poor people were "a real danger . . . [to] democratic republics." They ought to be broken up, he suggested, lest the mass of their poor and disaffected cause the sort of government managed by the sort of people approved by him and Tocqueville to "perish." After fragmenting the masses, "the government" could create "an armed force . . . independent of the town population, and able to repress its excesses."[27]

Next to weigh in was Ralph Lapp, the author of the bestseller *Must We Hide?* Merriam had urged hiding from poverty and Negroes; Lapp's apprehensions were directed not at the underclass but at what might come at us from overhead. Expressing his satisfaction that during the war the Plant Site Board of the Office of Production Management had ordered the placement of plants "away from highly industrialized areas," Merriam noted with approbation that these policies had been continued into the Cold War era, pressed forward by such eminent experts as General Augustin M. Prentiss, who wrote in 1951 that "the future development of urban communities should not be left to circumstances, but should be guided by definite plans . . . [for] dispersion of the population and industrial activities."[28]

"Circumstances" could have meant that aggregate of individual preferences expressed in unfettered markets; such preferences would have to be warped. Indeed, the argument was developing, those "definite plans" would have to be realized by "something more than . . . advisory committees." There would be opposition from those insisting that "Amerian public attitudes demand that it be done within a framework of our democratic institutions, that private mechanisms be utilized." So wartime measures would have to be camouflaged under more subtle devices.[29]

The masters of subtlety weighed in. Hearings on dispersion were held under the chairmanship of Senator Joseph O'Mahoney of Wyoming and by a House committee headed by Porter Hardy, Jr., of Virginia. O'Mahoney, consulting with Teller, enthusiastically offered legislation to "discourage the continued geographic concentration of industry." Hardy's district was as yet short of defense contracts. He proposed, and got, federal grants to put plants there and also federal "accelerated tax amortization." By such means, the nation could be spared "knock out blows" in a "sudden enemy attack." By 1955, however, the Senate Committee on Armed Services was hearing protests that the pork was going to the wrong places. Its response was that patriotism should prevail. "If industries are forced to disperse, [and] cities . . . prevented from growing," that was too bad, but "dispersion appears to be the only answer for reducing urban vulnerability."[30]

Lapp reported that after deliberation by the National Security Council and the Department of Commerce, Secretary of the Air Force Stuart Symington had forced the relocation of a Boeing plant from Seattle, Washington, to Wichita, Kansas. The mingling of patriotism with regional favoritism—Symington was from neighboring Missouri—did not go unchallenged. After the Chance Vought aircraft works had relocated from Connecticut to Texas, representatives in Congress from New England charged that "the Administration proposes to rip plants out of the northeast, and spread them throughout the prairie states." But they were running after a moving train: Senate Bill 1385, endorsed by the Truman Administration in 1946, called for the heavily subsidized distribution of industrialization and population to "areas of the United States . . . which heretofore have been without adequate industrial employment." Truman's successor, Dwight Eisenhower, had several things to say about grab bags, and about complexes using the taxpayers' general funds to divvy out "adequate industrial employment" where the votes were. But he admitted he had come too late to stop the train.[31]

The masters of subtlety prevailed, as Lapp had urged: "As old buildings obsolesce in the centers . . . they should be torn down and not replaced. The Federal Housing Administration should refuse to grant aid to those seeking to cram more buildings within the heart of a metropolitan area. Such measures will result in the gradual depopulation of the target centers and a build up in the outlying regions."[32]

Goodhue Livingston, Jr., a Republican gentleman of New York bearing a famous name, took up the Monsons' call for thruways to ream out firebreaks through cities, relating them to "fire-breaks used in fighting forest fires," and urged that "such fire-breaks [be] . . . carved out of presently crowded industrial and residential areas [whose current state no good citizen could] continue to view with complacency."[33]

These ideas were common currency at the time, but though espoused by planners, architects, and urban reformers of various political stripes, they did not carry the urgency of wartime experience behind them until they were focused into coherent and detailed policy by scientists still crowned with laurel and cloaked in purple. Carl Fisher and his Lincoln Highway associates had the "open road" going for them, but not patriotism. That was Edward Teller's contribution. With his assistance, a dispersion-industrial complex became interlocked with the political and industrial forces President Eisenhower dubbed "the military-industrial complex." A program of getting people out of old cities and into new ones along highways suited nearly everybody.

To keep track of how things were going, the Pentagon showed its propensity for body counting; it "pushed for more fine-scale information, and the Army funded in 1967 on an experimental basis a study to provide this information at the county level, which is now common practice." Only then did the Census Bureau do the work to provide estimates of "population change, housing change, or migration below the state level." In 1962, a group called the Southern Regional Demographic Group appeared under the sponsorship of the Oak Ridge National Laboratory. "The driving force for this was interest by the armed forces in demographic analysis, and a need for evacuation planning in the case of a nuclear attack"; Oak Ridge is still the place where LandScan data are compiled.[34]

SHAW LIVERMORE, EDWARD TELLER, AND JONATHAN EDWARDS

Soon after the death in 1958 of Ernest Orlando Lawrence, the Nobel laureate best known for his invention of the cyclotron, Edward Teller's Livermore Laboratory was renamed the Lawrence Livermore Laboratory. That was as it should be, for like Teller, Lawrence was said by Herbert York, that laboratory's first director, to have "wanted to do 'big physics.' " The origin of the name of the town, Livermore, lies in early California history, but in time folklore may well attribute it to a colleague of Teller's and Lawrence's, Shaw Livermore, who shared Teller's aspirations for "big" city planning. Shaw Livermore had another dimension, however, opening him to even larger considerations; as an economic historian, his interests bridged the gap between big science and environmental philosophy. He is a link between nuclear physics and religious cosmology.

In the early years of the Cold War, Livermore was among the economists who joined the atomic scientists in pressing for urban dispersion as a patriotic necessity. He was more than a theoretician, serving as a senior official of both the War Production Board and the Economic Cooperation Administration; he was later Assistant to the Defense Mobilizer, Security Programs, in the forefront of those urging urban planning to go "way beyond the old simple conception of civil defense." It wasn't enough, Livermore wrote, to "jump in a dugout, you know, or rush into a shelter." Instead, he pressed for "a wholly new idea like the Marshall Plan" to spread out population and industrial production. It was Teller-scale thought.

Livermore was one of the very few of Teller's colleagues who was capable of thinking on such a scale, and developing "wholly new" ideas. Perhaps that was because he was almost alone among them in being acquainted with grand old ones, including capacious concepts of the relationship of humans to nature. As such, he stood between Edward Teller and Jonathan Edwards, but he died before he was able to think all the way to an application of Edwards's broader view of human life to the consequences of a megalomaniacal technocracy as exploited by a dispersion-industrial complex.[35]

Teller came over Livermore's horizon during their defense mobilization days. Livermore encountered Edwards earlier, in his days as a historian at the University of Michigan. Edwards might also be said to have been capable of "big science" in the eighteenth-century sense of that term, as meaning "learning from experience and testing what is likely to be true." He had been as bold as Teller and Lawrence—bolder, indeed, in daring enough to seek an all-encompassing theology of man and nature. But Edwards's learning sprang from the fundamental premise that dominance by humans is delusory and its pursuit dangerous.

As a scholar, Livermore approached Edwards first through economics, becoming expert in the initial rupture of New England's theocratic communities during Edwards's lifetime, when a speculating class was coming to ascendancy in New England, treating the land not as a trust but as a commodity. I will have considerably more to say about this polarity between Teller and Edwards, about the contrasting ideas of these great men about man, nature, and limits, and how each of them learned from fire.

Those extended discussions will come along later. At this juncture, we pull out of this wayside map reading, to get back on the interstate.

5. TRUMAN, EISENHOWER, AND THE ROAD GANG

When Harry S. Truman of Independence, Missouri, was exposed to the wonders of European highway systems during his service in the First World War, there were already a half million automobile registrations in the United States. Truman observed the French disporting themselves in cabriolets along the Roman roads of their country, and heard tales of the taxicab army that was deployed out of Paris on newer highways during the first battle of the Marne. The French roads admired by Truman went from city to city, not within cities. Truman wrote his wife on May 19, 1918: "The French know how to build inter-city roads and also how to keep them up. They are just like a billiard table." After returning from the war and becoming county judge of Jackson County, Missouri, in the late 1920s, Truman pressed forward one of the nation's most ambitious county road systems. For his exertions he was elected president of a national road association, and was said to have taken Jackson County "out of the mud."[1]

Truman was a Wilsonian Democrat; Woodrow Wilson was the hero of Truman's youth; and to Wilson's example he was wont to return when his party regained power after three Republican administrations: "Our improved standard of living and vast economic expansion, which accompanied the tremendous growth of highway transportation over the past 40 years, are due in large part to the Federal-aid program first enacted in 1916, under a Democratic administration." As a good Wilsonian, Truman commenced his own presidency in 1945 by proclaiming that "our highway construction has not kept pace with the growth in traffic. . . . By any reasonable standard our highways are inadequate for today's demands. . . . To build highways that will meet these needs will require continuous effort over a long period of time and on an extensive scale." Even before the Great Depression, nearly 60 percent of American families owned an automobile. Like those of France, however, the public works programs of Wilson and Franklin Roosevelt were intended to encourage travel from one lively city to another, not to eviscerate those cites. That being the case, when Edward Teller and his allies talked to Truman's cabinet about dispersion, they emphasized linking, not gutting.[2]

Despite their fondness for road building as a way to put people to work, the New Dealers understood that home construction did so more efficiently, so highway construction funds were vulnerable to budget cuts. After the Korean War aroused fears of inflation, Truman, acting in accordance with the precepts of the Federal Reserve Board and his Treasury Department, put the clamps on highway budgets. In a famous letter to Dennis Chavez of New Mexico, chairman of the Senate Public Works Committee, on August 17, 1950, only six weeks after ordering the troops to Korea, Truman shut down highway construction. However popular it might be, he wrote, it was "in competition with defense needs." The interstate program took the largest cuts.[3]

This was bad news for Teller's crew, and it did not square with Eisenhower's sense of what defense needs might be. For them, the Korean War was a sideshow. The Soviets were not involved, and the Soviets as a nuclear power were the real threat. In 1948 they had blockaded the Allied-controlled part of Berlin and soon exploded their first atomic weapon. While the United States and China fought their proxy war in Korea, the Russians rushed through development of hydrogen bombs. In 1951 the United States Air Force announced that it could deliver atomic warheads in Atlas intercontinental ballistic missiles, and in 1952 the United States exploded Teller's hydrogen bomb.

During this escalation there was a split in Truman's administration as to highway construction. His Acting Chairman of the National Security Resources Board, Jack Gorrie, declared "industrial dispersion" to be "the simple military measure of using space for defense," but sought to broaden dispersion's constituency to include the Wilsonians and New Dealers, despite Truman's fears of inflation. Highway construction, wrote Gorrie, was "more than a defense measure. It is also an investment in the future welfare and progress of the nation . . . [promising] a healthier, more stable national economy," presumably in healthier and more stable places, and (tipping his hat to both complexes) was "essential to continued growth of private enterprise."[4]

This was the gospel according to the dispersion-industrial complex then nucleating in Washington. The Congested Areas Urgency Committee advocated reducing "the density of over-congested areas . . . to prevent a recurrence of overcrowding," and the administrators of the Housing Act of 1949, within the Housing and Home Finance Agency, used its provisions to subsidize the movement of populations out of the central cities. William L. C. Wheaton of Harvard, who had been at work in that agency during the Second World War, wrote confidently in 1951 that "a fifth or a third of our urban population with their factories" could be "relocated . . . in each decade."[5]

The factories were pelf, and resourcefully did the representatives of the Southwest and South go after them. Walter Rogers of Texas offered "plenty of fresh air and good wholesome living in his district," and plenty of dander as well. "No Russian plane," he promised, "is ever going to come near the Panhandle of Texas and ever get home again. We can do the job out there. We have oil and gas aplenty . . . and we are going to have the water." Oak Ridge, Tennessee, had a sparkling new lake nearby, thanks to a freshly built dam, and for decades it had had the services of Senator Kenneth McKellar, chairman of the Senate Appropriations Committee. The fortunate citizens of Oak Ridge can now state on their civic Web site that years before, McKellar, when challenged by President Roosevelt to slide some large sums in secret toward the development of nuclear weapons, "could assure . . . [him] that funds could be provided without raising suspicions regarding its use: . . . 'It can be done, and Mr. President, just where in Tennessee are we going to locate that thing?'"[6]

Hiding funds might be done, and one might even hide the purposes of plants as big as those at Los Alamos or Oak Ridge, but dispersing whole cities had to be done in the open. Most civic-dispersion plans were fully disclosed, as if their destinations were bomb shelters writ large. At the peak of the civil defense planning of the 1950s, a civic board in Memphis, Tennessee, contemplated relocating the city's entire population into its hinterland—thirty counties of western Tennessee, northern Mississippi, and across the Mississippi River in Arkansas and Missouri, "outside the main body of the . . . city."[7]

THE EISENHOWER YEARS—DISPERSAL GETS ITS THOROUGHFARES

General Eisenhower was elected president of the United States in 1952. He came to the office already persuaded of the need for a federal program of highway construction between cities—not through cities, however, and this was a crucial distinction for him. His observations of German successes in moving troops along autobahns had reinforced an earlier experience of his own. Just after the First World War, as a professional soldier with the temporary rank of lieutenant colonel, he had volunteered to participate as a Tank Corps observer in the First Transcontinental Motor Convoy, which took "various types of light and heavy motor trucks, touring cars, special makes of observation cars, motorcycles, ambulances, trailers, tractors and a machine shop unit" from coast to coast through bogs and sand, along desultory, rutted, single-track roads across wooden bridges, several of which collapsed under the weight of army vehicles.[8]

"The dirt roads of Iowa," he reported, "would be impossible in wet weather," and the convoy lost two days in Nebraska "in bad, sandy

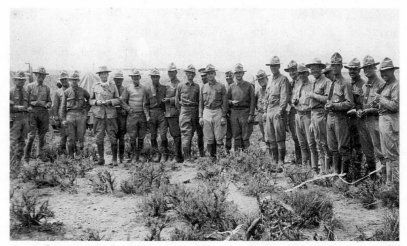

Lieutenant Colonel Dwight D. Eisenhower and colleagues of the highway reconnaissance, following World War I. Eisenhower later became "the highway president." (Eisenhower Library)

roads." Wyoming was worse, and the roads of "western Utah, on the Salt Lake Desert . . . almost impassable to heavy vehicles." The Great Basin highway was "one succession of dust, ruts, pits, and holes, . . . a track across the desert." That track was so narrow in many places that the "vehicles [had] to run one side off the pavement in meeting other vehicles, snipping the tire, the edge of the pavement and causing difficulty in again mounting the pavement."[9]

That experience, Eisenhower wrote later, "started me thinking about good, two-lane highways, but Germany had made me see the wisdom of broader ribbons across the land." "Ribbons" again. He was using the same term as Teller, but writing of highways, not of cities strung out along highways. Both men had become conscious of the virtues of target-dispersion during the Second World War, as the Germans were able to disperse the production of war matériel into small suburban facilities. And Eisenhower took to heart the success of the German high command in using their admirable system of autobahns to move their armies under cover of night and fog from one imperiled front to another, from Poland to France, from France to Russia, from Russia to Normandy, and back again.

The former Allied Supreme Commander in Europe became the Republican candidate in the presidential election of 1952. Among his attacks on his opponents was a rejection of Truman's evocation of the Democrat's achievements in highway construction. Eisenhower told the Hearst newspapers that "the obsolescence of the nation's highways presents an appalling problem of waste, danger and death. Next to the manufacture of the most modern implements of war as a guarantee of peace through strength, a network of modern roads is as necessary to defense as it is to our national economy and personal safety. We have fallen far behind in this task—until today there is hardly a city of any size without almost hopeless congestion within its boundaries and stalled traffic blocking roads leading beyond these boundaries."[10]

Teller had observed the woven red-and-white ribbons of a restaurant tablecloth, and had told Klein that the cities of the future should be gridded in that way, along highways. Eisenhower was fully conscious of the virtues of spreading out targets, but he was not a city-gutter, or a believer in large-scale, top-down urban reordering. He spoke of the roads themselves as "broader ribbons," especially after he considered the "appalling inadequacies" of the nation's highways to meet the demands of catastrophe or defense, should an atomic war come. As president, he took pride in the Federal Highway Act of 1956, and in an enormous increase in highway spending during his administration.

However, when he discerned four years later, during a campaign tour, that the interstate system was becoming an urban destruction program, he was dismayed; he was appalled when he found that Congress had finally approved his highway program only because urban destruction had been sold as a pork barrel program. It was, by then, too late. He was on his way out, but he called a meeting on April 6, 1960, at 10:35 a.m. The minutes have been preserved, recalling for some of us memories of the general when he was angry, his blue eyes fixed on those who had displeased him.[11]

THE YELLOW BOOK AND THE GRAB BAG

Eisenhower had appointed General Lucius Clay, a trusted wartime colleague and himself an autobahn aficionado, to achieve his intercity highway program. Clay and his colleagues struggled as their predecessors had struggled against the competing interests of short- and long-haul truckers, automobile interests, contractors, state governments, toll road advocates, interstate advocates, gas tax advocates, and sales tax advocates, endlessly bickering over tolls and allocation of taxes. Finally, they settled on promising great sums to urban congresspeople to tear down and build up, in a festival—indeed, a veritable orgy—of pork. It appears that they neglected to tell the president either about the pork or about bulldozing through cities and not just between them to create highways.

The president, having found out the truth, was not pleased. The tenor of the meeting became clear when one subordinate made the tactless suggestion that he and others had been at work on the matter since 1939. Eisenhower fired back that "while that might be so, he had not heard of it and that his proposal for a national highway program was his own; furthermore, that there was a tremendous difference between the present 90-10 Federal sharing type of program and any that had been considered 18 or 20 years ago." It was now a huge federal program, not a stitching together of toll roads and state highways. But it was not the cost-sharing device that bothered him, as the minutes of the meeting record. It was that "running Interstate routes through the congested parts of the cities was entirely against his original concept and wishes; that he never anticipated that the program would turn out this way."[12]

Eisenhower's anger became palpable as he told the meeting that "when the Clay Committee Report was rendered, he had studied it carefully," and had not found in it any "concept of using the program to build up an extensive intra-city route network. . . . He added that those who had not advised him that such was being done, and those who had steered the program in such a direction, had not followed his wishes." Whose wishes had been followed? That was becoming clear enough. Postwar America was becoming the post-urban expression of the ambitions of the dispersion-industrial complex for which Edward Teller and his colleagues offered intellectual respectability.[13]

The president's "disappointment over the way the program had been developed against his wishes" was both in its city-gutting effects and in its pork-barrel methods. Eisenhower told the gathering that he had not been shown the Yellow Book, a semi-secret volume produced in 1955 by the Bureau of Public Roads to convince Congress that a great deal of federal money would be spent not only in buying land from speculators in the countryside and building intercity highways, but also in tearing down "slums" and then building up highways. The president of the United States had been told, he said, "that this book . . . gave the legislative history of the Interstate System," and that urban congressmen had been assured of their share of the pelf "on a 'per person' basis in view of the taxes they paid; in fact, that they were to get more consideration since they paid much more in taxes per person and in total than persons in rural areas."[14]

The president added that he had been able to obtain a copy of the Yellow Book only "after several [broken] promises" and after the lobbying had been done and the process of gutting the old cities had gained its congressional momentum. Then, and only then, had the staff informed him "that this was what the Congress had been told, and that . . . the descriptions in the Yellow Book which they had before them when considering the legislation, were the prime reasons the Congress passed the Interstate Highway Act [of 1956]." Eisenhower had intended to ensure a balance between serving the military needs of the nation and providing postwar employment. The Yellow Book depicted a tilt toward urban replacement and removal, with lots of taxpayer money for everybody—except the displaced poor.

Though the president, in his final months in office, told his staff that he considered "Public Works per se . . . one of the biggest 'grab-

bags' for Federal Funds," he had been outflanked. All he could do after the fact was direct "an independent review to be made of the
Highway Program by someone who would bring him the facts."
When a president asks for an independent review, he is signaling his
intention to hold somebody responsible for a large mistake. But in the
case at hand, Clay stood between Eisenhower and anybody in particular, and beyond Clay—a sea of vague faces, many of them smiling
the smiles of the well-fed.[15]

Frustrated by an equivalent sense of impotence in curbing the
tightening grip upon defense policy of a "military-industrial complex," he left a warning against it in his farewell message. Though the
power of a dispersion-industrial complex had countervailed his in-
tentions for urban and transportation policy until matters "had
reached the point . . . where his hands were virtually tied," he left
to history its designation as such. Designated or not, it was successful; more than $300 billion was spent to build more than twenty thou-
sand miles of superhighways through cities, rather than between
them.[16]

Mark Rose's history of express highway politics from 1939
through 1989, *Interstate*, does not mention Edward Teller or the
atomic bomb. It does, however, describe in detail how the dispersion-
industrial complex, known to its charter members as "the Road
Gang," managed to resolve its internal jealousies to swing united support behind the Highway Act of 1956. Until then, so vicious had the
in-fighting been among them that they had delayed pelf for anybody.
But with an administration in power that had larger justifications in
mind, they all got something from that public works program that
Eisenhower had called "the grab bag." The Highway Act and its successors provided billions of federal dollars to state highway departments to be spent "according to local needs." The needs so served
were largely those of developers in new localities, not those of older
towns, which were bulldozed as "congested urban areas." Nor were
those needs localized down to the specific people forced out of their
homes. Only Mayor Robert F. Wagner of New York City was willing to

suggest that the highway acts pay to rebuild the urban areas destroyed as blighted or congested, and pay the moving expenses of the
people forced out of them.[17]

While the Highway Act of 1956 "increased automotive taxes" for
the public in general, it was said at the time that the small print provided generous exceptions for truckers, and differentially among
truckers. Lyndon Johnson, Majority Leader of the Senate, secured for
Texas, a "small trucker state," an exemption from any taxes for the first
thirteen tons of truck weight. Senator John Stennis, of largely rural
Mississippi, pleaded for more money for farm roads and less for interstates. Stennis was a potent figure in military appropriations, and was
skilled in country metaphor: without a comfortable subsidy, a farm-to-
market road would be like a "neglected calf," and so would the developer who planned to build speculative houses along it. Once the
truckers agreed with one another, the motorists followed, and the
gasoline suppliers, the cement suppliers, and the whole Road Gang.
William Norlag of the Central Motor Freight Association wrote in
March 1956 that his clients, who included "every red-blooded
trucker and his legion of allied industry and shipper friends," had
gone to work convincing Congress that it was a patriotic duty "to get
the big highway building program under way without further delay."
The general taxpayer picked up most of the cost.[18]

In retrospect, it may seem strange that so little attention was given
either to the larger social costs of gutting older cities or to the environmental costs of sending people helter-skelter into places where
they might be in danger of natural disasters. Many people believed in
"urban renewal through throughways." Some asserted that once better highways were built between central cities and their suburbs, nice
suburban people would hasten to flow into town: to offices, department stores, and cultural amenities such as a symphony hall. Others
described how much nicer the suburbs were, and predicted that the
flow would be out toward them. Neither were as shrewd as Edward
Teller and his colleagues in anticipating that the flow of traffic would
in fact be determined largely by combining housing subsidies with

highway construction. If enough government money went into making it easier to get a place to live outside the city than in it, as Teller predicted, cities could be evacuated and eviscerated.[19]

The results were impressive. It is no discredit to O'Mahoney, Hardy, Rogers, Wilson, or Edward Teller that an outward-spinning of population splattered some people into flame zones and flood zones. That was quite beyond their ken. Now that it has happened, however, and now that we know how it happened, we can set some controls on the spinning process. We can put up some splatter-boards, so to speak. One of them might bear the legend: PAY ATTENTION TO NATURE. THERE ARE LIMITS.[20]

THE DISPERSION-INDUSTRIAL COMPLEX RECONSIDERED

In the early days of American industrialization, the miller lived above the mill, which stood next to the waterfall. The steel plant was built as close to the coal mine as possible, because coal is heavy and expensive to ship. In the 1930s and 1940s, the construction of dams and power grids underwritten by the taxpayers financed a separation of power source from power use. This repeal of the ancient law of industrial proximity enabled separations of power from production and of production from population. In the 1950s and thereafter, Cold War mortgage insurance and highway programs encouraged that separation, as did individual preferences for more space. In addition, peculiarly beguiling climate conditions created the impression that the dry West was not as dry as it had been or would be thereafter. Thus psychology and climate moved in concert with transfer payments on an enormous scale. Billions of federal dollars were spent to induce millions of Americans to migrate out of cities and along highways into the suburbs and beyond—to the edges of natural systems that did not appear at the time to be as dangerous as they turned out to be.

Cold War policies were not solely responsible for these huge population shifts. Nonetheless, the arguments for dispersion laid out in detail in the *Bulletin of the Atomic Scientists* presented a straightforward, candid, patriotic, rational program, major portions of which were harmonious with the narrower interests of other influential people. Therefore Teller's own influence, while important, was only a contributing factor to a set of consequences going beyond even his globe-girdling ambitions. He and his colleagues were articulate about what they thought the government should do, and they had sufficient force to get the ball rolling, a ball that was subsequently kept in motion by the dispersion-industrial complex.

FEDERAL SUBSIDIES TO DISPERSION—HIGHWAYS

Those centrifugal forces were and are very potent, but not ineluctable. Cold War–era sprawl was an economic phenomenon, not a psychic one. Barry Checkoway of the University of Illinois was correct in writing, as early as 1980, "It is wrong to believe that postwar American suburbanization prevailed because the public chose it and will continue to prevail until the public changes its preferences. . . . Suburbanization prevailed because of the decisions of large operators and powerful economic institutions supported by federal government programmes, and ordinary consumers had little real choice in the basic pattern that resulted."[21]

True, that "basic pattern" was grounded in some public predispositions, but it was established by a series of specific and intentional programs, among them those propounded in the pages of the *Bulletin of the Atomic Scientists* in 1951. The first of these was for migration channeling along highways: federal aid for highway construction and other public works would be directed toward projects essential in carrying out the dispersal plan and would be increased in order to speed the rate of their completion.

City planners had been extolling dispersed and linear cities since the invention of the automobile. General Motors recruited the theatrical designer Norman Bel Geddes to make highways glamorous in his Futurama, in the GM Pavilion at the 1939 World's Fair. The exhibit astounded boys from small cities like me, who had no way of knowing that at the same time, Le Corbusier's sketches of French workers' high-rise housing along superhighways and Frank Lloyd Wright's plan for Broadacre City were making dispersion respectable among futurists. In the United States, advertising for automobiles, highways, and gasoline made "Automobiles for Everyman" the counterparts to coaches for kings.

In 1954 President Eisenhower's Federal Highway Act put nearly $2 billion into highway construction—enough to employ about seven hundred thousand people for two years. Then, in 1956, he signed another Federal Highway Act, creating the Highway Trust Fund generated by a national gas tax. The fund would pay for a $25 billion National System of Interstate and Defense Highways, 90 percent of which would come from *federal* taxpayers. This easy money quickly prompted *state* departments of transportation to plan for more than forty-one thousand miles of highways to pass through and connect America's cities. Mass transit and streetcars fell into disfavor. The Bureau of Public Roads approved construction contracts, and mayors got highway construction jobs at federal expense, though "the price federal and state highway planners exacted for those jobs was enormous. Each mile of freeway took away twenty-four acres of land; each interchange, eighty acres—acres that might otherwise have contributed to the tax structure of a city. . . . [Though] mayors knew their greatest need was for an integrated system of roads and mass transportation, not just Interstate highways tearing through their cities," they took the highways, the urban destruction, and the dollars they brought with them. Twenty-two thousand miles of highways were laid across cities, splitting neighborhoods, eliminating housing for the poor, and facilitating flight to the suburbs and exurbs. Over the ensuing three decades, Congress increased the fuel tax and added funds beyond those generated by that tax to the Highway Trust Fund, pouring $700 billion in 2004 dollars into freeway construction.[22]

The federal highway programs created conveyor belts between city cores and fire-prone, fragile ecosystems. Along the way, a lot of money went to the owners of fast-food establishments, hotels, and gas stations; builders got rich providing industrial parks and the huge spaces in which retailing came to look like warehousing—the "big boxes" of the trade.*

The automobile companies and the gas and oil industries prospered. An enormous transfer of wealth was accomplished between city real estate owners and exurban real estate developers, with the general taxpayers picking up the transfer costs. The gutted cities were stripped of tax dollars previously paid by industry, retail establishments, and middle-class residents, and were forced to raise taxes to cover growing municipal expenses. Those higher taxes drove more people out of town. Neglected city neighborhoods paid the price, with failing schools, rising crime, and a concentration of poverty. By 1990, industrial cities such as Pittsburgh, Cleveland, and Buffalo each had lost nearly 40 percent of their population. And the expense of fighting wildfires in the country went way up.

By 1980, the effects of the highway program upon both ends of the conveyor belt—at both ends of the geography of dispersion—were manifest. Firefighters were aware that their tasks were being made harder as ever more immigrants required rescue, though firefighting costs and the distemper of natural systems were not yet clear to the public in general. The cities were becoming sick. The countryside was already sick. And the taxpayers began to revolt. In 1991 the Intermodal Surface Transportation Efficiency Act (ISTEA, pronounced "Ice Tea") became law. It authorized $155 billion to be spent to balance better the benefits of taxpayer subsidies to transportation. More important, in the short term, the act provided a funding mechanism that cracked open the alliance between gas tax revenue, state depart-

---

*This is not the place for an extended discourse on the interplay of tax policy and transportation policy, but it is important to drop a flag on the field at this juncture to mark another Eisenhower-era innovation: accelerated-depreciation accounting as it interdigitated with highway subsidies. As the highways expanded, customers could get to big boxes by auto, and those boxes could be supplied by truck. Their developers could greatly increase their rates of return on investment because the actual revenues received were sheltered from income taxes by depreciation accounting that was not based upon actual physical depreciation rates but instead on much faster rates on a sum-of-the-digits or double-declining basis, after which the box could be sold to the next developer, with the capital gain again spared taxation at ordinary income rates by capital-gains treatment.

ments of transportation, and the highway construction industry. Federal gas tax funds could now be dedicated to other transportation options, such as mass transit, bikeways, and rail, and mayors could now use half their federal funding for highways or mass transit.

Decisions about how these funds were to be allocated were increasingly made at the state and metropolitan levels. There was even money to start rebuilding bridges and transit systems. ISTEA was also designed to meld transportation policy with environmental policy—though not yet in flame or flood zones. The Congestion Mitigation and Air Quality Program (CMAQ) directed federal funds to transportation projects that helped to improve air quality. In 1998, the success of ISTEA was affirmed as the $217 billion Transportation Equity Act for the Twenty-first Century (TEA-21), with $36 billion for transit and $162.7 billion for highways. Some light appeared at the end of the long tunnel; nature, out there where the light shone, was going to get some relief. For a few more pages we should stay in the tunnel, though, to observe other dispersion prognoses in a little more detail.

FEDERAL MORTGAGE SUBSIDIES

The prescription offered by the *Bulletin of the Atomic Scientists* for the use of federal subsidies to disperse the American city also included these provisions for the directed use of mortgage insurance programs (emphasis mine):

- *FHA mortgage and GI insurance* would be granted only to housing built in accordance with the plan [of dispersal].

- *FHA public housing* would be built only in accordance with the plan, [with priority to those] displaced from slum *or other* central city areas being cleared.

- *Federal slum clearance loans and grants* would be given only . . . [when] fitted into the dispersal plan—i.e., . . . reduced the density of an overcrowded area.

Since these recommendations were made, ten times more building was subsidized by federal mortgage programs in suburbs and exurbs than in central cities. This was not the result of Cold War dispersion policies alone; there was a dispersion inclination in policies inherited from the New Deal and also from the Republican administrations preceding it. As Jane Jacobs noted in *The Death and Life of Great American Cities*, "virtually every wise man of government—from right to left—was in favor of the objectives. A few years before the enactment of the Public Housing Act of 1934, Herbert Hoover had opened the first White House Conference on Housing with a polemic against the moral inferiority of cities and a panegyric on the moral virtues of simple cottages, small towns and grass." In the 1940s, some home ownership programs came out of bitter memories of the Bonus March and Hoovervilles. The New Deal used home building to provide employment, and both Republicans and Democrats in Congress thought it wise to mete out expenditure of accumulated wartime saving into mortgage payments rather than "binges" or "squandering." This somewhat paternalistic view of veterans' rights offered mortgage insurance in the place of bonuses.[23]

More than $5 trillion in mortgage loans has been guaranteed by the federal government since the Great Depression, most allocated after the Second World War, under the umbrella of the GI Bill of Rights. These guarantees are subsidies, reducing the cost of borrowing by shifting some of its burden from the homeowner to the nation as a whole. Lenders charge borrowers less because they know that the public will pay part or all of what the borrower fails to pay. On the upside, by the year 2000, 68.2 percent of our citizens owned their own homes. There is a downside to all this, however: many of the homes built with public help are in very dangerous places, from which more public aid will be required to rescue their inhabitants.[24]

By the time the war was over, the GI Bill became another suburban developers' subsidy bill and, in effect, a tax on urban homeowners. Most GI mortgages went to applicants whose actions accelerated the flight from cities. The effects of this were enormous: after many ad-

Highlands Ranch, Douglas County, Colorado, 2001. (Courtesy of
Alan Berger)

justments upward from original limits, such as those of the Public
Housing Act of 1934, the Veterans Administration, acting through
bankers, "thrifts," and mortgage bankers, had by 1996 guaranteed to
veterans more than fifteen million home loans totaling over $565
billion—with very little of that stimulating construction in the old
cities. Lending and insuring has become so standardized, remote, and
generic that many loans were and are insured by GNMA, FNMA, and
FHLMC without any insuring official or agent of those bodies seeing
the property insured. If the database said that the street, or the town,
had good loans, and the appraisal looked reasonable, the loan was—
and still is—made.[25]

Another honeypot of taxpayer money could be reached by the developers in the countryside: the Farmers Home Administration. By
1980, despite its name and its location in the Department of Agriculture, it had become primarily an urban-dispersion agency. It was
"flexible." It was not required to make or guarantee farm loans. Its

guidelines merely stated that it might loan money to "public bodies and not-for-profit corporations" in "rural" areas to construct or improve needed "community" facilities. Projects such as water and sewer systems, fire and rescue vehicles, fire stations, hospital improvements, and other facilities were eligible.[26]

Thus was created an enormous vacuum pump sucking population out of the old industrial cities and depositing them into fire-prone extremities. Post-urban America was born of Cold War policy, myth fulfillment, a hankering for open space, a dislike of dirt, crime, congestion, and neighbors of a different hue, and concerted promotion that began with a little cavalcade along Route 40 outside Indianapolis in 1913 and culminated in the triumph of the Road Gang—and its formidable allies.

PART THREE

At the End of the Line

6. MANAGING WILDFIRE

On July 6, 1994, in South Canyon, near Glenwood Springs, Colorado, fourteen young men were killed fighting a wildfire. Secretary Dan Glickman of the Department of Agriculture and Secretary Bruce Babbitt of the Department of the Interior went to the scene, assembling there key people in their departments who had been trained to understand fire behavior and, equally important, human behavior in the presence of fire. The report issued by these professionals dealt with what had gone wrong in South Canyon. Lessons from that disaster led to the Federal Wildland Fire Policy of 1995, which substantially improved the ways in which wildfires were thereafter fought on the ground.

This was real progress, enough to ask of any set of officials besieged with managing a government, meeting daily crises, and answering summons to testify by dozens of overlapping committees of Congress. In this busy epoch, nobody, Republican or Democrat, could be expected to do more. Nobody now can pause for a summer's brooding over large questions, as John Adams was able to do during his presidency and Thomas Jefferson during his. That is why those of us who are out of office—and some of us who will never again be in office—should do the constructive brooding.

The Wildland Fire Policy and its successors (to the time of this writing, the summer of 2005) dealt *only* with fire policy—not with people-and-fire policy. Though some of these directives address the troubles that ensue from the pernicious people-and-fire policies of the past, they fall short of any encounter with those policies themselves. So things get worse by the day as the climate gets warmer and drier and more and more people, those induced to settle in flame zones and others rescuing those settlers, are endangered. At the end-point of policy, at the delta, so to speak, of a river of migration, there has been improvement. The firefighting on the ground was made smarter after 1998 by information gained from a better-funded Joint Fire Science Program, and by practice refined in 2000 into the National Fire Plan.

The "Healthy Forests Initiative" arrived in 2002, aptly named an initiative rather than a program. In the judgment of Stephen Pyne, the nation's preeminent scholar of fire and its human relationships, that initiative "stumbled because it sought to link the National Fire Plan, with limited targets for thinning in select forests, to the Northwest Forest Plan, which might revive serious logging in places most Americans do not want it. That coupling proved toxic, akin to tacking an abortion rider onto an appropriations bill."[1]

Though population was moving and ecosystems were changing, policy was not—or not enough. Public agencies were getting increased budgets to fight fires, but most of the money was going for equipment and outsourced services provided by contractors comprising what *The Economist* called a "fire-industrial complex . . . the large centralized technocratically-based . . . structure that constitutes fire suppression culture."[2]

THE FIRE-INDUSTRIAL COMPLEX

Putting out wildfires that threaten human communities is desirable, politically necessary, and good business. Looking at the high, dry West as an investment opportunity, it is manifest that there are big wildfires every year somewhere between the Pacific shore and the

Mississippi. Such predictability delights investors, and the scale of the opportunity is large; wildfires generate annually between $.5 billion and $2 billion of government spending. Outside the defense, health, and education budgets it is difficult to envisage so juicy a market. In 2000, for example, federal agencies employed 30,000 people, many of whom were not employees of those agencies, to fight more than 120,000 fires, and spent $1.3 billion. While the front pages celebrated the heroic efforts of firefighters, the business pages noted all the money being spent "transporting crews and compensation for hazardous work and overtime," and a report from ECO-Northwest for the Ford Foundation described how "hefty" were the "contracts for aircraft, bulldozers, and fire engines [that] account for a large portion of the fire-suppression tab."[3]

In May 2004, *The Salt Lake Tribune* reported a statement by Senator Larry Craig, Republican of Idaho, that firefighting had "pulled $2.7 billion from other nonfire accounts in the past five years. The practice also is forcing the cancellation of $540 million in public land improvement projects that had been appropriated by Congress." That $2.7 billion was paid to get necessary work done. No one wants to leave people and buildings unprotected. Yet there is little doubt that a substantial amount of that money went to elevate the profit margins of the contractors doing the work. Profits are often engines of good works. In this case they may also be engines of good policy, drawing attention, as they do, to possible opportunities for those who pay them to look to other means. For example, big profits scored every year by the fire-industrial complex suggest that the taxpayers would save tax money if Congress were to register the predictability of an annual orgy of "emergency" funding and replace it with anticipation and prevention. At that juncture, a new investment opportunity would open in the preventive (or "prescriptive") fire market. As Pyne predicts, "it is only a question of time before outsourcing extends to the burning itself." But prevention is always cheaper than panicky alleviation. The market will have its role in the fire business. But in the American system it does not have all roles.

The nation has made other choices in other spheres, such as distributing the mail, defending its shores, and enforcing its laws.[4]

Meanwhile, those of us who are watching matters unfold, and making recommendations, should remain clear that the problem is not fire dynamics but the dynamics of population movement. It is not *what* is out there in the woods, but *who* is coming into the woods— more people all the time, while their destinations get drier and hotter. Pyne is correct in saying that "our failure is how we live on the land. . . . All over the country, Americans are recolonizing their once-rural landscapes with former urbanites, powered by urban expectations, urban economics, urban aesthetics." The woods into which many of us have settled, and want to settle, do not behave according to urban expectations. The problems they present cannot simply be left to the fire department.[5]

There is no national fire department. Not yet. And what is wrong in leaving things to the market through outsourcing? *The Salt Lake Tribune*'s account of Senator Craig's statement included the comment that the largest difficulty with that resolution of the problem is that safety standards often slip. "Monday's abrupt decision by the agencies to ground the fleet of 33 aging slurry bomber aircraft [essentially tankers with dumping bays] due to concerns about airworthiness" recalled the discovery by the National Transportation Safety Board that "maintenance and inspection programs were inadequate for the air tanker fleet, which is primarily composed of vintage military planes operated by private contractors. Seven people were killed in three tanker crashes from 1994 to 2002, each caused when the wings separated from the aircraft fuselage due to structural fatigue."[6]

Whether the crews are government or corporate employees, sending them above flaming landscapes in obsolete aircraft is just one of the unacceptable outcomes of sending people into the places that are burning below. The entire system is a disaster. It needs to be changed. The haste and waste should come to an end. We should stop subsidizing the land rush into fire danger. It is time for a good, healthy taxpayer revolt. An enraged and enlightened citizenry should rise up to demand an accounting for the waste, inefficiency, and risks to firefighters who are sent into mortal danger after the accumulation of fire load and people load.

After slowing down the rate at which things are getting worse, the revolt could require Congress to deal straightforwardly with the mess we are already in. That would require reversing the ratio between "mitigation" (diminution of inflammable materials, or fire load, where people are) and "suppression" (putting fires out after they have started). Mitigation is before the fact, suppression comes after. The current relationship between prevention and desperate response has improved little since the fire-related budget for 2001 was allocated into these ratios: 70 percent "allocated to suppressing fires, getting prepared to suppress fires, building fire facilities, and establishing an emergency contingency fund to cover fire-suppression costs"; only 14 percent for fire-load reduction (and much of that spent on remote locations); and 8.5 percent on restoration of burned areas after the fact but with preventive effect. The rest went to state and local governments, largely for suppression.[7]

The fire-industrial complex can sort out its own business opportunities in this mess. The rest of us need to understand it better so we can make things better. Three factors explain much of it: (1) normal bureaucratic intractability; (2) the aversion in any society to anticipating trouble; and (3) the generosity of Americans when presented with the troubles of their neighbors—a generosity that is seldom anticipatory. Inertia, anticipation-aversion, and compassion have played into the hands of two sets of interested parties: the dispersion-industrial complex and the fire-industrial complex. Offsetting these, however, can be the wondrous self-corrective resilience of the American people. It has responded to worse challenges than this. It is not beyond the capacity of the American public to keep clearly in mind that what matters in all this is what happens to people—and to all the other species with which we inhabit the earth.

HOW THIS INQUIRY BEGAN

President Lyndon Johnson used to call some disasters "teaching opportunities." The Los Alamos/Cerro Grande Fire was a missed teaching opportunity, but if we now give it proper attention, it can become one. National policy and practice created unnecessarily dangerous circumstances in the forests into which the Los Alamos National Laboratory was inserted. Circumstances have been created similarly throughout the fire-prone regions of the nation, and not just in the West. Only after the drought of the 1990s produced fires even more frequent than those of the every-decade-or-so pattern of the preceding thousand years did Congress authorize any substantial work to make the town and the laboratory safe for the people placed in the flame zone. That set of facts went without discussion in the immediate aftermath of the fire. Instead, reputations were destroyed, pensions docked, and deception and false witness rewarded.

There was no national park near South Canyon, so I had no role in the events that brought Secretaries Babbitt and Glickman, and Jack Ward Thomas, Chief of the U.S. Forest Service, there in 1994. As director of the Park Service I signed on to the Glickman-Babbitt report along with the chiefs and directors of the other federal land management bureaus. Pledging ourselves to the "code of safe practices" it contained, we affirmed that we held "our managers accountable and expect[ed] them to hold their subordinates accountable." We asserted that we would "take action when performance is not acceptable," and we promised to create "a management and institutional environment that fosters safe behavior, personal responsibility, and actions based on sound assessment of risk."

I have been troubled ever since—as have several others who signed the document—that it did not go further. It did the honorable thing, taking responsibility and pledging accountability, but it stopped there. It did not reach beyond fixing responsibility where fire was already loose and lives already at risk. We did not yet fully understand that whatever might be done in each firefight, the work of the people who fought it was made much harder because the political process had induced people to settle in dangerous places. No one wanted to face the fact that the lives of the firefighters of South Canyon were put at risk as a result of subsidized intrusions of settlement into a fire-prone landscape.

Slowly, these admissions have been coming. They would have come faster, and lives would have been saved, if the press and public had not been distracted into searches for scapegoats. For that delay, public officials bear responsibility, and so does the press.

Immediately after the South Canyon Fire, Secretary Babbitt, Governor Roy Romer of Colorado, Director of the Bureau of Land Management Mike Dombeck, and Chief Thomas arrived in the nearest large town, Glenwood Springs. As Babbitt later recalled, "Four smoke jumpers from Missoula, seven Prineville hotshots and a helitack team had been caught in a firestorm as it exploded up the mountainside. Some had made a run for safety over the top, others tried to deploy their fire shelters." When rescue workers reached their bodies, one was found "still clutching a melted chain saw; another had made it partially into a shelter, a protruding leg and axe handle were completely incinerated. The two members of the helitack team had got a head start on their run up a nearby slope; they were finally located, their charred bodies huddled under a rock outcrop in a burned-out ravine."[8]

As a Forest Service press officer "began to read the names: 'James Mackay, smoke jumper, Missoula, Montana,'" Babbitt related, "she choked up, composed herself, then proceeded through the list." Thomas, who also remembered the events of that day, picked up another strand in the story: "There was a feeding frenzy going on with the press. All the questions were predicated on who messed up and who was going to suffer for this. It was discouraging, if not disgusting. We had left the bodies there, briefly, for the investigation, and some newspaper people sneaked in and took pictures of those kids. I was never more angry and disgusted."[9]

Jack Thomas is a large white-haired man, solidly built, pugnacious and purposeful. He came to Glenwood Springs knowing what it was like when natural systems exploded in the face of human systems not prepared for them: "You've got trees blowing up and helicopters and rocks flying through the air—it's hazardous. It's like a war." On that hot July afternoon in Glenwood Springs, he did what he could to console the Prineville crew chief who had seen seven young people die, and went to meet with the family of a helicopter crew member who was still missing. "They wanted me to tell them that we'd find him, but I figured there was almost zero chance we'd find him alive. It was very emotional for everyone." At this moment, another set of people obtruded—observers to whom it was all a "story," something out of a movie, something verging on entertainment. Thomas recalled: "As we were leaving, there was a press guy who called out, 'Hey, Chief, you got your cover-up under way?' I went after him, and the security guy with me grabbed me and said, 'You don't want to do that.' 'Yeah,' I said, 'I really do.'"[10]

There is no doubt that Thomas "really" *did*—I have seen him demonstrate his unrepentant old-fashioned sense of the dignity of public service with a glare, an expletive, and, on one or two occasions, a barely restrained fist. On that day, he had in mind the firefighters, "people in a tough job that doesn't pay very well, and there's not much room for advancement. . . . No matter what you do, you're wrong. The press beat on you, and you try to make your case for the way you did it—you have to explain why you didn't fight a fire this way or that way, and what do you hear? 'Well, didn't you make a mistake?' Yeah, it's real easy fighting one of those fires from a distance, sitting on your butt with a cold one in your hand."[11]

One of the parents of a firefighter who died on the South Canyon ridge struggled to find words to respond to Babbitt's sympathy, and was able to say, "I hope that you are going to change things." Thomas promised to "learn from the experience and not have to repeat it." He did, and so should the rest of us: there will be fewer disasters such as that at South Canyon once the primary lesson of that experience is, in fact, learned: the "things" most important to fire management are not about fire. They are about people. There are too few trained and professional firefighters, Thomas has written; they are "strung out. There is too much fuel building up out there." He is correct—and there are also too many people "strung out" in a different and more prosaic sense—strung out geographically, too far into perilous places. More than fuel has been "building up." People have been building up into canyons and down into floodplains, and some have even returned to planting the wrong crops in the Dust Bowl. They have been induced to do so by government policies that have richly rewarded a few people in the real estate business, but have proven enormously expensive to taxpayers. These policies have also become murderous to those who have died where they were induced to build, or who were sent to rescue those persuaded to settle in harm's way.[12]

Too much fuel? Some of the fuel—the combustible wood in brush and trees and fallen timber and sawdust and lumbering slash—must, no doubt, be removed. But the problem is too many people in flame zones, with more arriving every day.

7. SCAPEGOATING AS DISTRACTION IN 2000

When the Los Alamos National Laboratory was built, it was thought to be safe from hostile humans in its politically remote location on the southwestern verge of the Pajarito Plateau. "The Lab"'s highly explosive materials and rare talent were, however, placed in an area that had been subjected to wildfire every five to fifteen years for many centuries, in an especially fire-prone portion of a larger inflammable ecosystem. Between 1960 and 1975, the yearly average for fires started by lightning in the Southwest as a whole was 2,371; of these, more than a thousand took place in all but two fire seasons. Though fires were vigorously suppressed after 1920, "the number of lightning fires per year . . . grew by more than 50 percent from 1940 to 1975; the mean annual acreage burned in the Southwest has increased continuously since ca. 1960."[1]

Until the 1980s, fire suppression on all public lands was organized as if it were a military campaign. Indeed, fire was treated as an insurgent force, in wildlands treated like urban neighborhoods. The National Forest Service acted as a national fire department, with Gifford Pinchot as fire chief as well as Chief of the Forest Service. This scion of urban mercantile wealth—educated at Exeter, Yale, and in both France and Germany—became Theodore Roosevelt's chief forester, and convinced his old friend the president of the need for fire suppression everywhere—no exceptions, and right away. (Smokey the Bear was not Pinchot's mascot, however, for the stately Pinchot was not a man for mascots; Smokey was not summoned to the scene until 1944, after Pinchot's policy had been in place for three decades.)

By 1920, the ill effects of no-exceptions fire suppression were already obvious; Pinchot's policy roused the western historian and novelist Stewart Edward White to write in *Sunset Magazine*: "We are painstakingly building a firetrap that will piecemeal, but in the long run completely, defeat the very aim of fire protection itself. The only question that remains is whether, after accumulating kindling . . . we can now get rid of it safely. In other words, if we try to burn it out now, will we not get a destructive fire? We have caught a bear by the tail—can we let it go?"[2]

Around Los Alamos, Stewart Edward White's bear—the feral cousin of Smokey—was growing in ferocity from 1943 through the 1980s. One-size-fits-all fire suppression permitted fallen branches and pine duff to accumulate thickety growth in the national forests around Los Alamos, and virtually nothing was done to reduce such fire load within the boundaries of "the Lab." Next door, the landscape of the Bandelier National Monument was less dangerous to people both because new residences for new people were not being constructed within the park and because fire load was being systematically reduced, tract by tract, by a series of prescribed fires conducted by the monument's management. The tragedy for that management and for national fire policy was that a "destructive fire" did, in fact, break out in 2000, just as they were finishing their job.

The United States needed a "secure lab," as that term was used by nuclear scientists in 1943. The immediate necessities of scientific warfare were imperative, but the long-term imperatives of protecting the place and its people from natural hazards were ignored. The place was not biologically secure—but biology was not the business of the scientists at Los Alamos in the 1940s. Soon, however, they became aware that they were situated in a tinderbox. George Cowan, who directed some of the laboratory's most important research, has told me that card games among scientists relaxing at the end of the day were several times interrupted by fires on the adjacent hills, permitting famous physicists to get their exercise helping out the fire crews. There was, however, no systematic effort to protect "the Lab" from those fires, nor did the congressional sponsors who put this national asset in such peril follow the initial construction budgets with commensurate continuing allocations for fire protection.[3]

Despite the great fires of 1954 and 1977, the laboratory received huge appropriations to make bombs, but almost nothing to protect its people. Every fire manager in the region knew that it was virtually certain that wildfire would strike again, as it had in five thousand places across the Pajarito Plateau since record-keeping began. No human intervention was necessary; three-quarters of these historic fires were caused by lightning. On average, the Bandelier monument was hit by eleven lightning fires every year. In ancient times, those natural fires were augmented by the people living there—the valley of Bandelier Creek was heavily populated for three centuries after A.D. 1200. Erratic weather caused dense settlement where growing conditions could be steadied by drawing upon springs and streams; the plateau was urbanized by eight or more pueblos of one thousand rooms or more, some of them, on its western flanges, persisting until the coming of the Spaniards. The inhabitants made use of controlled fire for driving game and to encourage growth of desired plants, and they further reduced fire load in the landscape by gathering wood to use in their fireplaces and pits for cooking and heating.

This rough balance was disrupted in the sixteenth century by the Spaniards. They arrived on horses, animals by then extinct in North America, bringing with them other exotic animals—cows, sheep, burros, and hogs—exotic plants, including wheat, and exotic diseases such as smallpox. The exuberant grasslands of the plateau attracted herdsmen, at first for sheep, a few cows, and goats. In the 1880s, the railroad arrived, providing access to markets without thinning the animals on the way. Herds of as many as twelve thousand cattle grazed the meadows and mountain-slope savannahs of the Pajarito, consuming the grass that for millennia had provided the natural fuel for frequent light, purging smaller fires. Cattle provided food and hides to humans, but their net effect upon the land was to make it more dangerous to humans and to all other animals. The Indians had cleared and burned the firewood, making way for grasses. Now the sheep and cows ate the grass down to the roots. Only when on the verge of starvation would they consume the unappetizing species of trees that replaced it, so today most of the grass has been replaced; eroded and dusty slopes are punctuated by stunted junipers and piñons, wherever these scrubby but inflammable trees can find water to suck from the land. Where some ponderosa pines survived, they crowd into dog-hair growth of little trees, turning to the sun like a cramped crowd of Times Square spectators watching an animated sign. They are there, gawking, when lightning strikes.

The arrival of federal land managers changed the ecology yet again. Fewer sheep and cows were permitted on national forest land, and ultimately all livestock were driven out of both Bandelier National Monument and the Los Alamos National Laboratory. Offsetting these opportunities for restoration was the cult of fire suppression, initially accepted by both the Forest and Park Services for political reasons, and given a meretricious immortality by the iconic image of Smokey the Bear. Areas that had been grazed or clear-cut, or both, grew up again in regiments of same-sized, tightly packed little trees, tangled with fallen limbs, the parched husks of bushes, and mats of resinous pine needles. When lightning came, or arson, or careless campers, this fire load was ready to burn.

All the ills of the inflammable West cannot be blamed on fire suppression. Some terrain does not function as a nursery for little stems, and in these areas neither "thinning" for a "Healthy Forest" nor prescriptive burning is necessary. However, it is certainly a blessing to the fire-prone West in general that in 1978, and more vigorously after 1985, federal fire policy shifted from fire suppression to preventive burning. Unkempt growth of dense and virtually uniform forests, which had been increasing for years, was demonstrably becoming more and more dangerous. Fires were getting worse, not better.

Since there was no surrogate for fire except a massive and continuous federal works program, and since the nation was not ready for that, policy shifted to controlled burning that could emulate quick, intense, purgative natural grassland fires while limiting their spread. After becoming superintendent at Bandelier in the early 1990s, Roy Weaver, a veteran of three decades of government service, encouraged his already seasoned staff of fire managers and scientists to step up the pace of controlled burning. For ten years, they conducted a regular process of setting two or three preventive burns annually, achieving the effects of a natural rhythm of small fires in a fifteen-year cycle. Fire load had been reduced on four-fifths of the monument by 1999. Whereas Los Alamos reduced fuel load on only 550 acres by the year 2000, the Park Service had by that time completed its work on more than 20,000 acres. No fire reduction was undertaken in the National Forest until 1996; it had no authorized fuel-reduction program until 2000.

Though they made every citizen aware of the dangers of man-made fire from the skies, the laboratory's proprietors refused to take wildfire sufficiently seriously. When they wrote and spoke of a possible Russian missile attack on the United States, everyone could recall the horrors wrought by fire upon European and Japanese cities. But sufficient time had passed since the great wildfires of 1910 that the same public had no way to recall that wildfire could be horrible as well. There was, however, an unintended benefit to the science of wildfire prevention from Cold War anxieties. The Forest Service had a lot of experience with fire. So those primarily interested in urban fire bestowed upon the Service generous dollops of additional funds from the nuclear weapons program. The funds escalated after the Cuban Missile Crisis. From those grants and the agency's own internal momentum came the research leading to "the Rothermel model of fire behavior that became the core of the national fire-danger rating system." The irony of a transfer to wildland fire management of systems grounded in urban experience doubled when the urban Rothermel model broke down in a place at the wildland/urban interface, where a more appropriate model was needed. Stephen Pyne has noted that Rothermel modeling failed to predict the burning of Los Alamos, thereby completing a circle "from the same Manhattan Project that erected The Lab in the first place."[4]

On Thursday, May 4, 2000, at 7:00 p.m., the now-famous test burn was started in a strategic corner of Bandelier. Several weeks earlier, the fire managers of Los Alamos and the National Forest had been informed that the test would take place, and they were briefed again on the plans that morning, at an interagency meeting in Los Alamos. The Park Service crew set the fire, observed it for an hour, and on the basis of well-established criteria made the decision that conditions were proper to allow it to continue burning. (Those criteria included on-site conditions and the confirmed availability of backup crews.)

One of the backup crews was reviewed at 11:00 p.m., and to the dismay of the fire managers found inadequate to the task. The crew was sent home, and at 3:00 a.m. on the fifth, a request for the second backup was telephoned to the interagency dispatch office in Santa Fe. The replacement did not arrive until after noon. By then, a helicopter was dropping water to slow the fire's spread into the forested area, and the Park Service crew had extended the fire down toward a paved highway, a fuel break parallel to the winds, and could concentrate on the eastern extremities of burning, beyond which lay the dense fire load on Forest Service land.

As suppression efforts continued, the Park Service fire managers consulted with their counterparts at the Los Alamos Laboratory, Los Alamos County, and the Forest Service. A fire-retardant aircraft was summoned, but it developed engine trouble and arrived three hours late. Nonetheless, by the close of day on Saturday, May 6, the interagency effort, its strategy jointly determined, seemed to be successful. The blaze was contained within previously established control lines and the highway. A backfire was set along the southwest control line near the highway. Suddenly, on Sunday, the backfire broke out as high winds from the west provided more oxygen. Thomas Ribe of

Santa Fe, the most assiduous and careful student of these events, continues the story: "The bottom of the west fire line smoldered into some logs, heated up and bang, it flared into the trees, ran along the highway as a sudden crown fire, jumped into the canyon then over the ridge and ran north toward Los Alamos."[5]

There was a two-day respite on Monday and Tuesday, but on Wednesday sustained high winds returned. The fire rose up as an uncontrollable, roaring wall of flame sweeping through the treetops on the ridgeline. It missed most of the town, Ribe writes, though "two crown fires touched residential areas, most houses burned from surface fires in heavy yard debris, from house to house, domino fashion, through neighborhoods."[6]

The history leading to these events was forgotten—the assumption of risk for an entire town, the failures to warn people of danger and to take action against it, the too-long-delayed efforts to reduce fire load in the surrounding woods, but not in the laboratory itself—as the firefighters struggled and the old air tankers and obsolete helicopters flew close to the flames. Householders gathered what possessions were portable and raced to get away. Among those evacuating with their families and a few cherished belongings were scientists who had precise knowledge of the risks these advancing flames presented, for they had done classified work on both fire and the limitations of fire suppressants. A few also knew just where, underground, there were explosive materials.

LOOKING FOR RESPONSIBLE PARTIES

As the fire raged and people suffered, the press arrived, avid to fix blame. A local newspaper editor accused unnamed "bureaucrats" of "arrogance and criminal incompetence."[7] The libel laws being what they were, the editorialist confined his charge to "astounding lack of common sense" on the part of "bureaucrats" within the Park Service. The state's senior United States senator, Pete Domenici, having uttered his own indictment of guilt in similar language, demanded an investigation by the General Accounting Office (now the Government Accountability Office). The verdict was in—let the court now convene.

This was not so disgraceful a performance as it seemed, though it was irresponsible enough: the senator was misinformed, and so was the press. The misinformation began with the communication to them of a non-fact, which was embellished in riffs from the press and politicians. Politicians, press, and public were led to believe that at an interagency meeting in the days immediately before ignition, opposition to the burn had been expressed by representatives of the Forest Service and Los Alamos. Further, it was widely believed that the Weather Service had offered another warning. In fact, no such opposition to the burn had been offered by the laboratory or the Forest Service. And there never was a warning from the National Weather Service.

While the Pajarito was still smoldering, the people of Los Alamos were just beginning to search through debris for things once precious to them. As if to encourage them and the public in general to demand more information about the relationship of fire and settlement in dangerous places, and to be dissatisfied with the "blame game" for the Cerro Grande Fire, six fires blazed up in the forests east of Santa Fe. In that direction there was no Park Service presence, and there had been no prescribed burns. The seventeen-thousand-acre Viveash Fire swept the Pecos River watershed, and the Spring Fire threatened the water supply of the city of Las Vegas. It was not in the interest of either the press or the politicians to connect events on the eastern horizon with events on the western horizon—so the six instructive fires went unheeded as the public read of more searches for *who*, not *what*, was to blame. Los Alamos began presenting the bills. Ultimately, more than $800 million was allocated for federal assistance, and no essential policy was changed to slow the pace of migration into fire danger.

Secretary Babbitt appointed an Interagency Fire Investigation Team on May 11. The team was directed to begin immediate interviews with those in the Park Service, the Forest Service, and at Los

Alamos who had participated in the fire management or who had advised that management. The team met for the first time on the eleventh. Assuring the waiting press that "the Federal Wildland Fire Policy is sound," it laid out its conclusions upon the unarguable principle that "the success of the policy depends upon strict adherence to the implementation actions." Thus the team confined its inquiry to hearing evidence of the degree to which the Park Service officials at Bandelier had strictly adhered to the policy they were given. Most of those giving evidence were exhausted, anxious, harassed, and subject to a natural eagerness to displace blame. Largely on the basis of assertions by John Romero of the National Forest Service and Dr. Richard Burick of Los Alamos, the investigators concluded that Park Service officials had been guilty of seven violations of that policy. Those conclusions were widely believed to be true. They still are—though three later and more careful inquiries concurred that they were not.

On May 12, the *Santa Fe New Mexican,* in an article headlined WILDFIRE BLAME GAME BEGINS, reported that Superintendent Weaver had been placed on administrative leave. "Pending investigation of the controlled burn he ordered," the press continued to report that "a series of errors by Bandelier officials caused the fire." A few days later, the *New Mexican* put the matter more directly: "The report places blame squarely at the feet of Bandelier officials." It did. But the later and more careful inquiries did not.

After the 2000 election, a new administration took office with no interest in awakening sleeping dogs. The larger circumstances of the fire went—and continue to go—unconsidered. The stage went dark again. At Los Alamos, it became bad manners to talk about how a large, natural, recurring horizon-to-horizon fire had become inevitable, though some people had, indeed, warned of it all along. Craig Allen, the resident fire scientist at Bandelier, and both William Armstrong and Claudia Standish of the National Forest Service had held public meetings at Los Alamos from 1995 onward to warn of fire generally, and of the perils of building houses in the midst of inflammable materials. Homeowners were urged to take responsibility for diminishing fire load—including piles of firewood—near their houses.

Allen is a chunky man of middle height, prone to contemplative silence and difficult to provoke into statements of more than a single sentence. I have never heard him raise his voice, though I suppose he must when he calls his dog. His style is sardonic; he explains but does not preach. Standish is a small, spare woman apparently without fear of taking matters into her own hands. Allen, Standish, and Armstrong are not the kind of people who would do well selling Fuller brushes or Avon products. That is not their style. But they did succeed in shaking the conviction held by most people in the disciplined and deferential community at Los Alamos that those in charge of their lives could not possibly have put them in harm's way. They went house to house, warning and advising the residents of Los Alamos who were willing to listen that they should reduce the fire load around their homes. On their own time, without encouragement, Allen, Standish, and Armstrong sought to convince the inhabitants to cut back the brush around houses, keep the eaves clear of dry leaves, and maintain water on hand for hosing down wooden roofs. Many people refused to heed them—surely, they said, if there was a fire problem they would have been told about it. Others, however, listened, and acted—and afterward had reason to be grateful. Allen, Standish, and Armstrong saved many houses, many precious belongings, and probably many lives.

THE GAO AND THE SCHENCK REPORT

When calamity struck in the spring of 2000, Senator Domenici's request to the General Accounting Office produced another report on July 20. The GAO limited its inquiry to allocating blame. It did not draw any larger lessons. It did, however, produce the unexpected conclusion that there was *no evidence* to support assertions made by "officials with the Santa Fe National Forest and Los Alamos National Laboratory . . . [to] the press that they warned Bandelier National

Monument officials beforehand not to set the prescribed burn." This was a shocker, and it followed a retraction by one of those officials, Romero of the National Forest Service, of his earlier claim to have administered such a warning. Another official, Dr. Burick of Los Alamos, had assured not only the press but also Congress, under oath, that a subordinate, Eugene Darling, had attended a meeting with the Park Service and Forest Service just before ignition at which he had warned them against conducting the test fire. Darling refused to back up Burick's claim, stating that no such warning had been issued.[8]

Conflicts of evidence were appearing. The GAO concluded that warnings from these other agencies had *not* been "communicated to Bandelier officials before they started the prescribed burn." Such a conclusion, broadening the range of responsibility and opening larger questions, was not welcome to those wanting the whole subject to settle quickly on scapegoats and get off the front pages. Nobody associated with the history of fire management within or near Los Alamos would come out well if that history were reviewed. And it was in no one's interest to tackle the role of "the Lab" in setting a precedent for locating large numbers of people at government expense in fire-prone areas, and leaving them without warning, without systems to meet fires when they came, and without adequate means to get out quickly.

Beyond those questions lurked all the others raised in this book—questions that powerful people wished to be left unasked. So scapegoats would have to play their assigned role, while everyone else went back to business as usual. It is no discredit to Anne-Kathryn Ziehe, of Senator Domenici's staff, that she was not the one to say, "Let's stop here and see what's wrong with the system!" The senator has been a staunch advocate of development in the high, dry West, and especially in his relatively impoverished state. Restraints on that development, even warnings about its consequences—not to mention withdrawal of federal subsidies inducing it—were the very last subjects he would have wanted raised in the flickering light of wildfire.

So Ziehe's response for Domenici to the GAO report was to insist that it included "a lot of damning things" about Weaver and his fire-fighters: "It says they really didn't know what they were doing." For many years, the senator had been the godfather of appropriations for Los Alamos; it would not do for people to think that neither he nor the management of "the Lab" had not known for all those years "what they were doing"—or leaving undone. There had been no senatorial or congressional support, or endorsement for the efforts of Allen, Armstrong, or Standish to make up, by their own efforts, for the absence of proper fire-load management on a government installation and in what was essentially a government town. And no thanks since.[9]

On May 27, a second interagency Independent Review Board appointed by Babbitt made its report. The board pressed no farther than the first into the sense of national *policies* that lead to the violent interactions of natural and civil systems. The board's task was narrower. *The Santa Fe New Mexican* headlined its story REVIEW REAFFIRMS BLAME FOR BANDELIER.[10]

Babbitt sustained a ban on Park Service preventive burns, offering his personal judgment that there were "serious systemic problems in the way the Park Service conducts prescribed burns. . . . Although the proper policies and procedures are in place, they are not being followed." Domenici informed the press that he was "happy that they've taken the matches away from the National Park Service." Fourth and fifth inquiries were then set in motion. The fourth, a Senate hearing chaired by Domenici, made no effort to engage with the root causes of the problems—that towns and buildings have been set in landscapes prone to recurrent fire. Nor did the Senate Committee appear to be animated by a desire to review the national fire policies in place. However, the hearing recorded testimony that could be compared with statements made at the next, and fifth, board of review, headed by William Schenck, the National Park Service Regional Director for the Midwest.[11]

Schenck is another veteran of many decades of service to the national parks, and a man of pronounced conservative political views.

The task of the group he chaired was to reexamine what had been said in "the blame game" about the events at Bandelier and Los Alamos. His board had more time and opportunity to cross-examine witnesses than either the investigative team or the GAO had had. This was because Denis Galvin, in charge of the Park Service at the time, drafted the board's directive.

In a letter written four years later, Galvin recalled that he had noted that "at the same time as Cerro Grande, a prescribed NPS [National Park Service] fire on the north rim at Grand Canyon jumped out of prescription and burned for weeks. It was the same weather incident that drove Cerro Grande. Right away I got skeptical about blame."[12]

What was different about the Grand Canyon fire, and the public response to it, from what happened at Bandelier/Los Alamos? Robert Arnberger, a tough veteran of managing big parks with big public constituencies, was the superintendent at the Grand Canyon at the time of the fire there. He later explained to me that he had been both luckier and politically more clever than his counterparts in New Mexico. He had no national laboratory or garrison town on the edge of the Grand Canyon to worry about. He could control his circumstances in an area with fewer people present. And he had the public outcry about the Los Alamos fire distracting attention. Still, his grasp of the politics of fire also helped, enabling him to provide an example for others.[13]

As Arnberger tells his story: "I saw the witch hunt forming up at Bandelier and the obvious fact that the superintendent [Roy Weaver] could not escape the stake." When the fire broke out at Grand Canyon, "we were in better shape for a lot of reasons. We had one of the best fire programs. No structures had been burned. Most of the fire was in wild country." So Arnberger pulled together "an expert interagency panel of about 10 experienced and noted firemen," which took barely a week to report only "a few minor mistakes in regards to the escape and solid evaluation of the fire program." And when Arnberger and Galvin sent their conclusions right to the Secretary of the Interior, "little came of it . . . some Arizona press, etc. The best defense is often a good offense." Later, Galvin commented on Arnberger's story: "Ever hear of the Grand Canyon fire? . . . Probably not. That's the point." Galvin and Arnberger have also concurred on another point: if the discourse opened by a big fire event is limited to who is to blame, not much of value will be learned beyond managing the press and public perception.[14]

Galvin also saw the witch hunt forming up at Bandelier and the likelihood that Roy Weaver would not escape the stake. So he did what he could to make the process fairer by sending Schenck to his task with a novel set of instructions. The investigation was not a criminal one, but rather, a personnel action. (Personnel actions provide fewer protections for the accused than do criminal proceedings—the accused, who is merely going to be fired, does not generally have the right to confront hostile witnesses or be represented by counsel.) But with a witch hunt and a blame game far advanced, it was manifest that Weaver would get little mercy from press or public. So Galvin instructed Schenck to adhere to the procedures for criminal cases. A little unusual, but under the circumstances offering something closer to due process for Weaver.

The truth did finally emerge, and prevented further damage to those lined up for further scapegoating. That was all Galvin and Schenck could achieve. They were individual employees acting as the administration of one president of the United States was ending and another was about to take office. Galvin and Schenck had no authority to expand their assignment to include the long-term political—or natural—history behind the conditions under which firefighters at both Bandelier and the Grand Canyon worked. The assignment they had been given by the outgoing Secretary of the Interior had been to investigate a failure to follow specific procedures. Galvin and Schenck had no franchise to go beyond that to inquire into the conditions making those procedures necessary. John Romero of the National Forest Service was right, in the end: "It's basically blame." The press agreed: on June 10, 2000, it was reported that Roy Weaver had taken responsibility "for the decision to ignite the planned burn that erupted into the uncontrolled 47,000 acre Cerro Grande Fire."[15]

Not until October, however, did Schenck's panel hold its last hearings. The press was no longer paying attention when the panel stated its conclusion in a draft report: the hurried inquiry of mid-May, and by extension the press coverage based upon testimony from the same informants as those at the May hearing, was grievously in error, and had unjustly fixed blame upon Weaver and his deputies. A capitalized notation, "FACTS IN DISPUTE," appears at four crucial points in the draft. The conclusion of the Schenck panel was that the Investigation Team Report had been "produced in a remarkably compressed timeframe." Written in haste and under pressure, it "was not always consistent with the facts and, sometimes, inappropriately, measured performance against policy requirements." That pressure came from the press, the public, and embattled public officials. "The magnitude of loss . . . certainly influenced the swift reaction and call to accountability." Indeed. So swift had the reaction been that none of the accounts of this classic event in the history of human intrusion into natural systems sought answers to the question of ultimate accountability for the losses incurred. Accountability? Who was accountable for ordering some people, and encouraging others, to settle into a very dangerous place, and leaving them there so long unwarned and unprotected against known dangers?[16]

The report lay in Secretary Babbitt's office for a month. Then, on the brink of his departure from office, Babbitt sent it back to the Park Service for revision, writing the director of the Park Service, Robert Stanton, "Something is going on here. . . . It is our obligation to get the issues out into the open, deal forthrightly with the problem and get it fixed. From what little appears in the Draft, I suspect we have a large problem not unlike the interagency dispatch breakdown that preceded the tragedy at South Canyon in 1994. We must make every effort to understand these problems and get them resolved before there is another tragedy."[17]

There remained "a large problem." But it was not a problem the new administration decided to take up. When Babbitt handed the Schenck Report to Gale Norton, the new Secretary of the Interior, he urged her in his exit interview to pursue his request for a broad review of policy. Instead, the report as a whole was sequestered, with parts of it leaked so often over so long a time that there was little left that might be deemed newsworthy. In one conference call, the chief of staff to the Secretary told several dozen people that he had no desire to release the report. In Washington, when the bottle is left on the shelf and a little open, it is known that the fizz goes out—the press loses interest, and is less and less likely to ask for changes in policy. Finally, the Schenck Report was issued unchanged from the Park Service's Denver press office, accompanied by a covering memorandum not from the Secretary, not from the director, but from Karen Wade, the regional director. John Wright, spokesman for the Department of the Interior in the new administration, pushed the subject as far away as possible: "Of course," said Wright to the press, "you are well aware of the fact that this is a new administration."[18]

Of course. It was a new administration, with less interest in stirring things up than the old. The fire-industrial complex was doing just fine. So were the developers of flame zones. So were all the interested parties, except the people who awoke in the night to find their neighborhood in flames. And what of the young men and women sent to fight wildfires? Stewart Edward White's "firetrap" was baited with more and more subsidies every year. Meanwhile, as Harold Biswell of the School of Forestry at the University of California predicted not long after White's warning, "wild fire damage and the number of homes burned will become much greater. Suppression costs will continue to skyrocket . . . [until there is] a greater awakening to the fact that fire is natural." As Biswell told his contemporaries, "fire management professionals should be honored when they return blackened and exhausted from the wild fire wars," but must they fight those wars everywhere in the West? Must we anticipate that nothing will be done to diminish the likelihood that they will be fighting fires all over the East as the climate warms and dries there, too? Might it not be possible that someday soon we may honor those who are sent to fight fires by sending them only as the last, not the first, resort? And could we not honor those who begin to reduce the number of fire wars to fight?[19]

Must it get worse before we make it better? It is already costly enough in lives and money. As I was writing this book, *The Albuquerque Tribune* carried a near-final computation of the cost just in putting the Los Alamos National Laboratory and its supporting village in a fire battle zone and leaving it unprotected. Four hundred and three families lost their homes; the taxpayers paid more than twenty thousand claims made by victims on the Federal Emergency Management Agency (FEMA), totaling $546,000,000, plus $23,500,000 in cleanup costs; the state of New Mexico and local bodies spent $129,000,000 on "clean up . . . and continuing remediation"; and the taxpayers paid $350,000,000 for fire remediation through "the Lab."[20]

8. SCAPEGOATING AND FALSE REMEDIES

Two years after the Cerro Grande/Los Alamos Fire, and six years after the South Canyon Fire, another broke out, a hundred miles to the southwest of Los Alamos on the Mogollon Rim of Arizona. It became known as the Rodeo-Chediski Fire, with "Chediski" pronounced by the local Apaches as "Shed-Sky." It burned across the Mogollon Rim, a ravaged land, part of which was being bravely nursed back to health by a very poor Indian nation, the White Mountain Apaches, as they sought to build a tourist economy grounded in a healthy environment. They had been moving in that direction by refusing to permit further overgrazing or more rounds of profligate timbering after the land had suffered from four rounds of unhealthy forestry.

When the Apaches migrated onto the plateau in the fifteenth and sixteenth centuries they found it well forested, though evidence of fire must have been visible because the archaeological record tells that wildfires had often struck the Mogollon. The Spaniards, next to arrive, rejoiced in magnificent stands of fire-tolerant ponderosa pines in parkland as elegant as an English estate or a German managed forest. The grasses were as high in midsummer as a mounted horseman's stirrups. But after overgrazing and over-timbering, most of the grasses and big trees were gone; despite all the Apaches could do, it was ready to burn disastrously. It did so just as respectful forestry was beginning to show its virtues, in much the same way that the Cerro Grande Fire erupted when the fire managers at Bandelier were nearly done with their prescriptive burning.

When the fire came, it burned 460,000 acres and destroyed four hundred houses. Forty thousand people were evacuated. As the embers were still smoldering, Jane Hull, the governor of Arizona, and Jon Kyl, one of its senators, took turns directing public indignation against scapegoats; the real history of the place and the real causes of the fire went unmentioned. Still, they did a service to history by using certain phrases that were so grossly misleading as to draw attention to the very history they were so assiduously failing to discuss. The governor in particular insisted that there was "nothing to learn" from experience in the Midwest and East, coupling that assertion with a call to solve the problem of fire by turning the still-recovering timberlands over to lumber companies for further cutting. Even the least curious of observers could legitimately ask, If lumbering is the cure, then how did lumbering work elsewhere—East or West? And here on the Mogollon Rim, how much lumbering had there already been where the burn occurred? The answers to these questions suggest the outlines of what might be a genuinely healthy forest plan.

THE FIRE AND THE SLASH

Two-thirds of the area burned on the Apache reservation lay within its heavily logged portion. Those areas worst hit were still littered with lumbering debris, with old logging roads everywhere. A hiking guide says of the Mogollon that "you can't hike a quarter mile without hitting a road"—twenty-two hundred miles of roads, three miles of road per square mile, built for timber extraction.[1]

Any forest professional knew what was likely to happen. The scene was set for "a big one"—yet people kept coming to live there, putting their life savings into houses in the midst of the firetrap. Then it went up in flames, confirming the judgment of the Forest Service that "timber harvest, through its effect upon forest structure, local microclimate, and fuels accumulation, has increased fire severity more than any other recent human activity." That had been a settled doctrine recently reaffirmed to Congress jointly by the Agriculture and Interior departments: "The removal of large, merchantable trees from forests does not reduce fire risk, and may in fact increase such risk." One of the founders of the Forest Service, T. S. Woolsey, wrote after the great fires of 1911 that "it is after logging that damage from fire is greatest." Lumbering encourages the growth of brush and little trees by permitting sunlight to reach them directly after the big marketable timber has been "thinned." Lumber companies have no reason to bother with such low-quality stuff, so they leave it in place. It then serves to provide ladders of flame from ground fires into the treetops.[2]

Senator Kyl and Governor Hull paid little heed to such matters as they moved from scapegoating to urging a speedy return to lumbering as the way to avoid further wildfire. Their scapegoating was endorsed by the *Lewiston Morning Tribune,* which laid the blame for the distress of the refugees and for the destruction of their homes on "granola-crunching, crystal-worshipping . . . environmentalist wackos and their socialist allies" who had prevented the Forest Service from commissioning lumber companies to crop the land, presumably thereby diminishing fire load.[3]

The senator and the governor, and several newspapers, followed up with other allegations that those environmental "wackos" had done their dirty work by suing to make certain that any timbering contracts on Forest Service land complied with the Endangered Species Act. Had environmentalists only allowed the Forest Service to ignore the law, the argument went, the lumber companies would have gone in for what they wanted, plus the brush, and the stumps, slash, and sawdust, leaving the place spick and span. In the Cerro Grande case, the scapegoats were federal officials. In the Rodeo-Chediski case, the "wackos" took their place, leaving the "feds" to enjoy a respite, cast in new roles as advocates of lumbering. Gale Norton, though Secretary of the Interior, joined the *Lewiston Morning Tribune* in asserting that the "environmentalists were to blame for recent wildfires because they had gone to court to block the federal government's proposed thinning projects."[4]

The governor's style was more colorful, but her message was the same: the guilty parties were "radical environmentalists . . . [who] would rather see the forests burn than to see sensible forest management. . . . The policies that are coming from the East Coast, that are coming from the environmentalists that say we don't need to log, we don't need to thin our forests, are absolutely ridiculous. Nobody from the East Coast knows how to manage these fires and I for one have had it." Her solution? Succinctly, it was this: "Health can be restored to our forest by thinning. . . . If somebody makes a profit on the deal that's even better."[5]

Neither the diagnosis nor the prescription was persuasive locally, where everybody knew that the worst of the fire, and nearly two-thirds of the acreage burned, was on Apache land, not Forest Service land. No lawsuits had been filed to stop the Apaches from timbering. The "wackos" had not wasted their paper and ink on enforcing the Endangered Species Act on the reservation. Instead, they had spent that paper and ink on suits affecting something less than one-twentieth of the remainder of the area burned on Forest Service land.

The scapegoating had a familiar ring, but the words used led some people to wonder why politicians were so eager to send the press on a wacko chase rather than in pursuit of understanding. What indeed has been the American experience with lumbering and wildfire? Why was the governor of Arizona so eager to convince her listeners that "nobody from the East Coast" knew anything useful about "how to manage" wildfires, forested land, or lumbering?[6]

Was the East Coast truly without any experience useful in the Southwest? How about the Midwest?

LESSONS

The killer fires in the East and the Midwest have broken out on cut-over land. With more than two hundred years of experience with wildfire, residents from Maine to Minnesota have learned in tragedy after tragedy that people will die unless lumbering is done with very great care and at a safe distance from towns. The lesson has been that death and pain and loss often come upon those who rush into the sawdust and stumpage, unaware of its dangers.

In October 1825, lumbermen pressing into the North Woods of Maine left stacks of slash and piles of sawdust that might be ignited by a lightning strike. The inevitable occurred. The ensuing fire burned three million acres, showing no respect for the state's international boundary with New Brunswick.

In October 1871, 3,780,000 acres burned after lumbering was done in Wisconsin and Upper Michigan. Thousands of homesteads and five towns were burned and fifteen hundred people killed, five times as many as in the Great Chicago Fire of that year. In the annals of the Midwest, the Great Peshtigo Fire is remembered as the consequence of both promiscuous lumbering and the failure of railroad companies to remove the fire load produced when they cut their way into the woods to log lumber-carrying rails. The death toll would have been much worse had fleeing settlers not been able to find refuge in two rivers and in Green Bay. An eyewitness, Peter Pernin, described the ferocity of the blaze: "Large wooden houses [were] torn from their foundations and caught up like straws by two opposing currents of air which raised them till they came in contact with the stream of fire." Not everyone who died was burned to death. So ferocious was the conflagration that many died from suffocation after the fire consumed all the available oxygen.[7]

Three years later, a dry winter brought so little snow that spring log drives could not be floated down the St. Croix River between Minnesota and Wisconsin. Small boys waded it, bank to bank. By midsummer the stumpage was aflame again, generating heat "so terrific" that it burned "out all traces of stumps." In 1879, fires burned out the homesteaders around Grantsburg, Wisconsin; "Only when buildings in town were threatened did 'all the men and boys' turn out to fight it."[8]

In September 1881, a million acres of Lower Michigan burned after

A contemporary newspaper illustration of people fleeing the burning mill town of Peshtigo, in the overlumbered region of Wisconsin, during the fire in 1871. The Peshtigo Fire killed more people than the Great Chicago Fire in the same year. (Wisconsin Historical Society Digital Library)

"Spot fires" can be ignited by sparks and flying embers more than a mile in advance of a crown fire. But where the lumber, slash, brush, and other inflammable materials have been removed by firewise action, spot fires near residential areas can sometimes be confined, and the advance of the main forest fire slowed, before the two unite and overwhelm civic defenses. (USDA, photograph by Bob Nichols)

lumbering. One hundred and sixty-nine bodies were counted. Some of the fire's survivors, and those who had lived through the Peshtigo Fire, were still in the woods in 1894 when the most profitable lumbering was being done across the St. Croix, around the Minnesota town of Hinckley. The getting was good. The total production between 1840 and 1912, "if loaded on to standard log cars would have required 2.2 million rail cars."[9]

A row of those standard log cars were lying on the railroad siding at Hinckley, "stacked with lumber higher than any of the buildings on Main Street . . . some said as high as the roof of the Congregational Church." Beyond the cars could be seen stumpage as far as the river, patched with windrows of sawdust and littered with dry branches. The town lay within a battlefield of "combustible cutover land." Summer had brought a baking Minnesota sun, and as the land dried out, a series of little fires spread from slash pile to slash pile, "all the way to the town of Pokegama, nine miles to the south." A little after noon, word came over the telegraph that Pokegama and all its inhabitants had been "engulfed in flames." At Hinckley "the volunteer fire department barely had time to deploy to the edge of town when the monster fire struck. A wave of scorching, overwhelming, heat swept over the fire fighters as building after building broke out in flames. . . . Hinckley [was] transformed into an island in a sea of flames."[10]

Several hundred people managed to board a train sidetracked beside the lumber mill but fueled and in readiness. "The heat was so great that the paint on the passenger cars was beginning to blister," but the train made it through "the blazing forest till it reached the town of Sandstone where it warned the inhabitants of the coming conflagration. The firestorm, however, was hard on their heels and within minutes of the train leaving Sandstone, that town was destroyed with the loss of forty-five people. When the train reached the trestle bridge over the Kettle River, they found it in flames. The engineer opened the throttle and the train made it across just before the bridge collapsed."[11]

When the fire had burned itself out, people returned to find the bodies of "dogs, cats, chickens and stock" that had inhaled the terrible heat and "died in their tracks without serious burns. In one instance a man was stricken down, but not burned enough to destroy his clothes, and in one of his pockets was found a small leather purse in which were four silver dollars welded together in one solid piece." Two hundred people had run for their lives up the railroad track; "as the flames gained on them the slow of foot perished one by one," but some had reached another train, which made a run for safety. It failed, but before it was consumed, it unloaded its passengers into a swamp, where they cowered until the timber and brush around them were consumed and they could return to the land.[12]

The fire wiped out Hinckley and other Minnesota towns—Sandstone, Pokegama, Mission Creek, and Partridge—and killed 413 people. In Wisconsin, across the river, the hamlet of Phillips had gone to the flames in July. Barronett burned on the same day as Hinckley; "the refugees of Barronett no sooner found shelter in Shell Lake than flames surrounded that town. Although more than fifty buildings burned, Shell Lake was able to save its mill and the lives of its citizens. Among the other mill towns devastated that fire season were Comstock, Benoit, Marengo, and Mason. An estimated 1.4 million acres of pineland and cutover were consumed by the fire."[13]

West Coast lumbering got under way seriously in the 1890s, and in September 1902, thirty-eight people were killed in a million-acre blaze in Yacolt, Washington. Meanwhile, lumbering in the East went forward, and in April 1903, six hundred thousand acres burned in the Adirondacks, in New York. Sporadic major fires continued in Maine—as recently as 1947.

In 1910, according to Stephen Pyne, farmers "around Manora, Long Island, battled to save houses from a wildfire that scoured the nearby woodlands," while others fought blazes threatening the towns of Ogunquit, Maine, and Plymouth, Massachusetts. Not all the terrain around Plymouth is rock; much of it is covered with resinous scrub pine. In New Jersey, in the summer of 1908, fire wardens in similar pine barrens had to be reinforced by volunteering "men, women, and children." Along Lake George, on the fringe of the Adirondacks, fires started early that year as lightning strikes set the interior of that much-burned area aflame, while the Catskills nearby erupted as well. By September, "there were fires in Maine and a yellow haze settled over New York State." Conditions were grave in New England from 1908 through 1910, but no graver than those that confronted the mayors of Santa Fe and Flagstaff in 2005.[14]

Pyne has drawn the following conclusions: "Almost all recorded big fires in American history, until the past few decades, occurred amidst landclearing, typically associated with logging. Partly that reflects a distortion of recording—the fires were registered because they affected people. But even in the 1910 Northern Rockies fires, the worst-hit sites were those recently cut, as along the Milwaukee Railway through the St. Joe Valley. . . . The same is true for Canada. The historic fire problem is a slash problem."[15]

In October 1918, the lumbering towns of Cloquet and Moose Lake, Minnesota, went up in flames amid 250,000 acres or more. Other sources say it was more than a million acres. We can be certain, however, that more than 450 people died, with many more imperiled as the fire leapt across the St. Louis River to come within two miles of the city of Duluth. The fire began in four hundred carloads of dry lumber along the railroad. As if in vengeance, it first turned its fury upon the lumber mills themselves. When they were gone, it went on to burn out the homes of the people who worked the mills.

As this chapter was in its final revisions in May 2005, a firefighting friend sent me an e-mail attachment of an Associated Press report of a wildfire that swept a hundred-square-mile cutover area of central Wisconsin, sending several thousand people to seek shelter beyond flames that had burned twenty houses and trailers. The fire was not far from the fire zone of the 1880s and 1890s, and about the same distance from the farmstead of Carl Schurz, the first Secretary of the Interior to make hazard planning part of a national agenda.[16]

President George W. Bush poses with one of the instruments of his "Healthy Forests" initiative. (Susan Walsh, Associated Press)

FALSE REMEDIES

President George W. Bush arrived in Arizona on June 26, 2002, while four hundred firefighters were still at risk. As he spoke to the press, aged slurry bombers and helicopters were above the fire line, passing over hundred-foot flames. The president thanked the firefighters and rejoiced that there had been no more buildings burned. He returned to Arizona a year later after another wildfire burned eighty-five thousand acres on Mount Lemmon, eighty miles south of the Mogollon Rim, in the Coronado National Forest. On Sunday, August 10, 2003, the *Arizona Daily Star* reported that as the president's airplane approached from his summer headquarters, a ranch in Texas, the supervisor of the forest, John McGee, issued a statement: "Recent thinning projects on Mount Lemmon weren't blocked by litigation and were even supported by local environmentalists. It was declining federal funding that kept the chain saws quiet. . . . We've not had lawsuits affecting us with our thinning projects." It appears that McGee was seeking to avoid another round of scapegoating, hoping that the president and his entourage would instead deliver more money to get rid of fire load: more money, he said, "will help the Coronado do its job." McGee underlined his message to the presidential party by noting quietly that over the preceding two years, the Coronado had ranked "dead last" in funding for thinning, despite the most perilous fire conditions in its history.[17]

Why was McGee apprehensive that the lessons of the Mount Lemmon blaze would be lost? Probably because his counterparts on the Mogollon Rim had returned from their firefighting to find that Governor Hull and Senator Kyl had developed their anti-wacko theme not in pursuit of greater appropriations for the Forest Service to do its work but, instead, to advocate "outsourcing thinning" to private lumber companies, according to the doctrine of a timber industry group, the American Forest Resource Council. Fires, said the council, waste crops. Those who put obstacles in the way of getting out the harvest should be discredited, and the nation should "turn over the management of these national resources to the professionals." This did not include the professionals of the National Forest Service, or the members of the Forest Stewards Guild, or the staff of the Forest Trust, who opposed a privatized lumbering response to forest fire. The "professionals" who should be heeded, said Chris West of the American Forest Resource Council, were not such people, but instead those who "live and work with these resources day in and day out" for lumber companies. The American Forest and Paper Association responded with enthusiasm to the call for handing over the fire problem to its members, but only after the call to duty was coupled with a guarantee of profitability—a subsidy that would require billions of taxpayer dollars. Getting out the crop is not, however, thinning. The crop for lumber companies is large, marketable logs.[18]

That guarantee of profitability has worked very nicely, though not explicitly. A former colleague in the National Park Service, still employed and therefore anonymous, informed me of one of the means devised of late to direct profits clandestinely and thus without arousing public outcry, a euphemistically termed "stewardship contracting" device: "They contract with a timber company to carry out the thinning and other fire hazard reduction management actions in the urban interface zone, and then 'pay' the timber company by letting them harvest larger trees, even old-growth, in the interior of the forest that is not a public safety fire hazard. The Government 'saves' money, there is no 'below-cost' timber sale recorded, and the timber company laughs all the way to the mill."[19]

In Arizona, the president of the United States had appeared at a still-smoky burn site to advocate such a program, though without stating its price, taking the occasion to instruct his listeners not about people in fire danger, or about fire, or about heroic rescuers flying obsolete aircraft, or even about fire losses, but instead about economic growth in general and specifically about employment opportunities working for lumber companies. "Any time anybody who wants to find work, who can't work, it means we've got a problem. So I want to talk about the job we have of making sure we grow our economy, so people can work." Apparently forgotten was the conclusion of the report of the National Forest Service after the wildfires of 2000: "It is after logging that the damage from fire is greatest."[20]

How can a society best organize itself to encourage both settlement and employment that can be sustained? There are lumbering jobs that can last, and can avoid irreparable damage to the resources upon which they depend. And there are also lumbering jobs that last only so long as one campaign—one profitable, unrestrained, clearcutting, road-ripping, slash-dumping season—and then are gone. Old-fashioned conservationists, and most of a new generation of environmentalists, favor sustainable forestry, based upon what fire has taught them. The governor of Arizona was impatient with that sort of restraint; it was too conservative for her. So she went for scapegoating and only one sort of sustainability—sustained ignorance of the lessons of fire—winding up her speech with her now-famous assertions: first, that environmentalists were "to blame for recent wildfires," and, beyond that—no lessons! "Nobody from the East Coast knows how to manage these fires."[21]

But what "policies coming from the East Coast" might commend themselves to the people of Arizona?[22]

PART FOUR

Learning from the
History of Fire

9. THE MENTORS: MARSH, GALLATIN, OLMSTED, AND THOREAU

Killer fires teach great lessons. There is wiser public policy than "Spread people out and let's see what happens." There are natural limits to settlement. Ignoring those limits will bring pain and death to humans, loss of homes and personal possessions, and irreparable damage to natural systems. As the National Forest Service summarized the experience of the nineteenth and twentieth centuries, "it is after logging" that fires fueled by slash, sawdust, and a multitude of brushy little trees will most easily sweep across dried-out landscapes and kill both settlers and those sent to rescue them.

These lessons were taught most emphatically where wildfires caused great losses of life—in New England, the Adirondacks, the Catskills, and then in the pine country along the Great Lakes. As lumbering and settlement moved westward, fire taught further lessons, and a succession of observant instructors assisted their countrymen to learn. There is a proud history in this country of writing and statesmanship grounded in understanding the interdynamics of human settlement and natural settings. In their differing ways, George Perkins Marsh, Carl Schurz, Albert Gallatin, Ignatius Donnelley, Frederick Law Olmsted, and John Wesley Powell put into words the lessons of fire, and wrote to warn about overstepping natural limits. Even the wry Henry David

Thoreau taught continental lessons while pretending only to talk about what happened in cutover and burned-over woodland outside Concord.

In the overlapping lifetimes of Marsh, Gallatin, and Thoreau, Americans experienced natural fire and Indian warfare as twin perils on the frontier. The conjunction provoked attention among thoughtful people, some of whom were more interested in fire than in Indians, but many of whom became interested in both. The Indians had used fire to prepare for both agriculture and architecture. That was a perception of considerable interest. Though at the time it was still generally believed among non-Indian statesmen that the Indians were doomed to extinction or amelioration, nonetheless, it was thought they might have useful things to say about fire and living within natural limits before they went. Gallatin in particular demonstrated how they might say those things with their architecture or in their languages.

European Americans had all along known that the continent over which they were extending their imperial sway had been inhabited by others before them. The remains of Indian architecture were too impressive and ubiquitous to be ignored; all the explorers and travelers who came over the Appalachians, including George Washington, observed with wonder ruins of earthen and stone buildings—and after wonder, with intense curiosity. Not until the 1830s and 1840s, however, did that curiosity lead to systematic efforts to record those ruins and, in the absence of written accounts of their creation, to record accounts in the spoken languages of living Indians. Men of more capacious interests, such as Gallatin and Marsh, began to learn what might be learned from Indians about how fire had been used and might be used within natural limits.

Marsh was born in Woodstock, Vermont, in 1801. As a student at Dartmouth College, on the nearby Connecticut River, he began studying the environmental theology of Jonathan Edwards, who had lived along the same river. Edwards had revived a tradition that placed living harmoniously with nature foremost among virtues. It was therefore natural that Marsh would assert that "the destruction of the woods" through the promiscuous use of fire was an imperial act, "man's first physical conquest, his first violation of the harmonies of inanimate nature."[1]

It is wonderful to observe how a desire for harmony may, in fortunate cases, actually be followed by actions to restore it. By the time Marsh encountered the doctrines of Edwards, overgrazing and the misuse of fire by humans had made a wasteland of the landscape around Woodstock. Another two centuries have gone by since Marsh's birth. Today, the fire-ravaged, overgrazed face of Vermont has been largely repaired. So sweet and seemly does the Woodstock Valley now appear that it is scarcely possible to imagine it as it was after the Great Fires of the winter of 1803–1804.

There is a photograph taken in the 1860s, from a perspective that might have been that of the front verandah of Marsh's house, now known as the Marsh-Billings-Rockefeller Mansion. Where today bask the fat cattle and sheep of the Rockefeller model farm, and where repose the landscaped grounds of the Woodstock Inn and Resort and golf course, there opened in the 1860s a scene like one of the battlefields of those years. Beyond the valley rose hills pockmarked with charcoal pits, stubbled with blackened stumps, and crisscrossed by the eroded trails of thousands of sheep.

In the eighteenth century, in Edwards's time, it must have been a very Eden in springtime. The great trees of Mount Tom sheltered deer; the valley streams swelled into ponds behind beaver dams, mirroring the great trunks of white birches; and the lowlands, earlier cleared by the Indians, were free of brush through controlled burning. The map of New England is dotted with towns named in commemoration of Indian forest management and agriculture. Greenfield, Deerfield, Springfield, Hatfield, Westfield, and Enfield were ready for the newcomers who took them, renamed them, and made somewhat more demanding use of them than had their previous occupants. Few of these immigrants from Europe in the seventeenth and eighteenth centuries pressed the carrying capacity of the land much beyond sustainability. Traditions of husbandry had permitted these immigrants' ancestors to remain in the same places over many generations, and they were not quick to abandon those ways. Slowly at first, however, and then more rapidly in the nineteenth century, husbandry was replaced by commercialized agriculture, gearing up for more and more production as prices fell lower and lower.[2]

The land paid the difference. After the great fires, it was struck in its weakened state by the merino mania. The Duponts smuggled a ram named Dom Pedro from Spain to their estate in Delaware, encouraging more landowners in their circle, including President Jefferson himself, to import these Pyrenean sheep with the long, silky wool. In the 1820s and 1830s, merinos were brought to New England, and for a time, the craze swept all before it. Even after the merino mania subsided, herds of other hungry sheep invaded eroded slopes and devoured down to its roots what grass remained. Though most of the merinos had died off by 1840, there were by then ten times as many sheep in Vermont as there were people. Though farmers did not have to file quarterly earnings reports like those in agribusiness today, they were pressed to produce fast results by international competition. In the 1850s and after the Civil War, railroads extended the markets for lamb, mutton, and beef, vastly increasing the damage done to the land as relatively light-footed sheep were replaced by overgrazing cattle.[3]

The Woodstock slash-and-burn fires of 1803–1804 showed dramatically the perils of lumbering without cleanup, forewarning what would happen in the cutover lands of Michigan and Wisconsin from 1880 until 1920, and more recently in the West, including Arizona. Lightning does not come as often to Mount Tom as to the Pajarito Plateau or the Mogollon Rim, but it strikes often enough. And even in winter, when there is less lightning, hunters get cold in remote places. Sometimes they build fires to keep warm and are careless amid the slash. The most terrifying childhood memory of George Marsh was of a fire set by a hunter on the cutover slopes of Mount Tom. Marsh was just learning to walk. His family was lucky—they had not yet left their old house near the river to build a cottage on the mountainside. We are lucky, too, because had the Marshes made the move earlier,

Man and Nature might never have been written. We would then have been deprived of its final line, one of the lessons of fire: "The great question [is] . . . whether man is of nature or above her."[4]

Marsh escaped from the destruction of Woodstock's forest and the contamination of its streams to another world. He married a woman whose family had grown affluent in trade and real estate in Burlington, and as a lawyer, diplomat, and Whig congressman, he was insulated from the delayed effects of fire and overgrazing until the 1850s. Marsh and his wife were able to hold on to a house on the hill longer than their neighbors, until, at the nadir of Vermont's ecological history, like many others they had to sell. The house and stump fields were purchased by Frederick Billings, the son of another local man who had lost his home earlier.

Billings had immigrated to California, made his first fortune as a railroad and mining lawyer, and moved on to New York. There he joined forces with Jay Cooke of the Northern Pacific Railroad to make a second fortune as a promoter of settlement in the Great Plains and the Northwest. Once back in Woodstock, Billings was able to begin the long process of restoration sustained by his granddaughter Mary and her husband, Laurance Rockefeller, who presented the Marsh-Billings-Rockefeller mansion to the National Park Service in the early 1990s. I recall Mrs. Rockefeller on a Sunday morning when we were staying in the house. She sat where her mother and grandmother had sat, in a north-facing window seat in the front parlor, reading to us from her Bible. I was reminded then of my great-grandfather Winter's Bible, back home. That home was not in Vermont, though he had been born there. Vermont meant for him shame, cutover, sterile hillsides, hungry sheep, bankruptcy, the loss of home, and fire. His story is interbraided with that of Frederick Billings.

PRIVATE IMPROVEMENTS

After Jay Cooke's financial collapse in the Panic of 1873, Frederick Billings became president of the Northern Pacific, but was forced out by another promoter of even greater genius, the German journalist-turned-railroad-speculator Henry Villard (Ferdinand Heinrich Gustav Hilgard). Villard outflanked Billings by securing investors willing to provide him a war chest, his famous "blind pool," but he did not last long as the railroad's president. He lacked two fundamental skills: he had no idea how to run a railroad, and he did not understand the importance of securing government land grants to induce migration to populate a region. What the Northern Pacific needed was an experienced manager like Billings, or like Edwin Winter, who brought the railroad out from a second bankruptcy in the late 1880s.

Winter's tenure is noteworthy chiefly because he did understand those devices now known as "public-private partnerships." He noted Cooke's success in persuading Congress to make a national park of the Yellowstone Basin, which lay along the Northern Pacific line. Then the Great Northern made the case for its most glamorous station stop in Montana, and Glacier National Park was created in 1888. On taking office, Winter deployed the Northern Pacific's lobbying power to secure national park status for Mount Rainier, on the tracks not far to the east of their terminus on Puget Sound. (The Santa Fe Railroad did not secure national park designation for the Grand Canyon until 1919, though its tourists and the Harvey Girls had been visiting the canyon as a national monument for more than a decade.)[5]

The Marsh-Billings-Rockefeller National Park came more than a half century later in the Woodstock Valley, which had already learned something about sustainable forestry and agriculture from Marsh, and had benefited from Billings's program of "permanent improvements." During Billings's lifetime, the stumps and char of the Great Fire were still visible on the slopes behind his mansion, but were disappearing into the shade of the exotic spruces and larches he planted after the sheep were removed. His larches have not survived, but his spruce now seem to be as native as the local pines among which he had them set. As Marsh said, "It requires a very generous spirit in a landholder to plant a wood on a farm he expects to sell, or which he knows will pass out of the hands of his descendants at his death. But the very fact of having begun a plantation would attach a proprietor more strongly to the soil for which he had made such a sacrifice."[6]

MARSH AND HUSBANDRY

Marsh's insistence that the financially fortunate show "magnanimity" in their "self-forgetting care for the moral and material interests of . . . [their] own posterity" was a useful injunction for a Billings or a Rockefeller, who could operate on the scale of a European landed magnate. Marsh was writing, however, to a broader audience, including many farmers and woodlot operators in New England who understood the distinction, as a Woodstock farmer once stated to me, between those who "want to marry the land" and those who "want to rape it and run." Abraham Lincoln had put it more gracefully as a choice between "cultivation" and "locomotion." A transition was under way from diversified and sustainable farming to the industrial-scale cultivation of single crops for sale in distant markets. Squires such as Marsh saw that transition in one way; dirt farmers who suffered through it saw it in another. Neither gentry nor yeomen were able to resist it, though all saw it occurring at what are now called the "interfaces" between garden, field, woodlot, and wild, where nature, too, resisted. Fire is to forest what dust is to field. This point is amplified in later chapters.

George Perkins Marsh was famous for urging private citizens to take better care of the land given into their charge, but beyond his native Woodstock, his chief influence was as an advocate of *public* husbandry. Like Carl Schurz—who took Marsh's admonitions to heart as Marsh took Edwards's—Marsh observed public subsidies channeling migration of private persons onto public lands. Like Schurz, he urged that Congress apply the same logic to the opposing process—reserving public land from private use.

From the first days of the republic—indeed, from the first days of the Confederation that preceded it—public lands had been granted and withdrawn, to serve public purposes. Parks as precious places were one outcome of "reservation." So was keeping land out of private hands to avoid troubles to the public that would come from promiscuous settlement. This deliberate apportioning of the nation's common store of land to be used in specific ways by private citizens, and the deliberate withholding of some portions of that common store, was a public expression of a European "tradition of sustainable husbandry" that succeeded that of the Indians. As the environmental historian Brian Donahue has shown, forestry and agriculture have been indistinguishable in New England. Both are essential to the area's agrarian heritage. In Donahue's view, which I share, husbandry "was our conservation birthright," though in many places "we have cast it aside and scorned it." Nonetheless, in many others "it is still alive throughout rural America."[7]

Husbandry is alive as well in community forestry, on some Indian reservations such as that of the White Mountain Apaches, and around some traditional towns, such as those of northern New Mexico and northern New England. It has never died out in some family-owned timbering operations in the same regions. It remains the basis upon which both agricultural and forest husbandry can be encouraged today. As Marsh reminded his readers, "public advantage" does not stop at the rich man's gate. While some of those behind the gate might show "magnanimity," Marsh did not expect everyone to do so. "Self-forgetting care" is not so widespread as to provide all that is needed for the long-term health of the earth. To make that point, Marsh dropped his passage about "magnanimity" and "self-forgetting care" from the 1874 edition of Man and Nature, and substituted a call for government to enter the picture. The well-disposed might "render the creation of new forests [or parks] an object of private interest as well as of public advantage," but public advantage might also require keeping old forests healthy. In the West, after public land had been used to advantage by the railroads, those railroads, through their assistance in creating parks, helped set aside land for public advantage.[8]

And after new or old forests have been set aside from settlement, how should they be managed? Marsh brought silviculture in the German fashion and the French regard for watershed protection to the attention of men such as Billings. Sustainable forestry was as natural to German and French peasants, who had wrested their woodlots from the aristocracy, as it was for German and French aristocrats schooled in treating their land dynastically. In America, without a peasantry or an aristocracy, the question arose in the 1840s: How should one look at the landscape with an equally long view? A good way to begin would be to look at what had happened to it over extended periods of time. Over the centuries, what, for example, had actually been the experience of humans in North America with the controlled use of fire?

GALLATIN, INDIANS, AND LIMITS

Marsh's associate in pursuing these inquiries systematically was Albert Gallatin, Secretary of the Treasury for Presidents Jefferson and Madison. Marsh's interests were primarily environmental, Gallatin's anthropological; they overlapped in pursuing what archaeology could reveal of Indian history, and what that history could suggest to their successors. In the 1840s, Gallatin was approaching his ninetieth year, but still expanding his vision to include *The Great Colorado and the Semi-Civilization of New Mexico,* while Marsh was beginning his deliberations on reports of "the remarkable mounds and other earthworks in the valley of the Ohio," contained in William Henry Harrison's *A Discourse on the Aborigines of the Valley of the Ohio,* published in 1838 at the same stage of Harrison's trajectory toward the presidency (1840) as was John F. Kennedy's *Profiles in Courage* in his. (Kennedy won the Pulitzer Prize for the book in 1957, and the presidency in 1960.) Harrison had asked some of the intriguing questions that Marsh amplified about "the difference between the relations of savage life, and of incipient civilization, to nature." However, as a man who had made his political reputation by killing Indians, he did not have quite the same interest in their past achievements as Marsh, who went on to examine their deliberate use of fire to clear and maintain not only cropland but ceremonial space as well, as a preliminary step toward astounding achievements of architecture and engineering.[9]

Why, Harrison, Marsh, and Gallatin asked, had all the skill and energy leading to the creation of immense earthworks ceased? The absence of a history to tell them whether the builders of those earthworks had exceeded their natural limits, or had killed one another off, or had died of disease, spurred every explorer of the region since General Richard Butler sent a copy of his *Indian Vocabulary* to his commander in the Revolution, George Washington, with similar speculations attached. Washington congratulated Butler for having "exerted . . . [himself] to throw light on the original history" of a country Washington had himself visited many times, urging that those exertions led "to some useful discoveries [about] those works."[10]

Gallatin and Marsh together provided the impetus to the publications of Ephraim G. Squire and Edwin H. Davis's *Ancient Monuments of the Mississippi Valley*, the first major study of Indian architecture and engineering. Gallatin also picked up where Butler had left off, with a monumental study of the *Indian Linguistic Families of America North of Mexico*, admired—and regularly used—by John Wesley Powell a generation later.

EMERSON AND THOREAU

Even Ralph Waldo Emerson wondered in print how the Ohio Indians might have cleared the land for their earthworks, and Thoreau wrote in his *Journal*, in 1857: "Why, then, make so great ado about the Roman and the Greek, and neglect the Indian?" And his dying word was "Indians." Yet though Indians had much to teach about fire and living with limits, Thoreau himself did not have the energy in his final years to undertake a study of those lessons. He was a strange fellow, presenting himself as a man who might travel far in speculation while remaining physically close to his native Concord, Massachusetts, yet driven to seek both knowledge and a release from the tuberculosis that was slowly killing him by undertaking a 1,500-mile trip to Minnesota. There he walked in the neighborhood of ancient mounds in St. Paul and St. Anthony (later Minneapolis) with the state geologist-archaeologist, Charles Andrews. Thoreau left his ruminations on such matters for later development; his journal carries only jottings on other presumably vanishing species as "bison last seen east of the Mississippi in 1832 and last beaver killed in south part of Wisconsin in 1819."[11]

The Sioux were still there, however, and on June 17, 1861, Thoreau took a chuffing shallow-draft steamer up through the shoals and sandbars of the Minnesota River to watch five thousand Dakota and Santee Sioux dance at the Lower Sioux Agency (nine miles from the present city of Redwood Falls). There he met Little Crow, who a year later led an uprising that drove white settlement back downstream. Limits can be established in many ways.

As the steamboat bearing him passed prairies that had plainly been set afire often enough by sparks from steamboat boilers, Thoreau may well have been moved to speculate about contained fire and wildfire, about fire as servant and fire as master, but he was never able to pull his thoughts along that journey into another book. He was tired. Had he had enough energy left, he might have considered, as well, the implications of two uses of fire by the natives of the Mississippi, Ohio, and Minnesota river valleys. Thoreau's predecessors, from the Ohio correspondents of George Washington and Thomas Jefferson onward, had noted that the Indians cleared with fire the fields they planted and used to attract game, and they also used fire architecturally. Carbon-dating was still to come, so all that William Henry Harrison and other early observers could know was that many generations of trees had apparently come and gone since the Indians had burned to prepare the plazas about which they built great octagons, circles, and squares of earthen embankments. By the end of the nineteenth century, archaeologists' observations had confirmed the likelihood that the Indians had also paid final fiery tribute to ritual places they could no longer use. They burned the wooden palisades surrounding those plazas, and then piled earth atop the embers of those sacred, purging fires.[12]

Thoreau was much interested in fire, however arch and indirect his treatment of it may have been. Its unpredictable role—requiring due respect—is the subject of three of the self-mocking parables in which he depicts himself as foolish in treating fire as if it were merely domestic in the home or tamely amusing outdoors.

When he went out, leaving a fire in his hearth at Walden, Thoreau wrote, "my house was not empty . . . It was as if I had left a cheerful housekeeper behind. It was I and fire that lived there; and commonly my housekeeper proved trustworthy." Commonly. Yet one day, when he returned from splitting wood to provide for that fire, he found that it had gone feral. A spark in his bed was threatening to burn down the cabin. He put it out, and left the point to his reader—when would we know that fire might not choose to be a housekeeper?

On another occasion, he and a friend carelessly left a campfire burning in grass; it spread to the woods and burned a hundred acres, a large area in Concord. "It was a glorious spectacle," he wrote, "and I was the only one there to enjoy it." But it seems he did not wholly enjoy it, for it provoked from him a little essay on due respect for fire in lighting it properly, tending it properly, and putting it out properly. His third parable was the subtlest of them all. The white, nature-defying church was the very symbol of Yankee conquest of nature, and even it could be threatened by a fire gone wild—even in Concord. Thoreau wrote of how his neighbors would "follow the sound" of a bell telling of fire "to see it burn, since burn it must." But they knew they must "see it put out, and have a hand in it," otherwise it might destroy "even . . . the parish church itself."[13]

GALLATIN AND INDIAN LANGUAGES

Still asking questions, Marsh, Gallatin, Thoreau, and Emerson came along after Washington, Jefferson, Butler, and Harrison, still trying to understand what had happened to the Indians who had created great works of architecture in the Ohio River Valley. Who were these mysterious people who had mastered the cultivation of plants, who had traveled thousands of miles on regular voyages in search of precious and beautiful minerals and objects (Marsh noted the presence of pearls in Ohio burials), and who had cleared sacred spaces in regular squares, octagons, and circles laid out according to the disciplines of the motions of the sun, moon, and stars—and then had ceased doing these wondrous things. Could they have become so estranged from their environment as to cease to be able to execute grand undertakings?

In an astringent essay published in *Ethnohistory* in 2005, Paul Nadasdy cleanses the palate from sentimentalizing some "ecologically noble Indian." He rightly urges more sophisticated diffidence in the face of what real Indians actually think and do, and less boxing them into categories of environmentalism with which neither their spiritual nor practical lives have much to do. Nadasdy does a service to those of us trying to learn from Indian experience with fire by getting the cardboard categories out of the way. Once the scene is clearer, it becomes possible to consider the likelihood that the Indians may have signaled failure in their use of fire to mark the end of experiments in living. Maybe their dense settlement of areas such as the Cahokia–American Bottom region in the central Mississippi Valley, the Four Corners of Utah, Colorado, Arizona, and New Mexico, and the Savannah River Valley pressed the limits of what nature would permit, though in all these places they made extensive and effective use of fire. Maybe they had to withdraw as the result of pollution, or diseases of crowding, or because they'd used up the supply of combustible materials. Perhaps their ritual fires were, so to speak, breaking one set of tools or knocking the bottom out of a ritually used pot.[14]

Marsh and Gallatin wondered if "the prairies were cleared by the same or similar people . . . while the restoration of the woods in Ohio may be due to the abandonment of the region by its original inhabitants." Could it be that all prairies should not be cleared, all crannies of the earth occupied? Are there limits to how much wood people can use for palisades against one another if they also need it for fuel and building materials? Such questions have been in the air, inviting scholarly inquiry, for a century and a half, since Washington, Jefferson, Gallatin, and Marsh asked them.[15]

Marsh learned humility in the face of nature, and in the face of fire in particular, when he was young enough to register the lesson, even before he studied Edwards. He did not know Indians as friends when he was young—as did Edwards, Thoreau, and Gallatin—but he knew about their use of fire as well as those three. It is one of the joys of knowing these inquiring minds to note in Marsh and Gallatin the coming together of two entirely distinct streams of thought about native peoples and nature—one stream flowing through the evangelical Protestantism springing from Edwards, the other through the militantly secular skepticism about some things and the equally militant sentimentalism about others set out in the music, poetry, and prose of Jean-Jacques Rousseau. On the threshold of that cheery coincidence is another: that Gallatin and Thoreau made their first Indian friends in the same easternmost corner of Maine. I doubt that the Abnaki had any special gifts of environmental evangelism, but there is always that possibility.

As a young man in Geneva, Gallatin learned from Rousseau's doctrines to be respectful of husbandry, and to be wary of patronizing those whom some might call "savages." In the rural landscape outside the city walls, he learned how his own countrymen had done better by the land than had the Greeks and Sicilians, whose environmental excesses elicited Marsh's most powerful warnings to his fellow Americans. In Switzerland, a mountain country where survival was precarious—indeed, it still is, outside an expensive hotel or a chalet supported by a substantial account in a private bank—husbandry had not asked more of nature than it was willing to concede.

Gallatin came to America in 1780 fervent in revolutionary doctrine. He became here a cool, sophisticated cosmopolite, offering arguments against overweening pride and exploitation in a prudential humanist vocabulary that made those arguments acceptable in an age when the cadences of Jonathan Edwards were increasingly treated as embarrassing. During the Civil War years, however, a more passionate rhetoric became permissible, and Frederick Law Olmsted, twenty years younger than Marsh and forty years younger than Gallatin, brought back to the discussion a passionate eloquence like that of Edwards.

OLMSTED

For Olmsted, Marsh, and Gallatin, as for Edwards, the earth and all its peoples were one. Respect for other humans and respect for the other creatures with which they inhabit the earth was the basis for the environmental and social policy of them all. They were all practitioners of practical politics, and enjoyed the uses of power, but they were not prideful technocrats. Olmsted brought into the middle decades of the nineteenth century a breadth of comprehension characteristic of the early decades of the eighteenth. He did not discourse on theology, making use instead of another set of symbols. His discourse on land policy did, however, arise from fundamental principles, as did Edwards's. In a single speech, Olmsted could unite discussion of the statue of Liberty atop the Capitol dome, the emancipation of the slaves, the destruction of the earth of the South by the plantation system, the prospect of equally disastrous destruction of the Yosemite Valley and the giant sequoias, public education through the Morrill Act, and homestead legislation.

Abraham Lincoln made the same associations, though when Lincoln and Olmsted spoke of "fire" in the crucial years of their dialogue they were unlikely to be thinking of wildfire. The nation was in the midst of a war, deciding, among other great questions, how the public lands would be distributed to private citizens, and how those citizens would make use of them.

Olmsted is chiefly known as a land planner and garden builder on a grand scale. New York's Central Park and the Vanderbilt estate at Biltmore, in North Carolina, are probably his most accessible works, though there are plenty of other examples, including his own house and demonstration garden in Brookline, Massachusetts, which is administered by the National Park Service as a counterpart to the

Marsh-Billings-Rockefeller site. His entire career was a demonstration that human intervention in nature can improve it. He knew a great deal about Indian uses of fire, and used fire for clearing his own land, always conscious that it was a dangerous tool. There is no irony in the fact that he first came to national attention with a report on what the planters had done with fire and other methods to destroy the fertility of the Southland, because he was as good on the defense as on the offense. His opposition to slavery arose from the conviction that it was bad for master, slave, and earth. Thus he linked man and nature five years before the publication of Marsh's book.

In 1859, Olmsted issued his famous report on the environmental consequences of the slave system. In the preceding seventy years, federal land-planning policy had made available to plantation slavery three hundred thousand square miles of farmland. Though half the states had abolished slavery during the Revolutionary War, and though half the land remaining in the federal domain lying north of the Ohio River had been spared the blight of slavery by the Northwest Ordinances of the 1780s and their successors, opening the South and Southwest to slavery was, in effect, a policy for migration and resettlement to accommodate a slave-based economy. The Southwest Ordinance of 1790 had no requirement as to the type of workforce permitted on the public lands sold to private citizens south of the Ohio River. Nor were limits set as to what could happen to the land.

The desolation of the antebellum Southland unfolded from those interrelated failures, as Olmsted demonstrated by offering the testimony of a Georgia acquaintance who had seen the process: when his friend first came to Georgia he was shown about by a real estate developer, who told him, "These lands will never wear out. Where they lie level, they will be just as good, fifty years hence, as they are now." Girdling, fire-clearing, and mono-crop cultivation followed, and "forty-two years afterwards, I visited the spot on which he stood when he made the remark. The sun poured his whole strength upon the bald hill . . . ; many a deep-washed gully met at a sickly bog, where had gushed the limpid fountain; a dying willow rose from the soil which had nourished the venerable beech; flocks . . . cropped a scanty meal . . . and all around was barren, dreary, and cheerless."[16]

That Georgian's observation was confirmed not only by Olmsted but also by De Bow's *Resources of the South*: "The native soil of Middle Georgia is . . . worn out, leaving a desolate picture for the traveler to behold. Decaying tenements, red, old hills, stripped of their native growth and virgin soil, and washed into deep gullies, with here and there patches of Bermuda grass and stunted pine shrubs, struggling for subsistence on what was once one of the richest soils in America."

The association of a pernicious social system with a pernicious ecological system was explained by another southerner: "It is positively bad economy for the Virginia planter to undertake the improvement of his estate. . . . It is a more profitable operation to emigrate with . . . [his] slaves to Mississippi and Louisiana, and there to employ their labor in raising cotton and *killing* land, than to attempt the improvement of the worn outlands at home."[17]

The plantation system killed land by a succession of blows—first fire, then erosion. Fire, used as a tool by many cultures, had more profoundly deleterious effects when used together with row crops, sodbusting plows, and cotton or corn grown without siblings. When the land cannot rest by rotation, fire does less good and more harm. Though it lays upon the soil's surface nutrients such as phosphorus and calcium previously stored in trunks, branches, leaves, and roots, as if they had been pumped there, these can quickly be used up or washed away. When the soil is deep, and has many nutrients to pump up, or is restored with new nutrients, it may produce crops for a long time, and fire can be brought back to do its pumping repeatedly. But that will not work if the land has been deeply depleted and eroded. In most of the antebellum South, fire was a sign of the advance of planters moving successively through the forests, scarcely pausing in the process: slash, burn, grow, move. Slash again, burn again, grow again, move again.[18]

WILDERNESS

Olmsted knew what man could do to nature unless limits were observed. Applying what he had learned about the past in the South to what might be done to prevent "killing the land" in the West, he followed Lincoln's lead in urging the protection of Yosemite and the Mariposa Grove. In the year *Man and Nature* received its first printing, Olmsted issued his "Preliminary Report on the California Interior." He was a canny rhetorician: he began the report with neither poetic evocations of waterfalls and big trees nor, at the other extreme of environmental writing, facts and science. Instead, he commenced with art and symbols.

Noting as "a fact of much significance with reference to the temper and spirit which ruled loyal people of the United States during the war of the great rebellion," Olmsted wrote that not only was there "a livelier susceptibility to the influence of art," but there was also an equal susceptibility to the influence of nature. The former, he said, had been shown in President Lincoln's direction that "the great dome of the Capitol" should be constructed during the war. "The forces of the insurgents watched it rounding upward to completion for nearly a year before they were forced from their entrenchments on the opposite bank of the Potomac; Crawford's great statue of Liberty was poised upon its summit in the year that President Lincoln proclaimed the emancipation of the slaves."[19]

Olmsted was clever—he knew the power of the complexity of meanings then drawn from the word "wilderness." "During one of the darkest hours, before Sherman had begun the march upon Atlanta or Grant his terrible movement through the Wilderness," wrote Olmsted, Lincoln had grasped the importance of preserving "the sublimity of the Yosemite, and of the stateliness of the neighboring Sequoia grove." Amid much greater perils, Olmsted noted, Lincoln could still envisage the need to protect a noble wilderness from becoming "private property and through the false taste, the caprice or requirements of some industrial speculation of their holders, [injuring] their value to posterity." Who else would have encouraged the imaginative reader to envisage the valley floor of a California wilderness as a battlefield in another kind of civil war?[20]

Who else? Lincoln may well have done so, for both ideas were being pressed upon him at the time he recommended to Congress that the Yosemite and the core of the sequoia forest be secured, in Olmsted's words, "against this danger," and be "segregated from the general domain of the public lands, and devoted forever to popular resort and recreation. . . . Portions of natural scenery may . . . properly be guarded and cared for by government . . . to be laid open to the use of the body of the people."[21]

The Yosemite Valley was withdrawn from settlement to protect it from desecration in the same years that other portions of the American earth were being desecrated by fraternal bloodshed, and still others being destroyed by the land and labor system that had brought about that conflict. As the Civil War came to an end, the people of the United States declared that slavery would cease its destruction of the land, while "great public grounds" would be held in trust "for the free enjoyment of the people." The duties of government, according to both Olmsted and Lincoln, included clear distinctions among the kinds of uses to be permitted on land made available to private citizens, and also between land to be allocated to largely private use and that reserved from development or settlement. Those determinations are the basis of migration policy as well as land policy. They remain among the duties of government.

10. CARL SCHURZ, FIRE, AND THE WISCONSIN EXAMPLE

In 1861, George Perkins Marsh almost despaired of securing the ambassadorship to Garibaldi's revolutionary Italy because his competitor for President Lincoln's favor was a far more colorful orator—Carl Schurz. Schurz lost to Marsh because he was *too* colorful; and, besides, he orated in a German accent. Nonetheless, he imbibed Marsh's theory of limits and passed it along, together with some practical experience with fire and land policy, to Robert M. La Follette and the statutes of their state of Wisconsin. The principle of setting limits to settlement was established in both federal and state statutes. Thanks to Schurz, La Follette, and other progressives, cutover lands that were known to be too susceptible to wildfire to be settled safely were withdrawn and set aside for forest restoration. Thus the way was made plain for the withdrawal of farming from places lying beyond natural limits and subject to other perils. Wisconsin and Minnesota learned limits from wildfire after lumbering. Texas and New Mexico learned limits from the Dust Bowl. The progressives' lessons for the arid West included the concept of setting limits at all levels of government, and for the nation as a whole those lessons blazed the way for the soil-conservation measures of the New Deal—which were, like the land policies of the Lincoln Administration, also migration policies.

For many years, the portrait of Carl Schurz hung beside that of Harold Ickes in the waiting room of the Secretary of the Interior. There was no such secretary in the cabinet of Thomas Jefferson; the functions later performed by Schurz and Ickes were instead within the portfolio of Albert Gallatin. Gallatin's portrait might go up in the waiting room, too, for there is a direct line of intellectual descent—though not one of office—from Gallatin, a soldier in the American Revolution, through Marsh, Schurz, La Follette, and Ickes to Russell Train, administrator of the Environmental Protection Agency under Presidents Nixon and Ford. George Perkins Marsh and Carl Schurz were essential links in that chain, forged in fire.

Marsh was a quiet fellow behind glasses, sober, earnest, "high-toned," "aristocratic . . . lacking a personal touch." He made stump speeches when running for Congress, but there is no evidence that he enjoyed it. On the other hand, Schurz, a happy warrior like Al Smith and Hubert Humphrey, loved crowds and sweat and applause. He was as tall as Thomas Jefferson and George Washington, as thin as Jefferson, and a first-rate pianist. He told tall tales as well as any politician since Abraham Lincoln. Schurz was probably the greatest orator of the party of Lincoln and Marsh—certainly its greatest in German. He had come to the United States in 1852 already famous as a revolutionary hero, and he lived to remind Wisconsin's German Americans that they had their own progressive past when he endorsed Robert M. La Follette in 1904. Two elements of that tradition were forest management, which came with the German immigrants from their homelands, and a respect for forest fire, which they had learned painfully in Wisconsin, Minnesota, and Michigan.

Schurz was the son of a village schoolmaster and the grandson of a tenant farmer. His parents managed to find the money to send him to a university, where his professor, Gottfried Kinkel, was stoking up the students to enlist in the revolution of 1848. Schurz was a lieutenant before he was twenty, fighting on the battlefield and in the garrison of the fortress of Rastatt. When it fell to the Prussians, Schurz led a party of his troops to freedom through a four-day ordeal in the sewers. Kinkel, however, was captured, and his wife implored Schurz to return to Germany and organize another great escape, this time from the fortress of Spandau, near Berlin. After two failures, Schurz got in and got Kinkel out, through an attic window. Once again, there was a flight through the woods and marshes, with the men dodging patrols and fearing betrayals. The way to Switzerland was blocked, so they made it cross-country to the port of Rostock, where they found a little sailing vessel to take them to England. Schurz left Kinkel there, and tried to reorganize his young colleagues from a base in Paris. The French authorities were not quite ready for another German war, so Schurz was deported as a dangerous alien.

He bought a farm near Watertown, Wisconsin, in 1856, but was not meant for seclusion. Before he was an American citizen he was back in progressive politics and nominated by the Republicans to be the state's lieutenant governor. He lost, but campaigned so success-fully for Lincoln across the German districts of the Midwest that when his party won the election of 1860, he was a prime candidate for the embassy to Italy. However, George Marsh prevailed, so instead of Garibaldi's revolutionary Turin and Rome, Schurz got the ministry to reactionary Madrid. He did his best, but was soon back in the United States to serve in the Civil War, for which Marsh was too old. Already a hero of escape dramas in Germany, Schurz became an American brigadier general and fought at Chancellorsville and Gettysburg.

SCHURZ IN HIS ELEMENT

The Wisconsin farm was far in the past when Schurz was elected to the United States Senate from Missouri in 1868 as a "Liberal Republi-can," a term coined at the time that described—and still describes—an endangered species; Schurz got only one term. He was still the leader of the German Americans, however, and a mighty voice on the platform; he was made Secretary of the Interior by President Ruther-ford B. Hayes in 1877, not then a major office. Schurz made it one, however, founding the National Geological Survey, which set in motion the preservation of the national forests. He selected Harry Yount, the last of the Mountain Men, to be gamekeeper for Yellowstone, charged with ridding the place of squatters and commercial hunters. Schurz instructed Yount to permit trapping and hunting only "for recreation or to provide visitors and residents with food." To enforce these ordinances, Yount had himself, a horse, and a rifle; Schurz and General Philip Sheridan inspected the results, and determined that sustaining so high a standard required the intervention of the cavalry. Yount was retired to the hall of Park Service heroes. (An award in his name is still presented by directors for service requiring pluck.)

It required more than pluck for Schurz to insist that forest reserves and, later, national parks be served not only by rangers such as Yount but also by scientists responsible to the public interest and not any corporate interest. That was the necessary precondition to the presence there a century later of people such as Dr. John Varley, who, on my watch as director of the National Park Service, startled the public by telling them the truth: fire is a necessary cleansing force in national parks. Murmurs were heard when Secretary Schurz forbade cutting down timber without permits in Yellowstone, a national park, and a roar of outrage came to the ears of President Hayes when Schurz inveighed against the lumbering of California's giant sequoias and redwoods. It was one thing to forbid the taking of commercial timber from the Yosemite Valley—though it was not yet a national park, it was a state one—but the groves of the other great trees in California were still in the public domain, treated as farmsteads by the timber barons by having them "homesteaded" and stripped of their timber.

SPOONER

Schurz did not accept the notion that eastern fire, timber, and settlement experience had nothing to teach the West. The lessons of the killer fires of the nineteenth century were being recognized in Wisconsin and Minnesota while he was in office, and he applied those lessons in his western policies. Back home in Wisconsin, the state supreme

The railroad builder and National Park promoter Edwin W. Winter, partner in real estate speculation with the senator and lumber king John Coit Spooner. (Courtesy of the author)

court was in the hands of Senator John Coit Spooner, described by the *Milwaukee Sentinel* as "chief of the corporation lobbyists," and later in life by *The New York Times* as "the ablest man in the [United States] Senate." Spooner refused to become Secretary of the Interior for President McKinley in order to lead the president's party in Congress, though by then he was a conservationist of a sort, and on good terms with Vice President Theodore Roosevelt. On the other hand, Lincoln Steffens listed Spooner among the "enemies of the republic," and Robert M. La Follette forced him out of politics.[1]

La Follette had quite another style from Spooner's flamboyance. He was a latter-day version of George Perkins Marsh, but with a considerably harder edge. Dry, tireless, relentless, humorless, undeflated by opposition and uninflated by adulation, he lacked dramatic gifts but was so convincingly in earnest when serving the interests of the small farmers that he could hold crowds of them afternoon after afternoon, in the baking Wisconsin sun, reading to them railroad rate tables and lumber company ledgers. They believed him, and endorsed his view that Wisconsin should lead the nation in showing how to act on the lessons of fire. In the 1950s, I campaigned beside a man who had debated La Follette, and he told me that it was a major achievement merely to endure the heat, the sweat of thousands of people in wool, and the stench produced by the horses tethered at the back of the town squares in which open-air, pre-microphone democracy was practiced. That was not a setting in which Spooner was comfortable.[2]

Besides, he had to defend those rate tables and those ledgers. From 1875 onward, until his death in 1919, the corporations he represented most consistently were those managed by Edwin Winter, first as General Superintendent of the Western Wisconsin Railway, as general manager of the Omaha, then as president of the Northern Pacific, and finally as president of the Brooklyn Rapid Transit Company. Winter was also Spooner's partner in Wisconsin real estate speculation. Their correspondence does not, however, show joint ventures in timberlands, which is odd in light of the special knowledge possessed by Winter as the carrier and Spooner as the producer of lumber. Instead they looked past both timbering and homesteading to the day when a transcontinental railroad might start at Superior, Wisconsin, or Duluth, Minnesota, at the head of the Great Lakes. So they bought up miles of lakeshore. It was a sound premise, but Superior failed to fulfill its obligation to become a metropolis. The fireplugs of Greater Superior remain to this day in open fields filling with second-growth scrub pines, though Spooner and Winter did better around Lake Phelan, in St. Paul. In success or failure, their politics remained compatible: Winter was once heard to say, while descending the grand staircase into the hall of his house at 415 Summit Avenue in St. Paul, "The only man who knows how to rule is the czar of Russia."[3]

As the Spooner era in Wisconsin faded into the La Follette era, and the state constitution was amended to encourage the declaration of "fire protection districts," the Forest Crop Law of 1927 embedded in Wisconsin statutes another set of Marsh's ideas. Recognizing that modest governmental encouragement would be enough to make sustained forestry more profitable than hardscrabble, fire-plagued farming, counties could dedicate tax-forfeited agricultural land to reforestation, remove it from their tax rolls, and receive state subsidies. Two years later, counties were also authorized to implement *countywide zoning*—to "encourage cutover settlers to move closer together instead of farming in isolation."[4]

Heeding its own experience and the exhortations of both Schurz and La Follette, Wisconsin was taking land out of settlement, helping farmers who had tried to make a go of living in the burned-over lands to find homes elsewhere. The state constitution was amended to clear away a decision its supreme court had made under Spooner's influence, which declared a "need to log" everywhere. The new constitution created instead "fire protection districts" where further logging was considered undesirable. Wisconsin's most distinguished historian of the politics of fire and settlement concluded that fire-protection districts—which in these pages are called "flame zones"—were "final" recognitions "that an unsuccessful farmer, settled on unsuitable land in an isolated place, was anything but a taxable asset to the county."[5]

LESSONS OF THE KILLER FIRES

Schurz was never fully tested as a farmer; the odds are great that he would have fared no better than many others, for the homestead he took up in Watertown, Wisconsin, was situated northeast of Madison, on the frontier between the grassland and the cutover forest. Sun Prairie lies just to the east and the timbered Baraboo Hills just to the west, much of them covered with trees dependent upon regular fires to reproduce properly. The great white pines of the sand plains reared up against the skies a little farther to the north, where in the 1840s William H. C. Folsom of Maine still saw "vast regions, densely wooded, in which the sound of the woodman's axe has never been heard, lying about the headwaters of the Chippewa, St. Croix, and other streams."[6]

By the time of Folsom's death, lumbermen had left those streams full of brush and slash, and federal migration policy, laid out in the Homestead, Desert Land, and Timber Culture Acts, had induced settlers to ruin their lives trying to make farms in the cutover. Wisconsin had already suffered so much from forest fires where the timbering had left the countryside strewn with branches and sawdust that in 1867 the state's Forest Commission issued a report entitled "Report of the Disastrous Effects of the Destruction of Forest Trees Now Going on So Rapidly in the State of Wisconsin."

In the fall of 1894, just before the great Hinckley fire, another Civil War veteran, General Christopher Columbus Andrews, presented a paper to the American Forestry Association in his role as fire warden of Minnesota. Entitled "Prevention of Forest Fires," the lecture offered Andrews's audience an estimate that fires were costing annually $25 million and many lives. It is a fair supposition that there was scuffling and scoffing in the audience as he concluded: "For the American people thus to allow such calamities to habitually occur, without adopting any adequate means for their prevention, causes our country to be regarded as in some respects only semi-civilized."[7]

One of Andrews's sub-wardens, George Goodrich, of Becker, Minnesota, put succinctly why his boss was going unheeded. "How an active sentiment can be awakened for preservation of Minnesota timber I don't know, as the present sentiment is to 'grab all you can' and no one cares about the future." The *Stillwater Lumberman* asserted with mock civic pride that none of the "first families" of that St. Croix River town had done anything so heinous as wildcatting timber: "But Lord, how those Minneapolis and St. Cloud fellows did steal!" A National Park Service St. Croix study tells us that "81.7 million feet of pine logs had been plundered from public lands, just between 1868 and 1876. One single case of trespass found that thirty-five million board feet, with a dollar value of over $75,000, had been stolen." So Schurz went to court, more than twenty-nine times in Minnesota alone.[8]

Andrews kept up the good fight until he was in his early nineties, arguing that the best means of preventing catastrophe when fires struck was to keep people out of the way of the fires. In accordance with that principle, he pressed for Minnesota to become better than "semi-civilized" by retiring large portions of the cutover from settlement to create the state and national forests that in 2004 covered seventeen million acres, one-third of the state. At his urging, in 1902 the Chippewa National Forest, nearly two hundred thousand acres, became the first federal forest reserve approved by Congress. One of the major reasons for its creation was a desire to reduce exposure of settlers to the consequences of "thinning" by contractors for big lumber companies, who—then as now—operated at such low margins of profit that they were unwilling "to take on the extra cost of piling the branches and brush left behind after logging and conducting a controlled burn."[9]

Progressives such as Andrews could rely upon public indignation stoked by a generation of Populists led by the magnificent Ignatius Donnelley, congressman, perennial candidate for national office, economist, Baconian scholar, and the author of both the best speculative inquiry into Atlantis and of *Doctor Huguet,* the first novel about what it would be like for a white man—in this case a middle-class, nineteenth-century southern physician—to wake up black.[10]

In the same season in which Andrews made his famous speech, Donnelley made another as chairman of a Minnesota State Senate committee investigating the illicit lumbering of state lands that held timber crops dedicated to supporting its schools. Writing for the committee, Donnelley observed the "seeming respectability . . . [the] outward show of virtue and piety, . . . [and the] pretensions of benevolence" of the big operators also responsible for leaving the land subject to wildfire. By perpetrating "the most gigantic fraud . . . upon the school fund . . . [these] Stumpage Thieves whose profession, whose every instinct is child robbery, and to whom falsehood is a stimulant and perjury a pastime" had been guilty of depriving future generations of education while imperiling settlers of the present.[11]

Easterners—from the perspective of Arizona—were learning the lessons summarized by the National Forest Service in its report of 1911, and again in its report on the wildfires of 2000: "It is after logging that the damage from fire is greatest." This has always been true when forests are opened to hasty and promiscuous lumbering, even though it is alleged that doing so will make them "healthy" by ridding them of fire load or counteracting insect infestation. When supervision and restraint are removed, legitimate operators as well as "Stumpage Thieves" are likely to have "their timber . . . cut by contractors squeezed into operating at a low margin of profit." This was how it had been in the 1880s and 1890s: the contractors "simply refused to assume the additional expense of controlled burns of the brush and branches left in logging's wake. Although a generation of experience taught them better, they left behind the fuel for future forest fires." The trap having been set, into these littered landscapes came the pioneer farmer, often working alone or with his family and lacking "the ability to contain a blaze once it began. He merely doused his cabin with water and waited for the fire to stop of its own accord. Hundreds of fires set in this manner swept over the upper valley each year between 1890 and 1910."[12]

A decade earlier, the attention of Secretary Schurz was called to the wholesale pillaging of the federal public lands, to the fires that followed, and to the deaths of many homesteaders who had been induced by real estate promoters, including the wildcatters, to try farming in cutover areas. After the fires, many continued trying to eke out a living on the sandy soil left charred by wildcat lumbermen.

The lumbermen and real estate salesmen had friends in Congress, so that body refused to provide the Department of the Interior with more than a total investigatory budget of $12,000. Schurz responded by going to the public, calling for "an end to preemption rights and homestead privileges for forest lands on the grounds the lands were not suited for family farms." A half century ahead of his time, he "advocated managing forestlands for sustained yield by keeping them in public hands and leasing cutting rights." "I found myself standing almost solitary and alone," he said proudly. "Deaf was Congress, and deaf the people seemed to be." I know the feelings—pride and anger, mixed—but of course Schurz was not left alone for long, for Ignatius

Donnelley and Christopher Columbus Andrews were waiting in the wings.[13]

Meanwhile Congress listened to the lobbyists. The Timber Cutting Act of 1878 authorized lumbering the public domain either by homesteaders or mining companies. Wildcatting lumbermen could cruise the public lands, pick the likeliest stands, cut them down, and pay a fee—after the fact—of $1.25 per acre. Then the poorest of poor farmers would come in and try to homestead there.[14]

Rutherford Hayes, a mild man, was in enough trouble already with Congress because he had backed Schurz on civil service reform. His fierce Secretary of the Interior was pressing too hard, so Hayes put the Division of Forestry into the Department of Agriculture. After Hayes, exhausted, decided not to attempt a second term, Schurz urged his Liberal Republican friends to support Grover Cleveland for the presidency. After the tenth try, the Forest Reserve Act (also known as the Creative Act) was passed in 1891, empowering the president to hew "forest reserves" out of the public domain rather than open those reserves to homesteading. During his four-year tenure as president (between Cleveland's two terms) President Benjamin Harrison tugged Schurz back toward the Republican Party by creating the nation's first forest reserve. It included more than a million acres south of Yellowstone National Park in what is now primarily the Shoshone National Forest, and later added another thirteen million acres in forest reserves.[15]

THE CREATIVE ACT AND FOREST RESERVES

The 1891 "Creative Act" was indeed creative. It placed on the record as firm a statement as those of the Homestead and Morrill Acts that the federal government could use its power as a landowner to favor one mode of settlement over another, and might even deny settlement in some areas when it was in the public interest to do so. The Creative Act repealed the Timber Culture Act of 1873, which had sought to induce tree planting by granting a homesteader 160 additional acres of land in the arid West if he agreed to plant a quarter of it in trees. This noble gesture did not keep its nobility long; the land went largely to speculators after a later Congress stripped out its tree-planting provision. The Creative Act counterpunched by repealing the emasculated "timber culture laws" and substituted language in section 24 providing instead that the president might "set apart and reserve, in any State or Territory having public land bearing forests, in any part of the public lands wholly or in part covered with timber or undergrowth, whether of commercial value or not, as public reservations."

Though the nation was not yet willing to give life to this provision by providing money for a Schurz-style civil service to manage the parks or forests, the principle was in place. Three years later, the Department of Agriculture prohibited the "driving, feeding, grazing, pasturing or herding of cattle, sheep and livestock" on the forest reserves. Common sense had coalesced around the idea that some places were good for some things, some for others.[16]

Science agreed; the National Academy of Sciences established its National Forestry Commission in 1896, issuing a report that set forth the principle of limits: "Steep-sloped lands should not be cleared, the grazing of sheep should be regulated, miners should not be allowed to burn land over willfully, lands better suited for agriculture or mining should be eliminated from the reserves, mature timber should be cut and sold, and settlers and miners should be allowed to cut only such timber as they need." That was husbandry.[17]

Though one of his more famous aphorisms was that there is nothing more unsettling to the public peace than a revolution left unfinished, Schurz was winding down. He might have been drawn to Theodore Roosevelt, with whom he became acquainted during their service with the National Civil Service Reform League, but he disapproved of Roosevelt's imperial war against Spain as Marsh had disapproved of James K. Polk's imperial war against Mexico. Roosevelt did please him by creating a full-bore Forest Service in 1905, but lost Schurz by striking up an alliance with John Coit Spooner. Before he died, Schurz, the old revolutionary, gravitated toward the hotter progressivism of Robert La Follette.

Many were the accomplishments of a generation that learned the lessons taught by fire. In Schurz's Wisconsin, the first report of the legislature in 1867 led to a series of withdrawals from settlement and provisions for sustainable state and national forestry. Thousands of lives and millions of acres were saved from further losses. Likewise, the worst eroded and burned-over areas of Minnesota, nearly a third of the state, are now protected in state and national forests. After the Midwest led the way, New England and the nation followed. Congressman John Weeks of Massachusetts secured passage in 1911 of the Weeks Act, authorizing states to recover watersheds so burned as to erode and send silt downstream to damage the ability of his textile-milling constituents to run their looms. From that legislation, with its extensions to permit federal acquisition of previously private land, came the White Mountain and Green Mountain National Forests. After limits were learned, lives were saved.

11. MIGRATION, FIRE, EROSION, AND JOHN WESLEY POWELL

William H. C. Folsom first came to Minnesota in the 1840s. The sound of the woodsman's axe had been heard in Wisconsin ever since lumbermen were led into its pinelands by Jefferson Davis. In 1829, more than a decade before Folsom drew the timbering possibilities to the attention of his fellow Yankees, the future president of the Confederacy, then a lieutenant in the United States Army stationed at Prairie du Chien, took a squad of men up the Chippewa River Valley to cut timber and shingles. His and Folsom's reports of endless forests of marketable pine did not go unheeded. Some southern planters such as Wade Hampton II appeared personally at Wisconsin land offices to diversify their businesses into white pine. Some northerners, such as Folsom and Christopher Columbus Andrews, came as refugees from the expiration of the lumber business in New England. Some Germans, such as Carl Schurz, came as refugees from failed revolutions.[1]

Because architecture is historic literature worth reading on its own, and because the lumber boom of the nineteenth century produced so much architecture that remains in Minnesota and Wisconsin, it is still possible to sort out where each of these groups tried to settle. The St. Croix Valley is Yankee country. At Taylor's Falls, Folsom and his colleagues built four-square, white wooden houses on "Angels' Hill." Franconia, just down the river, was named after another lumber town, in New Hampshire; Minnesota's Franconia was not so pious as that portion of its Taylor's Falls situated above the taverns along the docks. Stillwater marked an eddy in the river where logs could swirl peacefully for a while until they became so numerous as to form jams; in a single year, 1890, the St. Croix Valley produced 450 million board feet in logs and lumber. The white villages continued down both sides of the river to Hastings, where the St. Croix, full of logs, converged upon the Mississippi, also full of logs, and the two produced the closest nineteenth-century equivalent to a rush hour afternoon in Los Angeles.

The German immigrants were not acquainted with profusion of this sort, nor did they understand what happened after trees were cut from sandy soils and cattle left to slice paths through the bare and vulnerable banks of rivers. They settled in southern Minnesota, along the Root, and beside the upper Mississippi, where promiscuous lumbering had eroded the sandy shores of lakes, leaving them "so filled with silt that they became more like swamps and muskegs. Alder took root where once there had been blue water." Above Little Falls, German remained the first language of shopping in some country stores well into my youth, though the land the immigrants settled was "charred . . . [and] cutover. . . . The forest was gone and nothing was left to hold the soil in place," and the Mississippi's tributaries displayed "banks severely eroded by . . . runoff and . . . log drives."[2]

Northwest of Winona, the Whitewater Valley was settled early in 1856 by Germans who knew no better than to lumber out the trees whose roots had held the soil that would soak up the rain. On the uplands, these settlers shredded the prairie turf by plowing up and down the hillsides. When the topsoil began to follow the spring freshets downhill into the valley floor, the farmers were delighted. It seemed like the Nile Valley—fresh soil every spring. But soon, all that came down was sand, filling the riverbeds and forcing the water up over the fields. Twenty-eight times in one year the Whitewater River flooded; finally, after the river receded and the sun came, the wind drove the dust into the air in suffocating clouds. More sand flowed down the hillsides past the stumps and the abandoned cornfields—sand and then mud. It is said by local people that one roadway, built six feet above flood level, was six feet below the level of the sand-covered fields a decade later.[3]

The Ellringers, Marnachs, Kieffers, and Majerus participated in the tragedy with Ira Card, whose farm lay under sixteen feet of sand and mud. Rylon Appleby finally abandoned his house when the mud seeped over the windowsills. Today, the limestone Kieffer farmhouse remains, four miles west of Altura, in the midst of eighteen thousand acres owned by the state of Minnesota, purchased in the 1930s and 1940s from farmers who could no longer survive in the devastated valley. The Nicholas Marnach "fort," a large, three-bay, two-story limestone house, had slots under the eaves for firing rifles in case of an Indian attack, which never came. The house surrendered instead to the mud, and it has fallen into ruin.

The Yankees and Germans came into this eroded, despoiled, and fire-prone land in about equal numbers and at about the same time. It is likely that both groups were drawn to the free states rather than to the South, dominated by the slave system of the planters, or the Southwest, threatened by that system until 1860. The deliberate direction of New England migration by the provisions of the Northwest Ordinance shows how early in our national history federal incentives were used to control land use. To that larger subject I will return, but now I only suggest in a preliminary way that the New Englanders often migrated as villagers, going as a group, or as veterans, bringing their families with them. Architecturally, their progress can be marked by white wooden houses, contrasting with the brick, Virginia-Kentucky style that can be found along the southern extremities of the region, from the Appalachian corner of Ohio all the way to Galena, Illinois.

The Yankees went west in a burst after 1820, when three-fifths of the increase in population in upstate New York came from lumbered-out New England; the Erie Canal sluiced Yankees westward after the cost of crossing New York shrank from a hundred dollars to five dollars a ton. By 1834, when my own people first traveled from the Connecticut River Valley to the Hudson, and then along the Erie Canal and the Great Lakes to the Illinois prairie, as many as eighty thousand migrants passed that way each year. As each new Indian "treaty" opened a new province to settlement, farmers, tired of plowing their ancestral rocks and searching in the woods for hemlocks to turn into tannin, went west. White wooden Yankee houses went up all across the southern tier of Michigan counties and the northern prairies of Illinois and Indiana in the 1830s; Silas Farmer of Detroit wrote that "it seemed as if all New England were coming" through. In 1837, when the pinelands of the Chippewa Valley were ceded by the Indians, Wisconsin's white population was 11,683. A decade later it was 155,277, and two years later, 210,546.[4]

German immigrants of Carl Schurz's political persuasion were not drawn to the slave-owning German Coast of Louisiana or the quaint villages around New Braunfels, Texas. The majority were as steadfast against slavery in the United States as they had been against serfdom in their own country. For them as much as for the Yankees, the Northwest Ordinance and the free-labor state constitutions that followed from it were a powerful incentive to go to the Northwest. By 1860, there were as many people of German birth in Minnesota as there were Yankees—roughly eighteen thousand apiece.

By 1870, the Germans outnumbered the Yankees in Minnesota nearly two to one. Their migration thither had many causes, among them the absence of slavery (cynics would add the absence of non-Europeans, free or slave). That absence was not accidental. It was another instance of land-use patterns deliberately instated by the federal government and affirmed in state constitutions, including that of Minnesota. Labor systems, free or slave, are patterns of land use. So are environmental regulations. The Northwest Ordinance is in this sense a direct precedent to the Endangered Species Act.

There have been more direct federal interventions to establish some land uses and disestablish others. When the Chippewa Valley was being "cleared of Indians" and the land so acquired was made available to settlement by new arrivals at $1.25 an acre in the 1830s, the government was determining in effect who could settle where. It was doing this again when it made federal mortgage insurance available in some places and not in others, and when it paid 90 percent of the cost of highways into exurbia rather than the cost of mass transit in cities. Of course, what the government gives, the government may take away. After 1866, portions of the Chippewa Valley that had been lumbered and settled in the 1840s and 1850s were withdrawn from settlement and turned over to reforestation. The purpose was to reduce the pain and suffering from fire. The effect was also to reduce the humiliation of attempting to farm beyond natural limits.

The message imported by the legislature of Wisconsin was clear enough. So is the message now being sent by nature itself to all states: it is time to cease subsidizing settlement into other flame zones.

JOHN WESLEY POWELL, FIRE, AND SMART GROWTH

The same instruction came from John Wesley Powell, the most thoughtful nineteenth-century inquirer into the ecological realities of settlement in the arid lands of the West. Powell, another Civil War veteran, had lost an arm at Shiloh, but remained a good shot with his remaining arm as he explored the canyons and deserts of the West. Powell's nine-hundred-mile journey down the Colorado, through the Grand Canyon, demonstrated—as Harry Yount had done farther north—that it was possible for white men to go where only Indians had gone before. Like Stephen Long and Zebulon Pike before him, he entered the High Plains along the shallow rivers moving through cottonwoods; these trees are not stately as are the English oak, the German linden, or the white pine of Maine. They do not age into giants of the forest but, instead, become disheveled, battered old geezers. The cottonwood is of little use for lumber. It burns easily; charred cottonwoods are almost as common on the plains of the arid West as charred ponderosa pines are on the flanks of the region's mountains. As agent of the General Land Office under Schurz, Powell became the first senior government official to take note of the effects of wildfire upon the forests and rivers of the West.[5]

In 1878, Schurz sent Powell's "Report on the Lands of the Arid Region" to the Speaker of the House of Representatives with approval. This took courage, for Powell recommended inhibitions on the development of that region for agriculture, grazing, and settlement, to take account of its natural limits. However, he did repeat one of the many myths of his time that seemed to justify mistreatment of the Indians: "in the main," he wrote, they were responsible for wildfires, and thus he permitted the inference that clearing out the Indians would do as much good as clearing out fire load. Later he repented: the primary causes of wildfires, he came to admit, were natural—heat, dryness, and lightning. Furthermore, like Thoreau, Mark Twain, and many other white people, he himself had once carelessly set a fire. Powell's fire swept tens of thousands of acres. Though lightning continued to set fires throughout the West long after the Indians were no longer present, Powell had given further currency to a general misperception that appeared in the press as late as 2005.[6]

Once Powell had passed through his scapegoating phase, readers of his later work could see more clearly his central perception: fire is likely to occur everywhere that is hot and dry. The fuel may be grass or trees, but where there is lightning, there will be fire. Many places in which this will happen frequently should not be farmed or settled, and Powell said so. He was a brave man in many ways. He had been proven so in battle and in exploration; now he was tested in politics. Disfavored among boomers and land hawks in the West, he urged that settlement not be encouraged except in relatively fire-safe, well-watered, and well-protected areas along rivers. The government was the owner of most of the land, provider of protection for settlers—by the cavalry and then by the police. It built dams, and later power lines, and constructed and maintained roads. It was the nation's most active developer—and on land it chose to sell to its citizens at very low prices. Instructed by fire, Powell urged the government to see to it that the settlement it made possible remained within natural limits.

Along Powell's route through northern Arizona were object lessons both on the gradual effects of inhospitable weather and on the more sudden effects of wildfires. Many abandoned pueblos lay in ruins along the Colorado River, some of them with corn, pottery, and baskets still in place. Evidently ancient peoples had attempted to live in harsh circumstances, but had had to abandon their homes when the difficulties became, over time, insurmountable. Some pre-Columbian migration was caused by sudden events, but the archaeological record indicates that more often the causes were temperature and rainfall so erratic as to defeat planning for planting or reaping. Forty discouraging years of the thirteenth century starved out the people of the Colorado Plateau and drove them to seek better-watered homes to the southwest and along the Rio Grande.

Corncobs left in pots in cliffside pueblos tell one story. The corncobs sticking out of hardened lava in a volcanic cone just south of the Grand Canyon tell another. Sunset Crater is surrounded by the hardened lava flows that were aflame in the winter of A.D. 1064–1065, after the entire top of the mountain blew into the air. Thousands of people had lived along its slopes. Many died of burns, and many more from suffocation. As volcanic dust settled over thousands of square miles, the sun was obscured for months, as the Hopi, who were there then and are there now, recall in their ceremonies. Sunset Crater was given its name by Powell because the red, pink, and yellow silica, gypsum, and iron oxide that formed from fumaroles along the crater's rim are the colors of a lurid western sunset. The corncobs in the lava and the evidence of human habitation give the word "sunset" another connotation. There are limits. All the world is not meant for occupation.

LESSONS OF CATASTROPHE

Powell's survey of the arid West led him to the conclusion already reached by Marsh in the well-watered East: nature will have its way.

Powell urged that "residences should be grouped" into communities where they can be protected. Where water is scarce, underbrush dense, mountainsides steep, and lightning strikes often, dispersed homesteads are unhealthy. In such places it is wise to heed the folk wisdom of Hispanic villagers and Indians living in pueblos clustered close to springs and streams. By attending to that experience and to those traditions, Powell argued, newcomers could "have the benefits of the local organizations of civilization—as schools, churches, etc., and the benefits of cooperation in the construction of roads, bridges, and other local improvements."[7]

The generation of conservationists of the 1870s, led by Schurz and Powell after the death of Marsh, attempted to sort through the consequences of the Homestead Act of 1862 and its successors, the Timber Culture Act of 1873 and the Desert Land Law of 1877. Each of these pieces of legislation enlarged the scale of the parcels that might be acquired from the public domain for agriculture or grazing. But Powell and Schurz, like Marsh before them, pointed out that some land should not be put under the plow in forty- or four-hundred- or four-thousand-acre units. Dry lands could not be farmed as if they were in Indiana or Iowa. Some dry lands were unfit for any kind of agriculture, and even some of that which might produce a crop was more likely to produce a fire. Merely enlarging the size of trouble does not make it less troublesome. There are limits.

12. SMOKE, DUST, AND THE LAND

The limits set for human habitation change as climate changes, or as the air above the land changes, or the waters about it. The land itself may erode or subside, may be engulfed or flooded, may accumulate dust or loess (windblown soil), may be overlaid by ash or lava, may gain silt in a delta or sand on a beach, or may be manured artificially or by the presence of animals. Humans change land and expand the limits of settlement by gardening, manuring, and some kinds of tillage. They introduce plants, animals, and microbes, some beneficial and some not. They also rip and ruin, contaminate and desolate. Thus they expand and contract their own limits by their own actions. History records a series of intended or unintended, reversible or irreversible consequences of political decisions on land use.

In the United States, political decisions have both expanded and diminished the extent of habitable land; the edges, or frontiers, of those expansions and contractions have frequently been expressed by fire, dust, and flood. The study of the dust frontier is useful because it has moved forward and backward for many of the same reasons that the fire frontier has moved, and also because some wise political responses to dust have come ahead of equivalently prudent responses to fire. Wildfire and dust have physical characteristics in common, and they have sent similar messages to humans when the limits of habitation and use have been transgressed.

Fire is a rapid combination of oxygen with another element, releasing heat and light. When hydrogen burns it combines with oxygen, producing water along with flame and heat—in a perfectly controlled laboratory experiment. In real life there is always something in the neighborhood that corrupts this stylish simplicity. Some unfortunate cow or tree or—horrible to contemplate but nonetheless possible— some human body that has not burned completely and breaks into tiny particles, which appear as smoke or as a yellow haze, like that filling the air over New York State in the parched early summer of 1908. That cloud of tiny and partially burned particles of trees, shrubs, fur, and skin came from flames that themselves were visible because among their luminous gases were similar particles still burning. As the summer drought continued, more forests and grasslands dried into tinder ready to be converted chemically into flame, smoke, gases, and, in nature's ironic way, tiny droplets of water.

Dust is a nonluminous cloud of particulate matter not so light as smoke but light enough to be carried in the wind and the jet stream. It is made of the same sort of stuff that goes into smoke; both dust and smoke are ghosts of former life. Dust may be thickened by inert or sterile matter—bits of quartz, for example—but it comprises mostly particles of previously living stuff, some of it partially burned, some of it torn apart and dried out. Burning can be seen as a chemical process, tearing apart as a physical one.

Humans have caused, enjoyed, and suffered from fire since they became human. They burned and were burned out of Africa and onto all the continents except Antarctica. These Prometheans marked their migrations with the fires they set, and still do. There are pyromaniacs and there are those, such as the naturalist and explorer John Wesley Powell, who ignited wildfires unintentionally. Powell confessed to setting a forest ablaze from mountain range to mountain range because he felt cold one evening and was hasty with a little warming fire. Over those 150,000 years, others among us have used fire to warm ourselves, as well as to cook, clear land, drive game, break open rocks to secure minerals, and frighten our enemies. Byzantine admirals used flame throwers of "Greek fire" against enemy fleets a thousand years before flaming arrows launched by marauding pioneers set thatched Shawnee villages aflame in Kentucky in the 1770s. Humans have not yet used dust as a weapon, so far as I know, though dust clouds set up by hostile horsemen have been simulated by desperate foot soldiers dragging mats and branches to convince their foes that they were more formidable than they were. And all politicians know the practice and the expression of "putting dust in the eyes" of an opponent.[1]

Nature may not be hostile when it sets up smoke or dust, but it gives notice that it has been affronted. Often that affront comes after it has been distempered by drought, and is smoky and dusty on its own, bothering no one if no one is there. To reiterate an essential point, people must be present for a disaster to be a disaster. Humans provoke nature to disaster as often as they suffer natural disaster. Sometimes they merely settle where they should not. Sometimes they put animals where those animals do not belong. Sometimes they rip away sod and replace it with crops that cannot hold topsoil. Then the earth erupts and fills the sky with smoke or dust or a combination of the two, as it did during the great drought of 1908.

By July of that year, the air was so hot and dry over the Catskills that raindrops evaporated between the clouds and the ground. This does not happen often in the East, but in the West the natives have a word for it—"virga." In 1908, in the Catskills, as in the Sangre de Cristo Mountains of New Mexico, the lightning did its work, and the tinder was there when the lightning came. Maine was burning, too, and the Adirondacks, once again, and the forested corners of Connecticut. Stephen Pyne has reported that New Yorkers saw that "smoke even wafted in from the vicinity of Atlantic City," and from fires in the brown little hills around the watershed of Jersey City, covering Manhattan in a "heavy gray pall."[2]

The skies over Chicago were sometimes dirty pink and sometimes yellow, depending on how the mix shifted between gray smoke from Minnesota, Wisconsin, and Michigan and red hematite-laden dust from Oklahoma. Farmers in the luxuriously wet prairies of Illinois cursed their Oklahoma counterparts for filling the air with the dust that had swirled into the air after their plows, as dust follows a horseman in the desert. In Kansas and Nebraska, clothes drying on lines turned red. That happened again in the 1930s, when John Steinbeck described it:

The dawn came, but no day. In the gray sky, a red sun appeared, a dim red circle that gave little light, like dusk, and as that day advanced, the disc slipped back toward darkness, and the wind cried and whimpered over the fallen corn.

Men and women huddled in their houses, and they tied handkerchiefs over their noses when they went out, and wore goggles to protect their eyes.

When the night came it was black night, for the stars could not pierce the dust to get down. In the middle of that night the wind passed on and left the land quiet. The dust-filled air muffled sound more completely than fog does. . . . In the morning the dust hung like fog, and the sun was as red as ripe new blood. All day the dust sifted down from the sky, and the next day it sifted down. . . . It settled on the corn, piled on the tops of the fence posts, piled up on the wires; it settled on roofs, blanketed the weeds and trees. . . . Horses came to the watering troughs and muzzled the water to clear the surface dust. After a while the faces of the watching men lost their bemused perplexity and became hard and angry and resistant. Then the women knew that they were safe and that there was no break. Then they asked, What'll we do? And the men replied, I don't know. But it was all right. . . . The men sat in the doorways of their houses. . . . The men sat still—thinking—figuring.[3]

Later, the nation as a whole did some figuring, and showed itself capable of recognizing that transgression of nature's limits in some dry places produces dust. Now the nation as a whole can do some figuring about the transgressions of limits leading to suffering from fire. Once again, there are people in the wrong places, doing the wrong things.

MIGRATION AND WEATHER

The earlier discussion of recent migrations of large numbers of people into flame zones needs a little expansion backward in time and forward into policy—policy grounded in some more "figuring." It doesn't take much of that to agree with Abraham Lincoln that Americans are much disposed to "locomotion," but it is the business of the Census Bureau to provide the figures. The 2000 census showed that the average American stayed home—"retained residence"—no more than ten years. That was low "sedentism" by anthropological standards. During the 1990s, nearly 40 million Americans uprooted themselves in an average year to move to a new home—out of a total population of about 290 million. Westerners, the most unsettled among them, moved from place to place nearly twice as often as northeasterners, the ratio being 21 percent against 12 percent annually, on average.[4]

Western restlessness probably has something to do with western weather. There is a difference between weather and climate. Folk wisdom takes weather to be a laughing matter—because it changes. Nobody laughs about climate. Its changes take a long time and last a long time. Westerners expect better weather than they get, and are slow to accept that what they are in fact getting is climate. They seem to take risks easterners would not because they are prone to believing that better weather or science will take care of them. They are often disappointed, and move rather than accept the unpleasant contrary: they are living in a fragile, unforgiving environment that will put up with them only when they behave.

When goaded, the arid West bucks, producing dust and something a bucking animal does not produce—fire. Fire comes with dry weather, and fire is frequent in dry climates. Humans can do nothing about the weather, and only slowly do things that affect the climate, but they can do a lot about their politics. Human activity continues to cause long-term, irreversible climate change. Like scapegoating, weather can be a distraction. Before 1860, it was generally believed that agriculture was impossible west and north of the forested areas of the Mississippi Valley, away from narrow stretches of irrigated land along such rivers as the Pecos and Rio Grande and those strips along the Missouri and the Red where the Mandans and the Caddos had demonstrated that farming could be practiced among the cotton-woods. Nineteenth-century explorers such as Long and Pike, brought up beneath large trees in the East, reported that there was no use trying. Partially as a result of their assessment of the Great American Desert (the name given in the first half of the nineteenth century to the area west of the Mississippi) as not worth much per acre, the first transcontinental railroads were thought to be justified in seeking immense land grants. They got them, and then, in the very nick of Wall Street's time, the climate seemed to intervene—a run of wet years induced a rush to buy land-grant property in Nebraska, Kansas, and parts of the Dakotas. The homesteaders pressed even farther from the tree line.

In a classic passage in his essay "Climate and Settlement in the Great Plains," C. Warren Thornthwaite described a land rush into the danger of dust during the early 1880s, using terms that might with only a few tweaks be applied to the land rush into the danger of fire in the 1950s and 1980s. "By 1890, a vanguard of settlers had pushed . . . into . . . Colorado. The majority had come from the humid Northeastern States, and previous experience had in no way prepared them for the climatic hazards they now encountered. The initial settlement occurred during one of the rainier periods, and the settlers were predisposed to believe that the climate was becoming permanently more humid."[5]

Nature responded with the droughts and blizzards of the late 1880s and 1890s. In the next great retreat from the plains, convoys of prairie schooners headed back eastward. The farmers blamed the bankers, the railroads, and the gold standard, but the real story was that the limits of prudence had been violated. Half the people of western Kansas left between 1888 and 1892. Two-thirds of the population retreated from its especially dry counties. Twenty-six counties of South Dakota emptied out. In 1891, eighteen thousand prairie schooners crossed the Missouri from Nebraska, going east, leaving behind a landscape as ravaged as the loess hills of Mississippi and the piedmont of Georgia after the plantation system had done its antebellum worst.[6]

The farmers remembered, but the rest of the nation settled into the next normalcy—the 1890s, big-business supremacy, white supremacy, Jim Crow, and an illusion of human supremacy over nature. The cooperative movement did not include cooperation between humans and other species. As the century turned, the Progressive era flowered in the compost of partly decomposed Populist reform, and the Forest Service was founded in 1905, under Gifford Pinchot, who asserted that man could control nature, including fire.

Then, in the early years of the First World War in Europe, another transient and unsustainable rainy period encouraged replowing the plains to satisfy the demands of war-torn Europe. Farmers pressed again across the natural limits. Plows broke the High Plains. People talked of "dust mulch" each time the wind was down. But when the war came to an end, demand collapsed. Farm income dropped from $17 billion in 1919 to $10.5 billion in 1921. Calvin Coolidge responded by opining that "the farmers have never made money. I don't believe we can do much about it." An environmental disaster was on its way along the high, dry agricultural frontier. Another is now on its way along the high, dry urban-exurban frontier.[7]

When the great drought ensued in the 1920s, and then the great blow-away of the 1930s, people responded as they had before: they moved. As Thornthwaite recalls, "the period from 1920 to 1940 resembled the earlier period between 1880 and 1900. . . . Each drought period set in motion an emigration that grew into a rout. In both cases the series of rainy years had been mistaken for normal climate, with disastrous results. . . . Overextension . . . led to in-migration, in-migration was followed by disaster, and disaster by emigration and . . . abandonment . . . , [and then leading to] the shift of ownership from individuals to loan companies." That shift is what the first chapter of *The Grapes of Wrath* is about.[8]

No leader of government in the 1920s sought to "do much" as one-quarter of the nation went on a stock-buying binge while three-quarters of families made a go of it on less than $3,000 a year—the Jazz Age for some and the blues for many. An environmental depression ensued from the farm depression, and the nation danced the Charleston. The New Deal got started after farm income, having caught up a little, fell in the early 1930s by another 30 percent. In the 1880s, nature had retaliated with drought and blizzards, but until the 1920s most of the grasslands were still intact in the West, and most of the overgrazed mountainsides were uninhabited. The Soil Erosion Service and the Civilian Conservation Corps had some success in withdrawing acreage from wheat production when nature grew impatient and withdrew topsoil. Between 1931 and 1934, the Dust Bowl blew the exposed surface of the plains into the mouths and ears and nostrils of the already defeated people of that region. The black wind came, and the yellow sky over Chicago.

It all seems so distant now, the stuff of forgotten novels and gritty grade-B movies, until we look at the sky above Denver and Boulder and Albuquerque. Now it is not dust but ashes. The sky is again yellow over much of the West, as it was in 1933. Nature is sending winds to drive fires across overgrazed and overlogged mountainsides as nature has sent winds across overplowed and overgrazed plains. Nature's response to our lack of respect in the 1930s and 1980s was to remind us of our limits. That was before we added a further transgression—situating ourselves where once we situated only our cows. In the 1880s and the 1920s and 1930s, herds and farms pressed beyond the legitimate limits of human domain in the West. Now, exurban developments do so. Once, illegitimate agriculture affronted nature. Now we provoke nature with illegitimate development.

A dust storm of the 1930s, the hot, dry decade in which there were
also great firestorms in the forests. The dust taught lessons about the
limits of sod-busting and settlement. It has taken us longer to learn
the lessons of the smoke. (George E. Marsh album; the National Oceanic
and Atmospheric Administration, Department of Commerce)

This shift in the battle line between humans and nature is likely to produce a new set of migrations. As nature refuses to retreat, humans will, as they once did in the face of dust and, to some extent, flood. That will happen in any case; the policy question posed by these events is this: Should the government of the United States continue to encourage migration into flame zones? Though some of that migration has been driven by misperceptions about weather, fire, dust, and flood, some, I believe, has been caused by government policies. Policies can be unmade by the same means that they are made. The democratic process permits reconsideration. Sometimes reconsideration is feckless because irreversible damage has been done. In the situation before us, however, some of the damage is reversible still, and more damage can be averted.

What can be done can be undone. Hugh Hammond Bennett showed us ways to accomplish that.

THE GENIUS OF HUGH HAMMOND BENNETT

Perhaps only those of us who began testifying before congressional committees in the Eisenhower era, which was also the McCarthy era— in open and secret session, with or without the advice of counsel, and under threat of both political and personal retribution—can fully appreciate Bennett's courage and theatrical genius. I thrill to write his name, as I do that of the magnificent Joseph Welch. Welch's great moment lives incandescently in the memories of those of us who had been attempting, with considerably less effect, in articles and documentaries to slow the assault upon constitutional liberty by Senator Joseph R. McCarthy. Welch brought all our work to a blow-torch point with a simple question delivered in a trembling voice: "Senator, have you no sense of decency?" Bennett had the same genius. Welch had saved up his question and his tremble for just the right moment; Bennett saved up a cloud of dust.[9]

Bennett's masterpiece of theater was for many years accounted to be mere folklore. Then the archives of the agency he founded as the

Soil Erosion Service (now called the Natural Resources Conservation Service) were ransacked by Douglas Helms, its chief historian. And there, for wonder and delight, were letters and minutes confirming the story's literal truth: In April 1935, Bennett knew that the Great Plains were suffering drought. Dust was flying up from fields once covered by a poultice of short grass that had in the 1920s and 1930s been grazed down to its roots and ripped apart by plows to plant wheat. The people of the West knew that wheat does not have the co-operative, mutually reinforcing relationship to seldom-watered soil that native grasses do, but Congress kept on subsidizing plowing and planting, despite the dust storms set loose in previous droughts, in the 1880s, and in 1908–1910. Professionals such as Bennett knew what was needed. The government would have to set limits and stop en-couraging farmers to plant the wrong crops in the wrong places. In-stead, it should offer help to return the soil to its age-old partnership with grasses that were shorter and more deeply rooted than wheat.

If the damage was so great that even that would not work, more aid would be necessary to help the farmers or ranchers off the land. Ideas like this did not go down well in a Congress dominated by the interests of big ranchers and corporate farmers, or by easterners who had no direct acquaintance with the conditions depicted by John Steinbeck. The grapes of wrath had been sown, but not yet reaped. *The Plow That Broke the Plains* had not yet been filmed, or scored by Virgil Thompson. The photographs of Dorothea Lange and Walker Evans had yet to appear. But the need for action was there, and some-thing had to be done to get the attention of a Congress that would not take seriously what they were being told about Oklahoma or Ne-braska in Franklin Roosevelt's Grotonian accent.[10]

Bennett knew he had Senate hearings coming up, and he had a dust cloud forming. So he dithered, dallied, and found reasons to be required urgently in the field, while he summoned reports from his agents tracking the eastward movement of the cloud, which billowed bigger and bigger as it gained reinforcement with each mile from new updrafts of dust from drought-stricken barren land and smoke from eastern wildfires. Once it approached the Appalachians, Bennett was ready to testify. As the dust cloud began to turn the setting sun Steinbeck's color of fresh blood, hearings were arranged before the Senate Public Lands Committee. On the day for which they were scheduled, Bennett got the report he wanted. When his testimony reached its most urgent moment, he suddenly asked for a recess and suggested they all go to the windows. The sky had turned an ugly orange-brown. The sun was obscured. But the truth—and the need for action—was revealed. Bennett wrote that "everything went nicely thereafter."[11]

Well, more nicely. The bureaucracy was not much interested in change, nor were many ranchers and farmers, still thinking as they had since 1901, when Secretary of Agriculture James Wilson scribbled along the margin of a memorandum mentioning the effects of overgrazing on soil, "All too true, but not best for us to take a position now." In Bennett's great year, 1935, his associate chief, Walter C. Lowdermilk, was left standing alone in a meeting room after all the cattlemen present had walked out. He had been guilty of using "the baleful term 'overgrazing.'" Some dirty words become clean over time; it is no longer bad manners to speak of overgrazing among cattlemen, though the term "overplowing" isn't much used in talks with farmers. Sometime soon, though, "overbuilding" will come into the lexicon as an analogue to these other terms, but probably not until new droughts come and new firestorms and new dust storms produce dust to mix with smoke.[12]

When that happens, it may be possible to relearn the lessons of the Soil Erosion (later Soil Conservation) Service, and to apply environmental science in a cooperative, rather than an authoritarian or technocratic, mode. In earlier chapters, I pointed to the mutual reinforcement that workaday dirt farmers practicing sustainable husbandry took from patrician theorists such as George Perkins Marsh. A generation later, Carl Schurz synthesized Marsh's improvers and the vernacular practitioners of husbandry into an anticipation of the Progressive movement. From there it was merely a half jump to the agriculture and forestry policies of Robert and Philip La Follette and the New Deal. The improvers and the Progressives might have been content to arrange matters for the farmers and community foresters on the basis of their own expert wisdom. But by the time Hugh Bennett founded the Soil Erosion Service, that technocratic impulse was ready to be moderated by including people of each locality in consultation about best practices and best experience. As the twenty-first century rolled around, that tradition, though not always consistently practiced, was sufficiently strong to support a rebirth of forest husbandry in community forestry.

Husbandry and technical assistance may be enough when environmental degradation has not been too severe. Where matters have gone badly, however, more help was and is needed. In the 1930s, the Civilian Conservation Corps supplied an army of young men to redeem some of the errors of what might well be called "dust policy." A new conservation corps could do the same for fire load. There are similarities between dust and fire. There are also likenesses between grasslands that have been overplowed and promiscuously grazed, and fire-suppressed and promiscuously lumbered forests.

GENERAL EISENHOWER'S BEST EFFORTS

Those similarities emerged clearly in the 1940s and, though it is not conventional to say so, during the Eisenhower Administration, from 1953 to 1961, when the nation achieved important progress in land planning for arid regions between the New Deal and the Farm Bill of 1985. I have a little personal experience with the emergence of farm policy, though I did not know that at the time. As an Eisenhower Republican, I campaigned in his entourage across the southern tier of farming counties in Minnesota, and listened to a lot of his speeches. Thereafter, I experienced both the pride and terror of introducing him to the crowd before the Minnesota State Capitol. While waiting around for the "go" signal, I talked with him a little about the places we had been. Eisenhower had experienced life on the plains, where as a boy he observed drought relief follow drought disaster in recurring cycles, with periods in between in which the federal government met wartime urgencies by encouraging plowing arid areas with thin soil. As a man temperamentally irritated by waste, he did what he could as president to break this cycle by introducing more humane and economical ways of dealing with farmers who were sometimes urged to do the wrong things and sometimes suffered for it.

The core of the Eisenhower program was to discourage planting the wrong crops in arid lands and to provide instead federal payments to farmers to convert cropland to grassland and keep it in grass for five or more years—in effect, a phased buyout. Eisenhower's Secretary of Agriculture made use of all the conventional tools of planning: "restrictive covenants and surrender of eligibility for allotments, loans, and [in this case government] crop insurance." (Had they been thinking of fire policy rather than dust policy, they might have added government mortgage insurance.)

The Great Plains Agriculture Council—as Republican a body as the leaders of the Agriculture Department who met with them—advocated "those practices which are most enduring and most needed." On June 9, 1956, Eisenhower signed a bill providing for the designation of dust zones in ten Great Plains states having "serious wind erosion problems." The designation would bring "changes in cropping systems and land use and conservation measures." Even the Farmers Union went along, despite its traditional opposition to "master plans." H. H. Finnell of the Soil Erosion Service in Amarillo, Texas, described the result as a "logical permanent remedy" carried forward by "men of stable character and more patience than those who ride on waves of speculation."[13]

EISENHOWER, WATER, DUST, AND FIRE

This sort of logical remedy is long overdue for flame zones as well. Fire policy should be similar to dust policy, both being responses to related natural phenomena of a desert climate. Eisenhower's Abilene, like my native St. Paul, Minnesota, is a place where the forests of the East still make an attempt to cope with dry conditions and trees are precious. Just a little farther west, only cottonwoods accompany the shallow streams of the short-grass plains. Those of us who grew up beside large Midwestern rivers in the 1920s, 1930s, and 1940s cannot think of cottonwoods and water without thinking at the same time of the Army Corps of Engineers—dams and locks and reservoirs and flooded towns. "Control by society over water resources and their use" meant something quite different to Eisenhower than it meant to the Corps, with which, in all its ways and wiles, he was thoroughly familiar. The Corps had inherited a tradition of thousands of years of hydraulic manipulation. Canal building and diversion had been carried on by the Native Americans, who were also seeking by controlled burns to manage fire-prone "resources." Then came John Wesley Powell, in the nineteenth century, to evangelize for dam building, and in the twentieth, the Corps was able to amplify Powell's ambitions immensely through the use of concrete, steel, and internal combustion engines for earth moving. The Corps owes Powell a monument, though it was Herbert Hoover, the "Great Engineer," who got one. As the Hoover Dam demonstrates, dam building on a huge scale had become the major public construction program of Republican administrations well before it was rediscovered by the New Deal. It was for Republicans of the 1920s the equivalent of the defense budget for the Republicans of the 1990s.

In the 1950s, Eisenhower was as skeptical of the Corps and its constituency as he was of the "military-industrial complex." He had good reason to understand the subtle power of both, and warned his countrymen about big dams as fervently as he did about swollen military budgets and swollen farm subsidies. He sought to rein in the Corps as he reined in his Secretary of Agriculture. Both dam building and crop price supports for cotton and grain grown in too-arid land were becoming costly and were diminishing productivity. Eisenhower warned against creating farm programs that benefited only real estate speculators in the same old-fashioned way that he resisted the excesses of the dispersion-industrial complex in gutting the old industrial cities.

By the end of his term in office, Eisenhower had developed a full and indignant understanding of the power of those lobbying for big dams, for big arms budgets, and for big farm subsidies. The grandiose plans of the Army Corps of Engineers for "big dams" aroused in him a desire for something better—and smaller. People he had known as a youth were suffering in flood zones. When he became president, Eisenhower supported instead little dams that would leave intact bosques, bogs, and wetlands as flood catch basins. He did not get much beyond that, though his dust policy recognized the importance of treating respectfully water underground as well as that flowing over the ground.

SPECULATION INVADES THE CAPITAL ACCOUNT

When Eisenhower took office, it seemed to many that "the centrifugal pump, along with cheap power from Texas oil wells and the hydro-electric plants at Hoover Dam," could make the desert bloom. All the worries inherited from explorers of the Great American Desert such as Long, Pike, and Powell seemed to be evaporating. It seemed possible to draw a bonanza of water from beneath the plains. The Ogallala Aquifer still is "the size of one of the smaller Great Lakes . . . expanding and accumulating its precious water, unmolested, since the last ice age." Donald Worster, the preeminent historian of water in the West, has provided another measure of the magnitude of the Ogallala: it held nearly three billion acre-feet of water under Colorado, Wyoming, Kansas, Nebraska, and parts of Texas and Oklahoma—more than the Mississippi "had carried to the Gulf in two hundred years."[14]

That underground lake was as attractive to midwesterners (though not in the same way) as an on-the-ground one in Minnesota, with loons and pickerel weed and water lilies. People from Cincinnati and Toledo heard the Ogallala's call, and responded to layoffs at home by packing up for the Oklahoma panhandle, as people in Maine had responded to forest fires and the Panic of 1837—during the first great epidemic of "Texas Fever." Many who might otherwise have been nervous about living in the desert were encouraged to think of all that water down there—way down. For a time, the water came up as required, and bankruptcies diminished. Many farmers followed the example of Frank Zybach. In 1948, Zybach built the first big-spider center-pivot rotating irrigation system near Strasburg, Colorado, setting lines of sprinklers rotating around a central pump that could be moved when its green-up circle was wet enough to start the cotton and alfalfa growing. By the 1980s, two and a half million acres of the dry plains had been irrigated for the first time—drawing on the capital account of the Ogallala. Other farmers, who had grasped the truth that all capital accounts are finite even if their assets are stated in acre-feet, sold out.[15]

The sellers were lucky. The buyers were not. Seeing green circles in a nice warm climate, they rushed into the plains, few of them pausing to read archaeological journals. Had they done so, they would have learned that often before weather-induced land rushes had produced disappointments on a massive scale when the rains stopped and surface waters dried up. Not until the early 1980s did the nation come to understand that the unlimited bounty of the West and its infinite tolerance for exploitation were, in the literal sense, fair-weather doctrines. In a region that, in the words of my old friend Marc Reisner, "has desert in its soul," fair weather means rainier weather. The collateral truth is that when the weather returns to its dry normal, water rationing must follow or water will be fought over. That is the inevitable consequence of people asking too much of nature's bounty by settling in the wrong places and doing the wrong things to the land—and with water.[16]

Aquifers constitute the vaults in which are stored the continent's liquid capital assets. Aquifers are replenished by rivers and rainfall, and depleted by wells and surface evaporation. The cash-flow account of nature's economy is fairly easy to follow. Aquifers do receive new capital, which seeps gravitationally from higher ground and from the surface, in the same incremental way that gold goes into the vaults at Fort Knox. But an aquifer holds water as gold—as capital.

Not all rain can be spending money. Some of it has to be allowed to seep through to replenish the capital account—as endowment managers permit some of the total return not to be disbursed but to stay in the fund to offset inflation.

During the relatively wet years of the 1920s and 1940s aquifers seemed to be holding their own, despite heavy withdrawals for irrigated cotton and hay farming. Then new farmers and new homeowners inserted hundreds of thousands of wells into the flanks of mountains like acupuncture needles upon the shoulders of the earth. For a hundred years, explorers and geographers such as Powell, Bernard De Voto, and Walter Prescott Webb had been warning that water was the lifeblood of the West, and that humans could not live where the water did not fall, or run, or lie below the ground within range of a pump. Perhaps for a time enough rain might fall, or streams might flow, or enough dark water might come up from aquifers to permit human habitation nearby. But when all these sources have been tried and all found wanting, humans will have to move out. Before that occurs, there is likely to be a contest for control of the wells, the streams, and the aquifers between expanding Sunbelt towns and agribusiness. It will not be a pretty fight.

Their predictions came true during the drought of the 1930s, when the rain stopped and the streams dried up and the underground water was not there for the wells. The topsoil of the Great Plains became dust, sucked up into the air, and "the Black Blizzard" moved eastward in suspension at ten thousand feet, making Hugh Bennett's argument.

Twenty years later, President Eisenhower's agriculture secretary picked up where Bennett had left off, advocating "restrictive covenants and surrender of eligibility for allotments, loans, and crop insurance." A new set of dust storms was once again scourging the High Plains after further intrusions into fragile short-grass prairies had been once more encouraged by federal subsidies. Withdrawing such subsidies in the face of dust seemed thoroughly reasonable in the 1930s and in Eisenhower's day. Withdrawing similar subsidies in the face of fire would be equally reasonable today.

THE COLD WAR TRUMPS THE SOIL SERVICE

For another three decades after Eisenhower left office at the beginning of 1961, the Cold War with the Soviet Union supervened all else in American public life, dominating even farm policy. The most dramatic demonstration of that dominance was the U-turn away from Eisenhower's dust-control regime, which was ordered by his successors to take advantage of the failures of Soviet farm policy. The loss of productivity in Russian wheat fields in the early 1970s was an invitation as seductive as the loss of a Soviet nuclear facility. Starvation in Russia weakened the Soviet regime, and in effect American farmers were mobilized to bring changes in the behavior of that regime, using grain as a weapon. To provide that weapon, the Dust Bowl was put back into production. The Cold War put the dust back into the air.

Russian agricultural policy had collapsed in the face of drought. The response of Earl Butz, President Richard Nixon's Secretary of Agriculture, was to expose the American West to the consequences of another drought. The "Soviet Grain Deal" became Cold War policy. Fragile new sod was broken. Big electric pumps pumped more and more water out of the Ogallala. Butz proclaimed one of the thousands of "new eras" that have flickered like fireflies across the American political scene since the First World War. This time, the combination of Soviet demand and hydrological technofixes seemed to justify abandoning control of land use. The dry-land farmer, declared Butz, was now "free to produce as much as he can," even if that meant taking the axe to the windbreaks put in place by the Soil Erosion Service and the Civilian Conservation Corps, and setting the cruel steel plows back into the reestablished grasslands. Between 1977 and 1982, wheat farmers put back into cultivation nearly 2 million acres of Montana, 750,000 acres of South Dakota, and nearly 600,000 acres of that swath of eastern Colorado lying within the high plains Stephen Long had called "the Great American Desert."[17]

Then an extraordinary thing happened. Though deprived of the stage management of Hugh Hammond Bennett, and without political power to countervail the influence of Butz and the international grain brokers he served, the farmers and ranchers of the High Plains took land planning into their own hands. "As stories of increased soil erosion spread," the Colorado Cattlemen's Association and the American Farm Bureau joined in support of a "sodbuster" bill in Congress, to discourage plowing and the replacing of grass with wheat. "Several counties in Colorado" passed "ordinances to prevent plowing on grasslands." The 1985 Farm Bill turned to New Deal, pre-Butz precedent because the framers of the bill "wanted to eliminate . . . commodity price support programs [that] encouraged poor soil conservation practices . . . on highly erodible land." They saw to it that farmers who wanted price supports and "eligibility for allotments, loans, and crop insurance" would have to "implement the conservation plan to stay eligible for government subsidies." To these "sodbuster" disincentives were added "swampbuster" provisions: farmers could not get these government subsidies if they drained wetlands. According to Douglas Helms of the Soil Erosion Service, this phase of that service's institutional life showed that conservative legislation might be "premised on the idea that some USDA programs induced the use of erodible land that would not have occurred otherwise." Learning from past errors, the Department of Agriculture moved toward a moratorium on those programs in dust zones.[18]

Why stop learning now? There are limits. Dust tells us that. So does wildfire.

13. URBANISM, DISPERSION THEORY, MIGRATION, AND FIRE DANGER

I share Garrison Keillor's Minnesotan disdain for the disdainful. Though we both have chosen to live in town rather than "at the lake," whether it be White Bear or Minnetonka or Wobegon, we don't think those who do are crazy. We don't think they have refused to learn. I think—I have not consulted Keillor on this—that they have just learned how to follow the government buck. With federally insured mortgages they bought houses to which they could travel on federally subsidized highways, and often worked nearby in office parks and shopped at big boxes, all of which enjoyed federal subsidies in the form of shelter from income taxes through the use of accelerated depreciation.[1]

David Brooks, the journalist du jour of dispersion theorists, writes with derision of our suburban fellow citizens, who, he asserts, have a "remarkably tenuous grip on reality." I don't agree. I think their grip is firm upon the reality of the subsidies rewarding them for dispersing from the old cities. Therefore, in my view, suburban America was not "formed by collective fantasy . . . born in a frenzy of imagination," but rather by rational decisions to take the money the government was handing out. The dispersion theorists write of a great dispersal as if it were a mad, lemming-like rush to extremities. Brooks depicts a sort of Children's Crusade intoxicated by a strange brew concocted of "the complex faith of Jonathan Edwards, the propelling ambition of Benjamin Franklin, [and] the dark, meritocratic fatalism of Lincoln— all these inheritances have shaped the outer suburbs." Goodness! If there is dark fatalism in the neighborhood, it is that of those seeking to convince the rest of us that we can never learn the lessons sent us by dust or fire—or, for that matter, by Edwards.[2]

Edwards! There's an odd choice. Edwards is too important an environmental writer to be discussed in less than a chapter, certainly not to be cabined within the same chapter as dispersion theory. Edwards will have that chapter, at the end, to provide a balancing entry to all the space given at the outset to Edward Teller, his polar opposite.

Now, what must be said about the disdainful apologists for sprawl? They have given significant aid and comfort to those who wish to believe that we Americans are too far gone in foolishness to redeem ourselves. In reply, we—those of us who do not accept any conjectural American compulsion to make cities uninhabitable and unsafe and then to do the same to the countryside—have an obligation to act on the contrary premise. We assert that given all the facts, Americans can be relied upon to slow the degeneration of the American land and to diminish the perils confronting people living in flame and flood zones.

We may have a continental-scale mess, but it is not because all of us hate cities, one another, and nature. Hopeless? The only hopelessness resides among the disdainful, the supine, or the willfully indifferent to the lessons of American history.

DISPERSION THEORY AND AMERICANS

Is there an invincible American aversion to cities and towns? Will neither fire nor flood nor dust nor any other natural threat deter the citizens of this insane republic from seeking their doom? Will nothing counteract the frenzy—no sense of community, no common culture, no religious ties, no reverence for one another or for nature, and no consciousness of limits? The answer to all these darkly fatalistic propositions is: no. We need not acquiesce in a new manifest destiny of mutually assured destruction with nature. The fundamental assertion on which centrifugal fatalism is based is wrong.

We Americans are not all urbanophobic. There is a strong and continuous countervailing hankering for village life in the American psyche. That hankering was patent in New England from the origin of the "Pilgrim" communities. They were villagers.

True, they were "easterners." Then are westerners different? Let's look at three varieties of westerners: Indians, Mormons, and Hispanic Americans. Are they anti-urban? Not in Arizona and New Mexico when John Wesley Powell passed through. Many Indians lived in pueblos tightly compacted along the banks of rivers. "Individual families owned their house sites and irrigated fields privately, but the grazing and forest lands that comprised the rest of the land grant functioned as a commons in which all residents of the village had rights."[3]

Twenty years later, when Frederick Jackson Turner was proclaiming the end of the frontier, it was conventional to associate that event with the notion that the Indians were disappearing, too. There was a sort of romantic extinctionism in the air. But neither the frontier nor the Indians have accommodated it, for once again, in 2006, much of the higher reaches of the Great Plains areas have become about as thinly populated as they were when Turner wrote. Throughout the United States, on the other hand, the Indians are growing in number. In 2006, there were more of them in the United States than full-time ranchers and farmers. That fact bears on the subject at hand because, amid all the talk about the American psyche, it helps to recall that Indians have psyches, too, and that many of them like to stick together and always have. In 1500, most Indians were living in villages. Few lived in teepees, and nearly all those who did, pitched them close together. In the centuries immediately before the Europeans came among them, those of the Southwest were becoming *increasingly* urban, aggregating into larger and larger pueblos. The pueblo people were the first New Urbanists.

The people who migrated after 1250 out of the region where Colorado, Utah, New Mexico, and Arizona now come together—the Four Corners—did not disperse into the countryside. Some moved in large numbers into new pueblos on the Pajarito Plateau, as the archaeology of the Bandelier National Monument demonstrates. On the southwest flanges of that plateau they built a dozen concentrated settlements, each containing a thousand or more rooms, larger than any towns built by Europeans in New Mexico for another six hundred years. Somewhat later, these same people congregated into existing villages along the Chama, Jemez, and Rio Grande rivers, gathering as their cousins in Arizona had done, and engaging in intensive hydraulic farming.

The "Seven Cities of Cíbola" sought by Coronado's raiding party in 1539 may have been somewhat romanticized versions of the pueblos built by these people, but the very fact that there *were* such cities demonstrates that the Ancestral Puebloans never relinquished their urban preferences even under intense ecological stress. They built new towns as they required them. They remained townspeople, farming beyond the town in groups, not as independent yeomen. As townspeople they still meet in kivas, as northeastern Indians met in "big houses" and northeastern Yankees meet in meetinghouses. These are urban phenomena. So are the ball courts of the ancient people of Arizona. These ceremonial spaces were built not as golf courses are built, on the edges of towns, but as the core of each town, like courthouse squares or plazas in front of cathedrals, among other city dwellers. And the ways in which Indian people have used both fire and water show how carefully and skillfully that must be done if we, too, wish to live within limits.

DISPERSION THEORY AND THE HISPANIC AMERICANS

The movement of masses of Americans from the North and East to the South and West has been recently matched in magnitude by another, Spanish-speaking migration from south of the border. Millions of people have come northward along the ancient *pacheco* traders' routes, which became the Spanish caminos reales of New Mexico and California. In California, New Mexico, and Texas, Hispanic communities have been reestablished where they flourished before 1840. This was Spanish-speaking and Indian language–speaking country until then, and now it is again, increasingly, as if the lines drawn by the Adams-Onis Treaty of 1819 were being reinstated.

John Quincy Adams was much derided for having conceded to Spain and Mexico all this territory in that year; by 1850, it had been conquered, and new treaties ratified those conquests. Now by sheer migration, the Mexicans are renegotiating incrementally, one by one, the territorial cessions made after the wars with Texas and the United States in the 1830s and 1840s. And not only in the Southwest. The slow infiltration of Spanish-speakers into Florida and the Gulf Coast has set brooding over this vast region the ghost of the Spanish empire as it was in 1802. The crown domains of the Spanish Hapsburgs and Bourbons were then said in Madrid to include Florida and the Gulf Coast, all the way around to the Rio Grande at Brownsville, plus the interior as far north toward the Missouri River as the King of Spain could prove it and Thomas Jefferson's armed explorers could not successfully dispute it.

The participants in this south-to-north migration do not bring the same experiences as those from the North and East. The "New American Mixing Bowl" was created in the 1990s. Frederick Jackson Turner was wrong in thinking that the frontier moved in only one direction, and only once. All Americans did not migrate east to west. Many of them have migrated south to north.[4]

The frontier of human occupancy has moved back and forth across North America many times; Turner's one-way hypothesis is therefore a poor guide to experience with fire and to traditional willingness to risk wildfire. The south-to-north migrants did not emerge from Turner's Indiana-like world. They did not encounter fire as it occurs either in eastern cities or on Indiana's solitary farmsteads. Very little of the third of the territory of the United States that in 1820 lay below the Adams-Onis Line was rural as Iowa was rural. Nor was Florida, when it was wrested from Spain by Andrew Jackson. In Florida then, as in Nevada today, a very high proportion of the population lived in towns. The Spaniards themselves were either city dwellers or villagers, by and large, though some of their flocks were tended by lonely shepherds from backward places. John Wesley Powell's prescription for urbanism along rivers arose from his admiration both of Indian pueblos and of villages established within Spanish or Mexican land grants to groups of settlers, who ran their cattle and took their wood from the commons. Because that tradition was largely uncodified, it left those commons unprotected against the new land laws reaching New Mexico with the rush of non-Hispanic settlers. As a result, by 1950, many a New Mexico "commons" had been wrested away from the villagers, and by 1990, much that had been in common had been developed into ranchettes for outsiders—and not because of the preferences of their inhabitants.

Before the ranchettes there had been ranches and farms. Their story is no happier, as told in a study entitled *From Conquest to Conservation: Our Public Lands Legacy*, by the former chief of the Forest Service, Mike Dombeck, and Christopher Wood and Jack Williams. It tells how the failure of the nation to continue to cluster in settlements led not only to the disruption of community but also to the transgression of limits, and thus, ultimately, "the net effect of these policies was to lead land hungry settlers into an impossible task only to experience failure." Furthermore, such policies put these people at increased risk of death by fire. Settlers are easier to protect from fire when they live in villages than when they are scattered in "isolated farmsteads." Perhaps that was one reason why Mexico's land laws had not pressed people to set themselves apart from one another, as did the Northwest Ordinance. The settlers of the Old Northwest were chaneled into scattered homesteads by government policy in the 1780s and financed to stay there by new government policy in the 1860s.[5]

In any case, south-to-north Hispanic migration has been from town to town as much as it has been from country to town. Most migrants into the United States from the south came directly into the overland receiving stations William Frey classifies as "high immigration metros," such as Dallas, Phoenix, Houston, and Los Angeles. Other points of ingress for Hispanic immigration have been New York and Miami, traditional staging areas for seaborne immigration. The 2000 Census showed some "spilling out" by Hispanics emerging from these antechambers toward other metropolitan areas and pursuing service and construction jobs. Hispanics have gone where the jobs are. While a relative few are still doing stoop labor in the fields, most have found jobs in towns. The "mixing bowl" is urban, as it was in the nineteenth century. It does not lie in the countryside, or even in the suburbs. Now, once again, America, the nation of immigrants, is being re-formed in its cities.

The people migrating from south to north bring memories and expectations that can support fire policies more prudent than those springing from life in Ohio or Nebraska. Experience is important. It is the ground upon which there can be a useful discussion about fire policy and planning policy in the face of fire. The previously Spanish, now American, Southwest discloses from the air the urban heritage of the people who lived there before the rush of Sunbelt migrants after the Second World War. Neither the Indians nor those considering themselves culturally Spanish were spread out in grid patterns like those ordained by the Northwest Ordinance. There were no sections and quarter sections along the Rio Grande, along the Gila, or in the Los Angeles Basin. In rural New Mexico the village remains both a living memory and a living institution. Even in the new mixing bowl cities such as Phoenix and Albuquerque, Hispanic newcomers do not seem to chafe at the constraints of city life or to rush for isolated farmsteads in accordance with someone else's "American Dream." Despite all the persuasions of government subsidies for them to find housing in the countryside like their non-Hispanic and non-Indian neighbors, despite mortgage subsidies, highway subsidies, tax subsidies, and a blare of propaganda in the interest of exurban development, they have continued to congregate in towns and cities.[6]

TWO MORE URBAN TRADITIONS

The ball courts of Wupatki exert very little influence upon the location and organization of settlement in that portion of Arizona today, or on town planning anywhere on the Colorado Plateau. It is often said that there is little town planning there anyway, but that rumor is repeated only by people ignorant of the power of the Mormon Church. The Mormon tradition is a powerful force from Flagstaff north to Boise, and that tradition does not accommodate an anarchic model of the "American Dream." The lone cowboy, or the lone pioneer, is not the ideal citizen of Mormon country. Joseph Smith and Brigham Young dreamed of "smart growth" before that term was invented.

Smith told his followers to live as a "compact society." His "Plat of the City of Zion" showed a model town in Missouri on a mile-square grid, reserving a church lot at the center, with the farming to be done on the outskirts. Salt Lake City grew from such a plan, arranged along the cardinal directions. After Salt Lake City, Mormon towns of similar shape appeared throughout the Great Basin and the Colorado Plateau, in major part because Young's successor, John Taylor, ordained that "in all cases in making new settlements the Saints should be advised to go together in villages as has been our custom . . . instead of carelessly scattering out over a wide extent of country." The price of carelessness could be high in a country beset by "horse and cattle thieves, land jumpers, etc., and . . . hostile Indians." There were positive as well as prudential reasons for Taylor's urbanism, springing from a tradition of civic life unrecognized by Edward Teller or the dispersion theorists: "Their compact organization gives them many advantages of a social and civic character which might be lost, misapplied or frittered away by spreading out so thinly that inter-communication is difficult, dangerous, inconvenient, and expensive." Among other things, they could get to church.[7]

The West was not, and is not, a region without an urban tradition.

The "traditional American system of pioneering" mentioned but not comprehended by some dispersionist journalists was more than an anarchic display of prowess by hardy axe-wielding solo operators. The great political geographer Donald Meinig of Syracuse University has all along told his readers that "romantic" individualism was "quickly overtaken by and in some areas essentially excluded by a far more elaborate American system of regional development. And this system, too, had its famous symbol: the instant town mushrooming on the frontier even before much of the forest had been felled or fields cleared in the countryside. Less romantic to a later age than the log cabin, the town was far more potent in the shaping of the nation." The testimony of Richard Wade in *The Urban Frontier* seemed iconoclastic forty years ago, but he and Meinig have made it acceptable today: "The towns were the spearheads of the frontier. . . . Planted far in advance of the line of settlement, they held the West of the approaching population." Meinig suggests Lexington, Cincinnati, and St. Louis as good examples. Others might be Pensacola, Albuquerque, Detroit, and St. Paul.[8]

Besides, as an Indian friend of mine once reminded me, if one lone pioneer after another had come over the horizon toward my friend's ancestors, or if a lone cowboy had come without a cavalry escort, "we would have picked them off one by one." Migration was considerably less dangerous when it was group migration.

The urbanism of the American tradition went along with group migration; people often decided together to pick up and move. The lone cowboy and the solitary axe-wielder were on the fringes, though government intruded from the beginning to favor individual settlement rather than villages. The Northwest imposed on the western land its apparently ineluctable and inescapable grid system; the railroads got their land grants in square blocks, and sold them as such; the Virginia and Pennsylvania legislatures accommodated speculators by allocating their western territories into rectangles that could be bought unseen. Yet despite all the pressures to live in lonely isolation, the urban preferences of many Americans have continued to assert themselves.

URBANISM AND CORRIDOPOLIS

In the nineteenth century, many of the old cities of the East and Midwest became shaped like wheels, with the traffic moving inward, not outward. Workers were drawn toward industrial hubs along turnpikes and, later, along trolley lines from the countryside. Some of the hubs were much older grid cities. The residential suburbs were often sliced into sectors as well, with radials for roads, streetcars, and suburban railroads. During the Cold War and afterward, out-migration moved along the radials, now widened into interstates, leaving many of these metropolitan areas with a husk where once there had been a hub.

More recently, the wheel pattern has faded into the extended grid pattern on a metropolitan scale. From horizon to horizon, from service node to service node, corridors of urban development struggle along the pavement like boa constrictors that have swallowed pigs too big for them. The wagon wheel cities are gone, replaced by the attenuated grid cities where two out of three Americans now live. Sending tendrils of settlement into dangerous places, the post-urban network of not-quite-cities is set in not-quite-country. Though by the year 2000, 70 percent of the American land *area* was still occupied by people farming and ranching, these were thin on the ground, so thin that some farm states had more senators than representatives—a fact so familiar as to be no longer remarkable. Less than 2 percent of the population in that year was composed of full-time farmers and ranchers. That would be a large enough change from the past, but its effect upon the life experience of Americans is matched by the equally dramatic reduction of people living within city limits, in which only about 5 percent remain. Everybody else is somewhere else, along a highway, in corridopolis. What is "city" and what is "country" when metropolitan Atlanta extends across an area bigger than the state of Rhode Island?

AFTER THE SECOND WORLD WAR

How did this happen? A major study of the movement of people in twentieth-century America conducted in 1997 concluded that the overall pattern of movement was "a massive concentration of population into cities, with a multiplication of places as urbanization spread and larger centers captured ever greater numbers." Concentration. Not dispersion. That concentration was nothing new. It sustained an American centripetal trend *out* of the country and *into* the cities. Ninety-six percent of the subjects of King George in 1774 lived in the country, but over the ensuing decades, country folk and villagers became city dwellers; it was easier to gain a living in town. America changed from a nation of farmers, ranchers, and hunters in 1800 into a nation of industrial workers by 1920.[9]

Even as the Yankee individualists came into the Northwest, and after the Northwest into the Great Plains, most of them came as villagers. It is difficult to find among their Pilgrim fathers any who came from independent farms; they cited the "City on the Hill" as the model for respectable life, and were apprehensive about being "bewildered" in wilderness. Their descendants for many generations lived in little cities strung out along the pockets of fertility found in the clefts of the New England hills. The meetinghouse was as urban as a kiva or ball court. Vermont to this day is not configured like Nebraska. That is not just because it has mountains; it is also because Vermonters have preferences. They seem to like villages. It's cold up there. When the Yankees could gather, they did.

The immigrants coming to America from continental Europe were even more accustomed than Englishmen or Scotsmen or Irishmen to think of cities as places free from harsh landlords. Ferocious anti-feudal sentiments were expressed by immigrants from Württemberg and Baden immigrating into Minnesota as late as the 1880s. These refugees from nasty landlords and rack rents were no more infatuated with life in serfdom than the Russian peasants who escaped to Manitoba, or the Chinese peasants who emigrated in increasing numbers in the twentieth century.

Big cities and small ones grew, as the countryside emptied and the mines played themselves out, as timbered hillsides could no longer support lumbering camps, and as agriculture turned from production of staple crops on large spreads to garden crops serving cities. Against this long-term trend as it continued into the 1930s, Cold War policies from 1946 onward arrayed programs for purposeful dispersal. At its extremes it has scattered single-family houses into flame zones.

In the 1980s, however, metropolitan areas resumed their growth while population shifts to non-metropolitan areas did not keep pace. This was unanticipated by dispersion theorists who had been asserting that there was no use attempting to resist "long-standing residential preferences for low-density environments." Practice upset theory, in the face of continuing federal subsidies that might easily have produced an appearance confirming theory. Those subsidies remained powerful, however, and by 1990 the pace of non-metropolitan growth caught up again.[10]

In a paper entitled "The New Urban Revival in the United States," William Frey and his colleagues recently brightened the prospect of changing migration behavior away from dangerous places by changing economic incentives, wasting no space on mythic or archetypal psychic analysis. Frey notes that Americans are practical—they live within a geography of opportunities leading to a geography of choice: "the rise of the global economy and improvements in communications and production technologies" have changed the places where work could be found and done. "Populations" have responded "to those changes" by making their own residential choices, aggregating into the great migrations of the twentieth century.[11]

Since these choices responded to incentives, and not to laws of nature, their adjustment was possible, and behavior changed. "The diffusion of 'urban' amenities to all parts of the country—including areas previously considered to be remote or rural," says Frey, "has extended the location options of both employers and residents." He goes on to say that the economic health of urban centers large and small is "dependent on how successfully these areas can adapt to rapidly changing circumstances." The same thing goes for individuals—they too can adapt. And they might well do so when their governments help them to discern the danger of wildfire.[12]

Our fellow citizens who choose to live in suburbia and beyond are not stupid. Despite what some say about the "deep structures" of their psyches, they do not migrate in a trance. They make intelligent calculations of the costs and benefits of finding jobs and locating homes. They are quite capable of making fresh computations when benefits and risks are brought to their attention. Change those factors and their decisions will change. Far from being peculiarly addicted to "sprawl," they might, after such fresh computations, reveal themselves to be less urbanophobic than people in other nations. Robert Bruegmann, in his way, and Stephen Pyne, in his, have noted that "all the industrial nations are going through a similar process, from Australia's urban bush around Melbourne and Sydney to communities in the Canadian Rockies to Provence and Barcelona."[13]

Frey has remarked that the "return to urbanization" of the 1990s did "not bear out the deconcentration theorists' prediction of a broad-based, continued population dispersal." That is good news from a firefighter's point of view. It is not hopeless to warn people against living in flame zones. Nor is it hopeless to seek changes in those public policies that induce settlement disrespectful of nature. Matters can be improved because Americans are not hell-bent on a dangerous life in isolated places.[14]

PART FIVE

Whereas . . . and Therefore . . .

14. LONGER AND LARGER PRECEDENTS

During the second half of the twentieth century, millions of Americans moved out of the northern and eastern industrial cities and into the countryside. Millions more migrated regionally, southward and westward, going where the jobs were, where cheap land lay, where mortgages could be procured, where the roads were being built, where big dams were making power cheaper, and where utility lines were being strung. Though some of these highly subsidized migrants complained of an intrusive government, they took its gifts. In John Steinbeck's words, that made their "figuring" easier. Having figured, they moved.

It was long believed in the councils of government that it was in the national interest—the national taxpaying interest—that these migrations should be encouraged. Accordingly, vast sums were transferred from one set of taxpayers to another, in programs intended to reduce the density of target cities by inducing mass movement out of them. The dispersion-industrial complex entered the scene and delightedly caught up the nation's flagging enthusiasm for Cold War dispersion policies, reanimating and enlarging them.

In dispersing cities and targets, the theorists and then the dispersion-industrial complex destroyed traditional communities and also placed in peril people who had little understanding of the natural conditions into which they were being induced to settle. Those with an economic, social, and psychological stake in traditional communities suffered. Those who lost life savings to fire and flood suffered as well. The suffering was not, however, universally distributed. Operators of new gas stations and sellers of fast-food franchises along highways prospered; old gas stations and mom-and-pop groceries back home went broke. Many automobiles were sold. Many jobs with streetcar lines were lost. Much steel and cement found purchasers. In the end, trillions were spent or promised to be spent and, as the old lobbyists' saying goes, "it ain't coming back."

So the United States now has a new frontier, the interface of settlement and wildland, where the in-migrants remain exposed to fire and flood, and where the taxpayers face a continuing obligation to protect and rescue them. That obligation is real—the taxpayers helped place the in-migrants at risk. However, that does not imply an equivalent moral imperative to encourage more people to go where the danger is. The artificial system that produced much Cold War migration is obsolete. It should be scrapped.

Those who are heavily invested in that system will use gold and guile to discourage the abandonment of these dispersion subsidies. They will find arguments to make it seem hopeless to try to do so, cheering columnists and tele-savants who assert that a land rush into danger is merely an expression of individual preference in a free market. These complacent observers of unnecessary pain and death argue that Americans are repelled by one another and drawn to extremes, pushed and pulled so powerfully by a strange centrifugal madness that they will disperse into danger, whatever may be done in public policy. This is nonsense.

The notion of dispersion as the product of an irresistible mass madness evaporates under heat and light. So does the dispersion theorists' assertion that even if the American psyche were to be cured of its madness, the American legal system is too sick to be healed, because land law is committed to the principle that there shall be no inhibition upon what a landowner may do on his or her property once he or she buys it. Once it's yours, it's yours. That's the American way, we are told.

It isn't. Obligations in this country run with the land. And the "free market" has never ruled the American landscape. The largest recent intrusions upon that market have been those of the Cold War era discussed in the last few chapters, but they were not the first. Not an acre of land has changed hands in the last half century without a part of the price being paid by another taxpayer. For several centuries that price was affected by the salaries of the troops who wrested that acre from its previous occupants. More recently, that price has been elevated by public expenditure on the roads and utilities to make that acre accessible and habitable. The beneficiaries of billions in taxpayer subsidies in the past fifty years have received transfer payments from all other taxpayers. These payments have artificially raised the market value of some land, while inducing population movements out of other people's land, and lowering its market value. The winners who played with a stacked deck now proclaim a right to more of the same. Because they have gotten, they argue, they should continue to get. Why stop now?

The reason to stop is that present dispersion-practice subsidies ceased long ago to do the job for which they were intended, and have become pernicious. They were justified as serving *public* interests, though their benefits were bestowed upon *private* landowners and speculators. That has often been the case. There were, to give an obvious instance, winners and losers from channeling migration toward the Northwest Territory: yeoman farmers won; slave owners lost. When the Bozeman Trail was put back in operation nearly a century later, the Sioux and Cheyenne were losers, the prairie schooner immigrants winners.

The federal government has tinkered with land markets since 1785; federal money, diplomacy, and military force have all along manipulated land prices, channeling migration and encouraging some land uses. Agriculture using free labor was favored by the Northwest Ordinance; slave labor was encouraged by Article III of the Louisiana Purchase Agreement. The federal government has used armed personnel to encourage some land uses over others, and some land users over others. Upon the Great Plains, the cavalry sided with newcomers against Indians, and a few decades later, federal marshals protected foreclosing landlords against rebellious homeowners.

THE GREAT GIVEAWAY RECONSIDERED

In his classic account *Land Use Policy in the United States*, first published more than forty years ago, Howard W. Ottoson identified as "the most fateful and basic decision" in the history of American land use "the one made at the outset and allowed to stand until the end of the nineteenth century: that the [nation's public] lands should be disposed of rather than retained in public ownership." That decision happened so long ago that it has calcified into one of history's false inevitabilities, rather than living on as an organic contingency. It was not inevitable. It happened for peculiar reasons, and it was revolutionary because sovereigns do not conventionally strip themselves of their fundamental powers in that way.[1]

Equally radical were its corollaries.

First, the land so privatized carried with it many obligations that otherwise would have remained with the government. Thus a break was made between the American experience and that of countries in which the sovereign retained much of the land mass. Accordingly, private obligations to use land under public constraints became more important in the United States.

Second, the lands retained were kept in public hands because they were exceptional, not because nobody wanted them. They were marked for important public uses. The choice bits of 1789 were not privatized, though the pressures on the Founders to sell them off were excruciating. Their new nation was bankrupt, and deeply tax resistant. Their primary means to salvage its credit was to sell land. They tried other devices, such as excise taxes, and nearly brought their experiment to a bloody end; rebellions broke out in Pennsylvania, Massachusetts, and Kentucky, and in New England and the West there were threats of secession. Had the Founders chosen to tax income or lay heavy capital taxes, secession would have become very likely—the land- and slave-owning classes of the South, especially, were already disaffected. Yet the Founders withheld from sale important pieces of public land. They took the risk of missing just that crucial portion of potential revenue that land sales might have brought in order to use public land for public purposes.

Ever since then, it has generally been conceded that the public interest includes conservation of natural renewable resources such as trees and fisheries, and also nonrenewable precious metals. British monarchs had reserved to themselves any gold or silver discovered in their colonies; "sovereign metals" were kept in the royal exchequer to back the public currency. Having dislodged King George from his seat upon those bags of precious metals, the Founders substituted the national government, adding lead and copper deposits to its real estate assets not to be given away, but reserved for public use—at least in part.

Coal was not so regarded; it could be mined out of the land without returning anything to the "sovereign." But coal was not important in the eighteenth century; the Founders did not treat it as they did gold or silver, and by the time its importance was established, their balanced view of the relationship between public and private benefits had been replaced by a hell-for-breakfast exploitive privatism. Had the recovery costs of strip-mined land been "internalized" into the prices paid for coal land, a Land and Water Conservation Fund would have been established earlier. The Land and Water Conservation Fund provides funds for land conservation derived from leasing offshore oil—when it is not raided by the administration for firefighting money. The "stateside" Land and Water Conservation Fund is merely a return to the principles established when thirty million acres of federal land was presented to the states to improve public transportation (turnpikes, canals, and wagon roads).

The Public Land Ordinances of 1785 and 1796 took account of the national interest in channeling migration to preserve the nation's store of metals, to improve education and public transportation, and to ensure industrial development. Mill sites were to be treated separately from farmland, and were deliberately set aside to nurture a diversified rural economy. The farseeing Founders also gave thought to the relationship of land policy to public health, providing additional acreage of lowlands to the states to be drained to reduce the danger of malaria. Under the Northwest Ordinance, the sixteenth section in every township was withheld for use either as the location for a school or to endow a school elsewhere. More sections per township were added as the value of each acre diminished as the nation enlarged itself into the dry, thin-soiled West.

From the 1920s onward, immense amounts of public land were held back from general settlement to subsidize canals, turnpikes, and railroads, with the result that migration was further choreographed. Along these privatized corridors, settlements were deposited and were given a deliberate character by further land legislation. In the 1860s, the Morrill Act reserved more public land to create the system of land-grant colleges and universities, over the strenuous objections of those who insisted that the entire public domain should be privatized.

Federal highways were built with the direct proceeds of taxes—without land grants—in part because there was not enough marketable federal land left by the 1950s to generate the huge sums necessary. But highways also channeled migration and determined settlement patterns, as they made some people rich and left others behind to struggle along, growing poorer and poorer.

FOUNDERS, FAMILY FARMING, AND THE FREE MARKET

Among the Founders, Thomas Jefferson has become famous for his therapeutic view of land as a nurse of virtue and a crucible for citizenship. For Jefferson, therefore, the first beneficiaries of what others called the "great giveway" of public lands should be yeoman farmers. "How much better," he wrote to Albert Gallatin, "to have every 160 acres settled by an able-bodied militia man, than by purchasers with their hordes of Negroes, to add weakness instead of strength." Gallatin was Jefferson's Secretary of the Treasury, and thus responsible for getting every last dollar out of land sales to pay down the national debt. Both he and Jefferson knew that "purchasers with . . . hordes of Negroes" had ample funds and that few "able-bodied militia men" did. Contrary to a widespread belief, the planters did not have all their money tied up in land and slaves. They were exceedingly active in land markets in the West well before the Revolution, and remained major players in markets as distant as Texas and Nebraska until 1860. In 1800, the South had at its disposal more minted gold than the North, larger silver deposits, and, unlike New England and New York, large deposits of coal and iron. Slave-owning planters would, therefore, have been likely to prevail in a free market if all public lands were put up for auction. The social preferences of Jefferson and, even more emphatically, Gallatin would be met only if provision were made to bias that market in favor of family farming. "Those who labor in the earth are the chosen people of God, if ever he had a chosen people," wrote Jefferson. There was "peculiar . . . virtue . . . [in] those, who . . . [worked] their own soil." Gallatin's entire public career, from the Revolutionary era nearly until the Civil War, was grounded in an abhorrence of slavery. Therefore the two could agree that family farmers should be favored in dispositions of public land.[2]

That was also the view of most of the other Founding Fathers, including Hamilton, whose natural sympathies were with men who had risen on their own talent and exertion. Contrary to a widespread impression, he was no uncritical friend to wealth; in his view, wealthy men might be useful to the state, but not necessarily because they were virtuous. He opposed measures that favored "an hereditary succession by right of primogeniture . . . [as] liable to this objection— that it refers to birth what ought to belong to merit only." Hamilton's great state papers of the 1790s present a two-track system for the western lands, one of which was a kind of proto–Homestead Act policy, offering a hundred acres to anyone able to pay a cash price of thirty cents an acre, and a parallel program intended to draw the rich into paying down the national debt by offering them deferred payment schedules for larger purchases.[3]

Jefferson's stated opinion that farmers were "God's chosen people" was not required to justify preferring them to planters in the disposition of public lands: Hamilton's colleague in the writing of the Federalist Papers, James Madison, a planter himself, joined Jefferson in advocating the provision of plenty of land for family farmers, though in less poetic language. As Madison put it, "A great majority of the people . . . without land . . . will either combine [against those who have it,] in which case property and liberty will not be secure . . . ; or what is more probable, they will become the tool of opulence and ambition." No palaver about natural rights; just dour and realistic anticipation of the infirmities of representative government: as they anticipated, the people's Congress has indeed been from time to time the tool of opulence and ambition, and the land itself has suffered.[4]

THOMAS JEFFERSON, GEORGE WASHINGTON, AND LIMITS

Jefferson was neither an uncritical democrat nor a slavish adherent to the determining of all land-use decisions by "market principles." His view of his fellow citizens was like that of Madison. Daniel J. Boorstin, the greatest American conservative historian of the twentieth century, shows in his pungent *The Lost World of Thomas Jefferson* that Jefferson often wrote of the need to direct traffic in the public concourse—ordinary citizens needed to be shown the proper ways to behave, even if they were being nursed by the land. Unless kept within limits, they would "forget themselves in . . . making money." When writing of direct popular election of the upper house of a Virginia legislature, Jefferson observed to his friend Edmund Pendleton that he had "ever observed that a choice by the people themselves is not generally distinguished for its wisdom." Specifically, the settlers in lands taken from the Indians in the Northwest would need a period of indoctrination and seasoning before they might become fit citizens of a republic. Jefferson was no advocate of unbridled license, confessing that "he would submit to almost 'anything rather than a mere creation by and dependence on the people.'" Law would be necessary.[5]

Jefferson did not, therefore, treat ownership of land as an unqualified right or as a mere speculators' commodity. In his peculiar and fascinating brand of animism, land was treated as a nurse, a therapeutic agent to make rough settlers into citizens. That is a noble calling for nature, and nobly would Jefferson have nature treated. Therefore he was averse to turning loose squatters and speculators upon the land to do what they would, however heedlessly.

Each of us has his or her favorite Founder. Mine is George Washington, for many reasons, including his preaching little but practicing what he preached. For example, in 1793, Washington wrote the English agronomist Arthur Young that he wished to convert his estate into what would be, in effect, homesteads, small holdings to be worked by yeomen—"to settle it with *good* [his emphasis] farmers." The slaves already at work there would be freed to be "hired by the year as laborers." Washington wished, he wrote, to provide for his old age and for his family from rental income "upon a solid basis in the hands of *good* [again, his emphasis] farmers." The antislavery provisions of the Northwest Ordinance were just beginning to be applied. As if anticipating the twenty-year debate over the Homestead Act a generation later, Washington wrote that "to exclude them [slaves] . . . is not among the least inducements for dividing the farms into small lots."[6]

Washington was the nation's great exemplar and teacher of the employment of inducements to alter land use. Every owner of plantation-exhausted land knew why it was "much better" for the land itself that it be settled by family farmers rather than by slave-driving planters. As Washington wrote to Young, the man with a large investment in slaves had to keep them working, and had the means to keep on buying land for them to work. So they took any "piece of land [that] is cut down," meaning stripped of its timber, and "kept [it] under constant cultivation, first in tobacco and then in Indian corn (two very exhausting plants), until it will yield scarcely anything" at all.[7]

As president, Washington had the congenial but immensely difficult job of putting such inducements into place on the public lands
ceded by the states north of the Ohio River, though the states had
actually only ceded *claims* to lands that were in fact held largely by
Indians. There is no need here to relate the sorry chronicle of how
Washington was forced against his will into a series of campaigns
against those occupants. Lost in that familiar tale, however, is its sub-
text, his deployment of the United States Army to enforce the prohibi-
tion of the ordinance against slavery and to counteract the assaults by
squatters upon Indian lands. When Kentucky planters strayed across
the Ohio, threatening to bring their slaves with them, the officers of
Washington's Revolutionary army who had settled in Marietta, Ohio,
complained to their old commander directly. This was, they said, "fla-
grant trespass" upon both the "rights of humanity" and the Northwest
Ordinance. They were ready to put on their old uniforms if Washington
sent the regular army to stop the planters, to protect the rights of the
Indians, and to see to it that until order was restored, there would be no
"further sale of lands there for the discharge of public debt."[8]

The Mariettans assumed, as did Congress, that the nation as a
whole had the right to inhibit practices on private land that produced
peril to neighboring citizens. Provocation of Indians then did so—as
provocation of fire now does. The nation can determine what sort of
land use it will encourage or discourage by the conditions placed on
the sale of public land. It would be fatuous to suggest that during the
lifetimes of the Founders the cause of freedom was uncontested or tri-
umphant. The slave owners who dominated the government of the
United States until the election of 1860 were as well aware as their opponents of how land might be allocated to serve economic interests.
They wished to induce another kind of migration through governmental action than that sought by the Mariettans. Prohibitions upon
slavery channeled family farming through the North, whereas an invitation to unconstrained land use extended the plantation system
through the South.

The slave-owning and slave-selling planters of Georgia and South Carolina resisted entry into the Constitutional Union until they had extracted two assurances from the other states: the Constitution would not be understood to free their slaves, and its "fugitive slave" clause would be read to require the return of slaves from the free states where those slaves had sought freedom. The republic was held hostage to ensure the market for slavery; Georgia did not give up its western claims until many of its slave sellers had completed their sales. North Carolina refused to give up its claims to what is now Tennessee without an explicit guarantee that slavery would be permitted there; and Virginia saw to it that its slave market in Kentucky was excepted from the provisions of the Northwest Ordinance. By determining what sort of migration would be permitted where, these were, in effect, migration-control devices.

Nonetheless, the Founders did establish a Constitution and a set of land laws that prevented the unrestrained operation of proslavery market forces. Congress did *not* seek "to maximize cash proceeds, rather than to promote migration and economic development." Instead, it set forth in detail what land uses it preferred and what kinds of development it sought. As a result, even though the tide was flowing toward unconstrained privatizing, "tallying the disposals through the year 1828, one finds that almost half the conveyances represented donations" to secure public purposes. The other half went to specific preferred classes of buyers at reduced rates, to induce those buyers to migrate and, at the end of migration, to do some things and abstain from others.[9]

The Homestead Act of 1862 expressed the culmination of this phase in the nation's life. Abraham Lincoln brought a new birth of responsibility to the land, as well as a new birth of freedom in the victory over slavery. His land policies produced the founding of the national and state park systems, and both the Homestead and Morrill Acts. In our day we should bring another new birth of responsibility to the land and to one another.

ENCOURAGING MIGRATION BY SEEDING THE LAND

The history of inducements to migration includes the precedents for the kind of channeling just discussed, anticipating the boards and bulkheads put in place through the exertions of the dispersion-industrial complex and the expenditure of taxpayer money during and after the Cold War. It also demonstrates how the people of the United States reserved within their public land certain sections that would be kept from settlement resulting from migration. Though generally committed to privatizing the public domain, successive Congresses have kept these places out of the game. Before independence, the British, French, and Spanish governments excluded settlers from fortified churches, trading posts, and barracks; after independence, both state and federal governments retained the most strategic locations within their control for public uses, such as forts, courthouses, and customs offices.[10]

These preempted spaces served as nuclei of towns, seeding territories and drawing migrants, just as the National Laboratory nucleated the town of Los Alamos. The Pajarito Plateau was thus deliberately seeded as the Romans had seeded the Danube frontier, as the Spanish presidios seeded Texas and California, and the palisades of St. Louis, Detroit, and New Orleans seeded the claimed dominions of the King of France. Western Europeans did not, however, build entire national cities as the Romanov dynasty did in Siberia and Alaska. Not since the early federal government planned twelve towns in Alabama, and the government of Georgia staked out four to dominate its four great river basins, has government been in the business of building towns—forts, bases, and laboratory towns being special cases.

Instead, it has been American policy to grant public lands to private persons with public obligations attached. The French, British, and Dutch all had done so, with seigneuries along Lake Champlain and manors and patroonships along the Hudson, as a part of a seeding process intended to attract settlement. The template of the Northwest

Ordinance—squares within squares—was anticipated in 1717 by Sir Robert Montgomery, Laird of Skelmorlie, for a marquisate of Azilia on the Georgia coast. The marquisate's garrison of battle-scarred highland veterans were to live as yeoman farmers with a constant eye to the southern horizon, where the Spaniards were busy building presidios and missions. The Azilia bubble burst at the same time as the South Sea and Tulip bubbles, in the 1720s, but the squares lingered on. A decade later, General James Oglethorpe made use of them to plan for Savannah and the other armed camps in his successful colony of Georgia.[11]

Oglethorpe's Georgia of the 1730s was no more to be settled helter-skelter than George Washington's Ohio would be in the 1790s; in both locations the citizen-soldiers were to accept restrictions on their behavior and movements. There were to be no slaves in Georgia or in Washington's Ohio, and no exploitation of Indians. Oglethorpe issued rules to prevent both speculative aggrandizement of individual holdings and the plying of Indians with rum to secure land cessions; for this purpose Washington created alcohol-free government trading posts. After Oglethorpe was attacked at home as a possible Stuart sympathizer, he could not remain in Georgia. The planters of neighboring South Carolina scented opportunity, and Oglethorpe's restrictions were demolished despite protests and petitions from his Highland clients, who continued to oppose slavery for another generation.

Before Oglethorpe's scheme fades from memory, it is useful to emphasize once more the intrusiveness of his experiment, like Washington's in Ohio. Land was made available for private use only if certain obligations were met to the commonweal, and only if the settlers adhered to the Founders' choreography: they were intended to move along, and to settle within, those grids, as many of them do to this day. On a summer day in the flatter parts of Washington's Midwest, you can see the dust rise from country roads cut along the township lines of the Northwest Ordinance. Farmhouses in Ohio sit where Montgomery of Skelmorlie would have had them had Azilia expanded that far.

The Armed Occupation legislation of the 1830s and 1840s produced the final appearance in the Southeast of the privatizing of home
defense through seeding a border with veterans: soldiers mustered
out of the United States Army in Florida were provided the land and
expected to hold off the Seminoles. Central Florida still has landowners whose ancestors got their first "stakes" that way.[12]

RESERVATIONS

The obverse of "seeding" is reservation. Forts, bases, training grounds,
and national laboratories are often surrounded by fences bearing
barbed wire and OFF LIMITS signs swept by searchlights. No private
settlers homestead in the state-size Air Force bases of Vandenberg in
California and Eglin in West Florida. The logic of reservation in the
public interest would permit placing OFF LIMITS signs on the edge of
flame zones still in public hands, once it had been concluded that it
was as important to save lives that way as it was to train pilots.

There were many precedents for preventing private citizens from
making their homes in large areas attractive to settlement. George III
got in trouble with the speculators of Virginia by presenting the
"Proclamation Line" of 1763, which closed off the frontier to colonial
expansion, but his reasons for doing so were perfectly sound. The
taxpayers of Britain were paying for Indian wars resulting from incursions beyond that line, and recovered nothing from the profits secured by speculators who hired private armies to make those
incursions. Purchasers of large tracts, sometimes millions of acres,
syndicated themselves as land companies, and took what they could
take. George Washington had been one of those speculators. After independence, knowing the game, he used the power of the presidency
to withstand speculative excess, resisting speculators, squatters, and
those who took Indian lands beyond treaty lines by "tomahawk title."
Those lines shifted, however, after Washington's restraints were no
longer in place. But dishonoring sound principles does not make
them less sound. Reservation was sound policy, and still is.[13]

The Founders were willing to go beyond simple reservation to representation, beyond protecting Indians from whites, and whites from Indians, to providing Indian tribes with representation in Congress. These proposals seemed bizarre to many at the time, and were lost in the rush toward exploitation and expropriation that followed, but in retrospect they had much to recommend them. In the midst of the Revolutionary War, the Treaty of Pittsburgh made provisions for an Ohio Valley reservation with congressional representation. There was a proposal for a Cherokee state with its own representative, and Alexander McGillivray opened such an opportunity for the Creeks in his discussions with George Washington. These were all devices to channel migration.[14]

Conceptually, keeping settlers out of places where they might be killed by the settled-upon, and keeping the settled-upon out of the reach of settlers, is like keeping people and fire apart. The state legislatures of Wisconsin and Minnesota recognized the wisdom of Indian reservations at the same time that they recognized the wisdom of fire reservations. The state forests were reserved from land previously privatized by federal land-disposition programs, and withdrawn from settlement because those legislatures concluded that it was too costly to the taxpayers, and too inhumane to the settlers, for those areas to be farmed. There were compatible reasons for the federal government to set aside from settlement national parks, national forests, and wilderness areas. As noted earlier, Carl Schurz prevailed upon President Rutherford B. Hayes to withdraw thirteen million acres of land from the "Great Giveaway," and more federal and state land has been withdrawn since. The point made by Schurz was that there were higher values than private profit, including public health and safety.

He was still making that point in 1894 when Congress permitted the Department of Agriculture to prohibit "driving, feeding, grazing, pasturing or herding of cattle, sheep and livestock" on national forest land. This provision was attacked as unconstitutional, on the argument that by then the public lands had become a "grazing commons," but the department's action was affirmed by the United States

Supreme Court in 1911. Thereafter, the public retained the right to determine which uses were proper and which were not; from time to time, all commercial uses have been banned from portions of the public domain, as they are in wilderness areas.[15]

Withdrawing use of public land has frequently been accompanied by withdrawing public subsidies to private landowners. Permitting use is the first step to seeking encouragement for use. The reverse is always possible, and increasingly desirable. The effect of taking away subsidies for plowing the Dust Bowl was in effect to withdraw six million acres of Texas from cultivation, because subsidies withdrawn from marginally profitable activity are as powerful agents of policy as land withdrawn entirely. Both are justified when that activity becomes too dangerous or the subsidies become disproportionate to the public good they were intended to underwrite. Federal inducements to grow crops in the desert were wasteful, stupid, and cruel. Having observed their effects on the people and the land, Congress put an end to them.

Congress will in time cease to induce homeowners to expose their houses and their families to the likely passage of hurricanes, floods, and wildfire. Subsidies to induce them to do so are equally wasteful, stupid, and cruel. They can be stopped, too.

The history of the West presents a series of such withdrawals—even when the subsidies wore cavalry blue and rode horses. In effect, settlers protected from nature by federal firefighters are like those protected from Indians by the cavalry in earlier periods, and the assistance provided to settlements in nature's proper territory—flame zones—is like that rendered to emigrant trains into Indian Territory. The analogy is instructive. The nation found that it was wise to cease encouraging emigration when it became too expensive to keep those mounted and uniformed subsidies in the saddle and to find replacements for those shot out of the saddle. The most conspicuous example of the withdrawal of such a uniformed subsidy occurred under treaties ratified by Congress on February 16, 1869. The Sioux had been resisting intrusions upon their hunting grounds and farms in the up-per Missouri Valley since the 1850s; recently Crazy Horse had wiped out eighty cavalrymen. The American nation and the Sioux nation were both weary of war. Crazy Horse kept the costs high, and the benefits of the Bozeman Trail and its three forts had declined. The trail had been used largely to bring miners from the crossing of the Platte River in Nebraska northward to the goldfields of Montana. As the Union Pacific neared completion in Utah, the miners could get to Montana without the trail and without the Sioux.

A Peace Commission was established to produce a truce with the northern tribes. It was also to make peace with the Navaho in the Southwest, who were becoming dangerous again after being forced into their own Trail of Tears, "the Long March" from Arizona to a parched desolate place along the Rio Grande to starve. The commission agreed upon a great North Plains reservation, including most of both Dakotas and Montana. The Navaho were offered a considerably smaller area in Arizona, close to their previous homes. The northern reserva-tion was proclaimed to be "unceded Indian territory," as if it had not yet been conquered, while that returned to the Navahos was called a "reservation," as if a gracious gift. In both cases the Indians were promised—once again—that the government of the United States would channel migration to prevent the seizure of Indian land.[16]

At that juncture, George Armstrong Custer's detachment, which had been sent into the heart of that reservation, found gold within its Black Hills. Though Custer was eliminated from the scene, the army of the United States refused to accept his Last Stand as final, and it mobilized the latest technology and a massive force to overwhelm the Sioux. Land was transferred in this case not by tomahawk title but by Hotchkiss gun title. The miners and settlers had their way; the north-ern reservation was broken into fragments.

This episode in the long history of reserving and un-reserving In-dian land is offered here to show how on occasion cost-benefit analy-sis has led the dominant power on the continent to deny parts of its conquered lands to general settlement. The costs of occupation and of the rescue of those non-Indians who might seek to take up occupancy against the wishes of those already there became unsustainably high. The Sioux, Seminole, and Navaho were expensive enemies. It is no wonder that many of them are still living where their ancestors were when the first white men probed their defenses.[17]

More tribes might also still be in place had the United States government not found in "allotment" laws a non-military device for breaking up Indian lands and enabling outsiders to intimidate or swindle Indian landowners one by one, reducing Indian-owned land from 138 million acres in 1887 to 48 million in 1934.

Wildfire is also an expensive enemy, differing from human antagonists, however, in that it cannot be cheated. In flame zones, whether reserved or not, feral fire will take for itself what it can take.

One further wrinkle in reservation policy is worth mentioning in the context of computation of costs and benefits. When the Founders deployed their armed forces to keep down the costs of warfare provoked by government-subsidized or government-protected settlement, they made no distinction between reining in private armies bent upon invading the dominions of the King of Spain and restraining squatters and tomahawk-title seekers from entering land reserved for Indian nations. In the spring of 1794, Washington's western commander, General Anthony Wayne, was about to open his successful campaign against the Indian nations of the Old Northwest, which culminated in the victory at Fallen Timbers. He was infuriated at being forced to divert his attention and a detachment to rebuild Fort Massac, near present-day Paducah, Kentucky. The problem was not that the Indians were troublesome in that quarter, but that certain Kentuckians had been stimulated by Edmond-Charles-Édouard Genêt, André Michaux, and other agents of the French Republic to contemplate assaults upon the Spanish possessions in the Mississippi Valley.[18]

The president issued a proclamation of neutrality, making it illegal to participate in such undertakings on behalf of the French or anybody else. His proclamation was soon written into the Neutrality Act of 1795. Private invasions, "filibustering," stirred up trouble because the government was expected to rescue the filibusterers. That trouble was more than the pillaged real estate was worth. So it is with encouraging settlement of fire-prone areas from which the settlers must be rescued, imperiling the rescuers.[19]

With some of the history in place, we can look to the future, assured that we have plenty of precedents for what must now be done to take the steam out of the engines now powering a land rush into fire danger.

15. TOWARD A HEALTHY FORESTS AND COMMUNITIES CORPS

Night after night, the fire season of 1985 produced television pictures of wind-driven fires striking settlements in Idaho and California, and demonstrating that wildfire is not just a western problem; 100,000 acres burned in South Carolina, several thousand of them perilously close to the city of Camden. Federal and state officials responded not only by the shift discussed earlier from fire suppression toward preventive burning, but also by forming what is now the National Wildland/Urban Interface Fire Program. In 1992, the advisory group for the program adopted the term "Firewise" to describe "the state of being knowledgeable and prepared for wildfire in residential or urban settings."[1]

After innumerable workshops, seminars, and intensive neighborhood-level work, "firewise" has lost its capitalization and entered the common lexicon. It has now become a generic term for purposeful reduction of fire load on a household scale—clearing pine needles from eaves and gutters, moving woodpiles off decks, raking duff from the ground, and cutting out brush. More remarkably still, "firewise" has also become more than a good *housekeeping* seal of approval; it has become a good *community-keeping* seal: entire towns can secure designation as firewise by coordinating and encouraging individual action by planning, building codes, and enforcement of compliance.

Stephen Pyne has written, "In the backyard only the small stuff matters." But it matters a lot. If the neighborhood is to become safer, each householder must provide fire-defensible space, "in which the land need not be stripped, only sculpted to dampen fire's ability to creep into, radiate toward, or hurl embers at the house. . . . This is properly the responsibility of a homeowner not only to himself but to his neighbor. . . . An errant ember can be extinguished rapidly if someone is present to stomp it out. . . . Once a house and immediate surroundings become defensible, a firefighter can swat out sparks, douse trickles of encroaching flame, protect a structure—and himself."[2]

"The shouting begins," writes Pyne, "when defensible space is expanded to the community itself, particularly where a hamlet abuts against public land, because it effectively extends the influence of private landholdings into the public domain." In other words, protection of private homes often requires putting out fires on public land that, absent those adjacent homes, might otherwise burn themselves out harmlessly. Firefighting is costly, sometimes in lives as well as dollars. The preventive, defensive perimeter around settlement must thrust salients outward because wildfires strike settlements along a "chain of combustion. . . . The power of fire resides in its power to propagate." The purpose of fire-load reduction is to reduce "the capacity of a landscape to carry flame."[3]

What would that mean in practice? How much sculpting should be done, and by whom? Those were questions much in the minds of the survivors of the great Hayman Fire on the Front Range of Colorado in 2004. One hundred forty thousand acres had gone up in flames between Denver and Colorado Springs, burning through a landscape that had burned many times before. As the people came back, unloaded their U-Haul trucks, and poked around their yards for trash that had once been toys and lawn furniture, they had good reason to look at the charred slopes around them and think about the carrying capacity of flame. When Forest Service polltakers came among them to ask what they wanted done, nearly all of them said they favored "mechanical removal of hazardous fuels" as well as "prescribed fire in combination with mechanical removal." Many of them knew that prescribed fire can itself be risky. That was the Los Alamos lesson. Nearly everybody knew it was also smoky and noisy. But just as citizens of Georgia and Florida have learned to live with prescribed burning, so the Hayman survivors acknowledged a high probability "that a wildfire will occur near their homes in the near future." That being a given, they favored reducing the "carrying capacity" of the forest surrounding their rebuilt homes by prescriptive burning.[4]

They also said they had "strong feelings of vulnerability from wildfire risks enhanced by the inaction of their neighbors." Though they accepted responsibility for defending their property, they also said that "all neighbors, including homeowners, the Forest Service," and their homeowners' association should be involved in "mitigating these risks."[5]

Involved? What if some refused to be involved? What if refractory or irresponsible people failed to clean up the fire load on their own properties despite requests from the homeowners' association? Even in libertarian Colorado Springs, when volunteering runs into irresponsibility, the law steps in. That is how it has been according to the Judeo-Christian tradition since that necessity was laid forth in the book of Genesis, since sustained in the Common Law doctrine of "nuisance." Under both canonical and common law, individual expression stops at the point where it affronts the common good. While the Taxpayers for Common Sense (TCS), fiscal conservatives averse to waste, advocate firewise measures and firewise education, they add that "education . . . will never fix the problem . . . Faster, firmer action is needed in the form of regulation from government."[6]

The National Association of State Foresters anticipated the TCS, endorsing zoning changes at the local level, including the *required* "use of firewise materials and methods, and the creating of defensible space." Were taxpayers and foresters ahead of themselves? Not according to a team headed by Brian Muller of the University of Colorado. Even in that anti-requirement state, "required use" is on its way. Firewise education, the necessary precondition to requirement, is gaining acceptance along the Front Range. The TCS report says directly that if state and local governments continue to duck their responsibility to make and enforce firewise ordinances, "while handing billion-dollar fire suppression bills to the federal taxpayers, then federal regulations should be considered."[7]

Beyond the range of volunteering and the neighborhood fire brigade, beyond the homeowners' association and the town fire department, fire-load reduction and putting out fires become the work of the state and nation—of people trained for these jobs, and paid to do them regularly, at the taxpayers' expense. Abraham Lincoln said that "a great amount of locomotion is spared by thorough cultivation." True—and a great amount of combustion can be spared by organized and professionalized prevention.

TOWARD A HEALTHY FORESTS AND COMMUNITIES ACT

Sooner or later, I believe, prevention—fire-load reduction—will require mobilization of a Healthy Forests and Communities Corps (HFCC). There need be no anxiety about that corps running out of work. The direction of climate change is toward job security for any force that reduces the likelihood of wildfire, and copes with it when it strikes human settlements.

Disaster relief is vastly more costly than disaster prevention. Besides, the fire duty now being performed by state and federal foresters pulls them, often insufficiently trained, from other important work. Fiscally conservative legislators who doubt the importance of this work can best address their doubts by dealing directly with them, not by avoidance through pretending that it *may* be done, in full knowledge that it will *not*, because there is no one to do it. *The Salt Lake Tribune* coverage of a statement by Senator Larry Craig of Idaho, a conservative who does deal with this matter directly, took note that firefighting had "pulled $2.7 billion from other nonfire accounts in the past five years . . . [and forced] the cancellation of $540 million in public land improvement projects that had been appropriated by

Congress." Should not the same Congress be asked by the public to face up to the annual recurrence of wildfire? Should not its next step be to professionalize the national task of firefighting? Of course it should. And it will, as soon as the public feels sufficient revulsion to sending insufficiently trained and badly equipped part-time crews to fight fires, and resents sufficiently the current tax-supported bonanza being enjoyed by the wildfire-industrial complex.[8]

The New Deal demonstrated with the Civilian Conservation Corps that the community's work on the commons should be done by the people of the community through their government—explicitly, budgeted to do what it does. No subsidies. No sleight of hand. No "euphemistically termed stewardship contracts." No buried treasure for those whose lobbyists know where the treasure maps are to be found. There is plenty of work to do, and much of that work will be using preventive fire to replace natural fire. (At the higher elevations, neither fire suppression nor "thinning" nor prescribed burns appear to have had much effect on ridgetop-to-ridgetop burning. But, of course, few people live on very high ridgetops—and those who do, choose to live there.)

Many people live where they have been encouraged to live. As the Taxpayers for Common Sense wrote in their report on the Hayman Fire: "In some cases, it may be better not to expand communities into these hazardous areas in the first place, but to take these factors into account and build homes elsewhere." In the American system, each individual makes the decision as to where to build or buy—unless that individual is assigned to live on a reservation, in a garrison, or a national laboratory. The question for tax-paying citizens, in a democracy, is whether or not they wish to pay for subsidies for the construction of buildings in places where those buildings are likely to burn, and also for their rebuilding.[9]

LUMBERING AS FIRE TREATMENT—THE BIOLOGY

Should the taxpayers, then, subsidize lumbering as an economical way to reduce fire load? No. Not for that, either. At Peshtigo, Cloquet,

Rodeo-Chediski, Cerro Grande, and Hayman, fires devoured the detritus of lumbering, whether of the conspicuously messy nineteenth-century type or of the somewhat more fastidious twentieth-century variety. So, by the end of 2004, an emerging consensus was stated by Mark Blaine in *Forest Magazine*: "There's an inverse relationship between the benefit of thinning for fire and the profit from trees harvested. Bigger trees resist fire better than little trees, but bigger trees offer more commercial value. In forests where mechanically removing fuels offers the most benefit, it's the smallest stuff that must go": close-packed little treelets, woody bits and pieces, stems and twigs, branches, sawdust, and miscellaneous lumbering slash—"kindling."[10]

No self-respecting investor would put money into a lumber company that tried to make fire load into a commercial product without a healthy subsidy, or without taking down big marketable trees. "Thinning" is *not* the same business as lumbering. Maybe someday biomass energy production will become a good business, but that day will come only when the prices of oil and other alternative fuels are a lot higher than they are today.

Besides, "in some places the effects of logging have a lot more to do with fire danger than the oft-cited crisis resulting from fire suppression." When forests such as those of Yellowstone National Park, dominated by lodgepole pine, are "adapted to burn infrequently but intensely, and depend on the heat of a stand replacing fire to function ecologically . . . thinning isn't an option for managing them." The difference between lodgepole and ponderosa is enough to require entirely different fire-load treatment in each system. And because "no variety of pine takes fire as does a blade of grass or a stem of sagebrush or chaparral, the lumbering/thinning prescription doesn't work on all sorts of tinder." The notion that one-time "thinning" would do the trick everywhere is unconvincing to anyone who has suffered the periodic conflagrations behind Los Angeles and San Diego. Chaparral has to be burned out or brushed out every year or it will feed a big fire.[11]

In *Tending Fire*, Stephen Pyne sums it up: "That fire management is simply logging in sheep's clothing is simply the Big Lie of the extreme environmentalists. That a revived forest industry can cure forest ills is the Big Lie of cutting's extreme partisans. . . . Proposals to revive logging may make a political statement, but they are not speaking to fire."[12]

The Forest Service professionals and mountain states foresters, led by Jack Cohen of the Fire Sciences Laboratory in Missoula, Montana, agreed that there is no need to return the deep woods to the lumberjacks. Jim Robbins of *The New York Times* reported their view that "the only thinning needed to protect houses—even in the most tinder-dry forest—was within a 'red zone' of 150 to 200 feet around the building." With these facts in mind, it is well to recall another basic truth constantly reiterated by Taxpayers for Common Sense. The problems masked by the Forest Service budget include not only the systematic diversion into recurring fire crises of many of its best people, but also the diversion of "nearly one-third of [it] to . . . [a] wasteful . . . commercial timber program." It is not only wasteful. It actually contributes "to the risk and severity of wildfire in the National Forests."[13]

After 4.7 million acres burned in 1994, at a cost of "$950 million to the federal taxpayers," and after the Forest Service alone spent another billion dollars in 2000 "to combat wildfires on 2.2 million acres of National Forests," other federal agencies spent $600 million more, and states at least as much again. The Taxpayers for Common Sense concluded that much of this money was wasted because it was spent "to log the National Forests to benefit timber companies, which contributes to the escalating risk of catastrophic fires."[14]

LUMBERING AS FIRE TREATMENT—THE ECONOMICS

The dollar costs of firefighting in the national forests grew, from $138 million in 1980, and $253 million in 1985, to $1 billion in 2000. Although the Government Accountability Office, the Park Service, and the Forest Service agree that a dollar spent on fire prevention is worth six or seven in suppression, and although these bodies have agreed with the TCS that "a concerted long-term fire-prevention effort" over decades will be necessary to "reduce fire risk [just in] the National Forests," funding priorities remain grotesquely skewed toward suppression. In any legislature, including the U.S. Congress, disaster trumps anticipation.[15]

An aversion to anticipation has been encouraged by both a wildfire-industrial complex and a dispersion-industrial complex. A lot of lobbying is done by those invested in things staying as they are; a lot of money is made from the status quo, however absurd, dangerous, deleterious, or expensive it may be. The lumbering lobby represents the primary beneficiaries of the current situation outside the refractory elements in the Forest Service bureaucracy (with which it is entangled). A billion dollars a year in subsidies to lumbering is a lot of money. While only a quarter of the timber product of the national forests of the 1980s is still hewn and trucked out, the budget allocated by the Forest Service to pay for getting it out has actually increased; unit costs of production have gone up from nineteen dollars a board foot to more than fifty-two dollars. The Government Accountability Office (then the General Accounting Office) set the average annual subsidy from the taxpayers to the timber industry as running at more than $300 million annually as late as 2000. John Baden and Pete Geddes, two Montana foresters, wrapped up this set of numbers with the comment: "Those trees are worth more standing than as boards, especially in the region's roadless areas. . . . [I]n most Rocky Mountain national forests the cost of managing timber sale exceeded the value of the logs by a factor of five. Most logging here was politically driven and the full costs of exploitation were ignored, discounted and obscured."[16]

As the Taxpayers for Common Sense pointed out, the lumbering subsidy to the Forest Service serves "no important national goal," and according to the congressionally funded Sierra Nevada Project, it raises firefighting costs: "Timber harvest, through its effects on forest structure, local microclimate and fuel accumulation, has increased fire severity more than any other recent human activity." General Christopher Columbus Andrews of Minnesota and Carl Schurz of Wisconsin understood that more than a hundred years ago.[17]

A chain of reports in the years 2000 through 2004 from the Forest Trust and Forest Guild confirm this view. The big trees that go out are fire-resistant, and the dense growth of little, uniform "hog-bristle" trees that spring up thereafter are prime "tinder." With the parasols of big tree branches gone, the sun bakes and crisps the grass, little trees, duff, and lumbering detritus. The people of Hinckley and Cloquet learned that, and so did the firefighters struggling with the Crooked, Ryan Gulch, and South Fork Nemote #4 Fires in Montana and Idaho in 2000; they, too, commenced in timber slash, according to the National Interagency Fire Center. As if to recapitulate the midwestern experience of the entire nineteenth century, the TCS report concluded that "commercial logging can exacerbate the problem. Moreover, a focus on commercial logging politicizes the problem and distracts from real solutions."[18]

Those solutions include putting fuel-reduction money where it is needed—where the people are. And, even more important, changing federal policy to decrease the number of people in such places—or at least to decrease the pace at which those endangered people are increasing in number. That is what was successfully achieved after settlement and cultivation exceeded their natural limits and produced disasters marked by dust and flood. There is no reason why the successes of the 1930s and 1980s could not instruct success in the 2000s.

16. TOWARD A NATIONAL FLAME ZONE ATLAS

As Senator Larry Craig suggested in the interview quoted earlier, the Forest Service should do forest service, not fire service, except in the direst emergencies. So should the Park Service. And before emergencies strike, where should fire service in the form of fire-load reduction be done? Where the people are, where they live, and wherever it is likely that a wildfire, once loose, is likely to reach them.

Let us start there, at the hearth, at the center of a schematic diagram of the circumstances of a fire-concerned citizen, around which appear a set of concentric circles. Slicing those circles roughly in half, and proceeding outward from the core, on one side are ever more remote wildlands; on the other, ever more remote institutions in the civil order.

Exploring the wildland half is like taking a backpacking trip that starts at the hearth and works its way outward through parks, forests, and ever wilder places toward wilderness, whether so designated or wild in fact. The most remote place in my imagining of wildland is a crag in Alaska—for me, Ultima Thule. Yet is even such a place remote? Even there, the air, moisture, and climate are affected by human action.

From the same hearth, people eager to improve fire management have a journey to take in the other direction. Depositing the backpack at home, they grasp briefcases instead and pass through backyard and neighborhood, town, county, and state jurisdictions to arrive in the Federal City. Then the route to their destination must pass through the lobbyists' hive on K Street Northwest before it rises up Capitol Hill to reach the uttermost opposite to that crag—the catwalk under the dome of the United States Capitol. The explorer-reformer up there on the cat-walk can now turn around to look back on the institutional landscape. I like to think that the Alaskan crag may actually be visible from there—if just barely. The scene figuratively before the traveler looks like a political map of central Europe during the medieval interregnum. Its complexity has arisen from two hundred years of efforts to cope with the demands and opportunities of trusteeship over 2.1 billion acres, the richest legacy of land of any nation in the world.

The National Park Service protects, preserves, and explains more than 375 places (the number grows almost every year) selected by Congress as being of special national significance. The Service began as a merger of the staffs caring for national cemeteries (such as that at Gettysburg), national monuments (such as those on the Mall in Wash-ington), national historic places (such as Independence Hall and the hulk of the battleship *Arizona* in Pearl Harbor), and places of out-standing natural qualities (such as the Great Smoky Mountains, or the Yellowstone.)

The Park Service is part of the Department of the Interior, as is the Bureau of Land Management, which manages land only in the West, generally at lower elevations than that within the national forest sys-tem, and with less marketable timber. The United States Fish and Wildlife Service, also a Department of the Interior agency, manages smaller "natural areas." In truth, even within the National Park Ser-vice the distinction between "natural" and "cultural" never made much sense, and is truly meaningless when applied to the Bureau of Land Management, whose effective jurisdiction includes cemeteries, battle-fields, monuments, waterfalls, geysers, and places in which the history of memorable people was made.

The Bureau presides over 130 million of the 160 million acres, largely grass and shrubland, subject to wildfire but of a different sort from the largely tree-covered terrain managed by the United States Forest Service, which is part of the Department of Agriculture. The Forest Service is responsible for about 230 million acres throughout the nation, though not in every state. About 190 million of these are said to be "forested," presumably with trees big enough to burn.[1]

RESPONSIBILITY—WHERE?

How does the interested citizen, with all this in mind, find out which of these agencies (indeed, which agency out of the thousands not named, but engaged in firefighting nonetheless) is responsible for dealing with wildfire at any particular place? Which of them maintains that part of the, so to speak, border patrol on the frontier between wildland and settlement? The answer is: nobody knows precisely where that frontier is. Though all these entities do what they do very well, the nation remains in need of a Flame Zone Atlas grounded in candid, consistent, and comprehensive data, to tell us where people are at risk from wildfire. A useful atlas would show graduated degrees of danger, from low probability of big fires to high.

The atlas would have to be revised regularly: these are dynamic natural and civil systems; the likelihood of fire alters with weather patterns and vegetation; population comes and goes. (In the West and Southeast, it has, in general lately, been coming.) In many places, the Flame Zone Atlas would inform local communities where conditions were sufficiently within the range of firewise measures to be safe for human use. A memorable color scheme should suggest how safe or unsafe a neighborhood is. Such a scheme is already available to private insurers, though it does not cover the entire nation. Without awaiting the atlas, however, we already know some important truths about the political geography of fire:

- Most wildfires *do not start on federal property*.
- *Very few* wildfires start in the national forests.

- Ninety percent of the settled areas threatened by fire *are not next to national forests.*

- And most of those now, or soon to be, fire-prone *are not in the West.*

Why are so few people aware of these simple propositions? Part of the confusion arises from political counter-naming or renaming. Examples of counter-naming would be denoting clear-cut forests as "Healthy Forests," dirtier air as "Clear Skies," firing professionals and calling that process "professionalization," calling disorganization "reorganization." Renaming may simply be a desire to keep people alert. That can be the only reason why the General Accounting Office was renamed the Government Accountability Office. Still, the GAO remains the GAO, and that is something, and it can still be heeded when it tells Congress, as it did on September 13, 2000, that "neither the Forest Service nor [the] Interior [Department] knows how many communities, watersheds, ecosystems, and species are at high risk from catastrophic wildfire, where they are located, or what it will cost to lower this risk. Therefore, they cannot prioritize them for treatment or inform the Congress about how many will remain at high risk after the appropriated funds are expended."[2]

After eight million acres of forest land burned in the West in 2000, the nation might have been instructed by its leaders where the fires were likely to come next. But despite hearing after hearing, press release after press release, task force after task force, the government of the United States and the governments of the wildfire-prone states still do not know the degree of fire risk in each of the nation's communities.

SMOKE AND MIRRORS AT THE WILDLAND/URBAN INTERFACE

In the *Federal Register* of August 17, 2001, the Secretaries of the Interior and Agriculture purported to provide such a list. It was headed

"Communities at Risk," but the small print confined those communities to those "in proximity" to federal land, thereby restricting the focus of risk reduction to federal property, especially to the national forests. Even smaller print admitted that a community would be placed on the list only if the secretaries agreed to put it there after the state submitting the information agreed to confess to its being at risk.

Without probing deeply, it was obvious that the coverage would be spotty; from the outset, everyone concerned knew that the list would be a composite of "whiteouts" and "balloons." "Whiteouts" were where developers controlled the process. Developers do not go to confession in the *Federal Register.* "Balloons" would appear where states scented the potential for federal dollars, and produced ludicrous definitions of need. Take the case of much-ballooned Georgia: it confessed to much need but includes little federal land, most of that in well-asphalted military bases and in fire-resistant swamps and bayous.

So eager for federal largesse were the ballooning states that when the United States Geological Survey and the Geographic Names Information Service took up the charge from the secretaries to find the 11,376 communities put on the final list, they could locate only 9,371 of them; the rest defied satellite searches for built-up areas or had never made it onto any existing list of real towns. Three-quarters of these infinitesimal or phantasmal hamlets were—or were said to be—in six states. When all the purportedly imperiled communities submitted by these states were located on regional maps, they peppered the landscape right up to borders on the other side of which were great white spaces, apparently and mysteriously unthreatened—the regions of whiteouts.

These purported safe havens were created by opting out. In the devil's dictionary of counter-naming, opting *out* is called opting *in*—or, sometimes, more ambiguously, "self-definition," which sounds as benign as voluntarism. Now, really, what town wants to proclaim to the world that it is likely to go up in flames? What meat-packing plant wants to say that it is full of food poisons?

APPROACHING ACTIONABLE TRUTH

The absence of a useful federal list of "Communities at Risk" does not mean that an objective list, applying uniform criteria, cannot be created. Three such lists exist. Because there has not yet been sufficient public outcry to require them to become the basis for public policy, they remain private, not widely known, and uncorrelated. Correlating them, and making the correlated information accessible, is not in the interest of developers who are seeking to sell property to unwary buyers, or who are concerned lest taxpayers cease to be willing to pay for more incentives to such buyers to accept undue risk. But sound information is the basis of sound policy, and sooner or later that information will be sought. When it is found, migration into such places will be discouraged, and subsidies for migration into them will diminish.

Therefore it is useful to establish from whence respectable information can come. The first of the three partial listings of communities truly at risk is a data bank in New Jersey kept by ISO. Once an acronym, now a corporate title (like 3M for Minnesota Mining and Manufacturing), ISO denotes a consortium of casualty insurers. It describes itself as presiding over "a GIS [digitalized geographic information system] product that combines fuel loads (from thirty-meter satellite imagery, interpreted to identify wildfire-prone vegetation), slope of terrain (using U.S. Geological Survey quads), and specific road-access hazards (essentially dead-end roads at least partially surrounded by fuels)." Its coverage is limited to nine western states, including California, but William Raichle of ISO is right in saying that these are the states currently with the most people at risk. That does not, of course, limit the potential applications of ISO's methodology, or its application to more and more communities as climate change puts those communities at risk. The beauty of this system is that the climate and vegetation data can be "overlaid with census and related housing/building information," as a necessary step toward a national Flame Zone Atlas.[3]

The second of these existing data banks of "Communities at Risk" covers more ground but less intensely. It was compiled by a team led by Volker Radeloff at the University of Wisconsin, and provides general guidance to neighborhoods at risk nationally, though not down to the household level. It uses satellite images to locate the interspersal of houses into wildlands. The third data bank was generated by a group in Colorado led by Greg Aplet, Senior Forest Scientist of the Wilderness Society.[4]

The following conclusions emerge from a study of these three data sets:

1. Only about 9 percent of the land area of the lower forty-eight states lies within any true Wildland Urban Interface (WUI), where human settlement is set in or near vegetation that might burn if the weather conditions are dry and hot enough. In 2006, other places may not yet have gotten hot and dry—not yet, so they may not be colored red. That color should be reserved for those areas where people live, where the vegetation is inflammable, and where the weather encourages wildfire. That color would appear on a relatively small portion of the land area of the United States. The problem is manageable.

2. Because 39 percent of the nation's houses would fall within that 9 percent of the national estate in the WUI, the problem remains primarily one of people management, not of fire management.

3. Only about the same percentage of communities—less than 10 percent—live in a WUI abutting Forest Service land. This simplifies matters further, except for politicians who want to bait the Forest Service.[5]

4. Broadening fire-load reduction to all federal lands—not just Forest Service land—would not do much more of the necessary job. Only about 17 percent of wildfires have started on all federal lands. Private, state, and tribal lands account for 85.12 percent of the total area of communities actually at risk from wildfire. Department of Defense property amounts to only 2 percent; the Bureau of Land Management manages only another 2 percent.

5. The "thinning" idea was launched by its proponents on the grounds that it could end the problem of wildfire if lumbering/thinning were permitted *on federal lands*. That was and is a bogus proposition, not only because of the economics of lumbering as fire-load reduction, and not only because of thinning's ineffectiveness in reducing many fuels, but also because less than a fifth of the acreage burned in the United States in recent years has been in national forests—probably no more than a third in forests of any kind.

Where, in fact, is the WUI? Most of it lies in the East and Midwest, including two thirds of both Connecticut and Massachusetts. Global warming and regional drying will make these areas, and the rest of the East and Midwest, more dangerous to wildfire, a prospect that may not seem very threatening unless one drives regularly between Boston and Cape Cod, where, during an average summer, traffic is slowed several times by dense pine smoke. More than once a summer, even now, residents of Plymouth with rooftop gazebos can see flames in the Myles Standish State Forest. New England is warming along with the rest of the continent; the fire load is there, including combustible structures, awaiting a little more sustained heat and a little less moisture.[6]

The seven states having the most acreage—not people—in the WUI are all eastern and midwestern. Only after them comes the familiar list of western states—Idaho, Washington, Colorado, etc.—noted earlier as being at the top of those also receiving in-migration. Of the eastern states at risk, Florida and Georgia are also high in-migration states. Though they do not now appear to be any more susceptible to fire than New England, they will suffer sooner as the climate becomes warmer and drier. The rapidly growing population in the Southeast, as well as the slower-growing population of New England, is pressing into private land and creating new flame zones. And in both regions, the relatively low percentages of federal lands make it especially silly to talk of lumbering the federal forests as a cure-all for their increasing fire problem.

DIFFERENT SIZES, DIFFERENT PROBLEMS

The foregoing discussion has treated all flame zones together. But, of course, they are not all alike, though some politicians and their economic allies attempt to assert this in order to justify a one-size-fits-all fire policy. As it happens, the particular "size" that is most televisual is also the "size" most coveted by lumber companies—big, charismatic conifers. Crown fires sweeping through ponderosa pines make for great pictures. Though lumbering big ponderosas can be profitable, the economics of the timber business do not correlate well with the economics of settlement of fire loss: most people in flame zones do not live in ponderosa forests. They live amid brush, piñon, juniper, or chaparral. Trailer homes in scrub far outnumber starlets' pads under ponderosa or lodgepole.[7]

The differences among the vegetation systems in flame zones are dramatically manifest in three ecosystems at gateways to national parks. In the region around Yosemite, 31 percent of the fire-prone area is covered with black oak and other hardwoods, 10 percent with grassland, 20 percent with chaparral, sagebrush, and other shrubs, and only 8 percent with ponderosa pine plus 7 percent mixed conifers and lodgepole pine. (The rest is in various mixes and small populations of a variety of species.)

On the Colorado Front Range, around Rocky Mountain National Park, 37 percent of the land is covered with ponderosas and lodgepoles, 17 percent with a variety of grasses, 11 percent with shrubs, 2 percent with aspens, and 4 percent with piñon/juniper forest. The rest, again, is covered with various mixes, with no single species predominating. Estes Park and Boulder have quite another fire problem from Yosemite's.[8]

In central Idaho, north of Sun Valley, one can turn north toward Glacier National Park or east toward Yellowstone from an environment in which sage, bitterbush, and other shrubs cover 44 percent of the ground; 13 percent is covered with grassland, 13 percent with ponderosa pine forest, 7 percent with Douglas fir forest, 7 percent with predominantly mixed hardwoods and conifers; the lodgepoles, familiar in Colorado, are down to 3 percent.

Though these are all western forested systems at roughly the same altitude, each is different from the others. No single policy can prevent wildfires from afflicting the people who settle into all of them, or cope with the differing kinds of wildfires that break out in them. As Volker Radeloff has written: "Even within a single state there can be stark differences, forests on the Olympic Peninsula will hardly ever burn, the Eastern Cascades are at high risk from crown fires, both areas contain WUI communities." These differences among fire-prone natural systems do not mean that it is impossible to produce standards distinguishing low-risk areas from higher-risk areas and these from the highest-risk areas, each such grade applicable only within each natural system—down to the zip-code level—being presented in a national Flame Zone Atlas.[9]

ISO does that already for the states it covers. Its FireLine system correlates across many ecosystems' six "fuel types." They range from WA for water and NF and Fo for other non-fuels for wildfire—such as downtown urban areas, deserts, bare rock, large roadways, and irrigated areas—through F1 (grass and scrub), F3 (medium fuels such as woodland and timber), and F5 (heavy fuels such as brush and shrubs). That final distinction is instructive to those advocating lumbering as the remedy for wildfire. The results are impressive when satellite data are ground-tested to distinguish rhododendron from chaparral—satellite photographs are not too useful in flower identification—and when slope is added as another criterion. (In California, "70 percent of the properties burned in the 2003 fires were in areas of moderate or steep slope," though only "24 percent of policyholders throughout the state . . . lived on sloped terrain.") The results were impressive, though depressing as well: impressive because satellite technology and computerized data assimilation can produce wonders of prediction and potential savings in lives and property; depressing because the political process is so far behind the capabilities of a technological society.[10]

Identification of dangerous places is the necessary precondition for protecting people. Digital technology and satellites have made this much easier, providing more precise tools, such as Global Positioning Systems (GPS), and advances have also been made (albeit painfully) in the science of fire management. We can now define the probability of repeated wildfires in precise, graduated terms. A Flame Zone Atlas could set forth where wildfire is likely to strike. Once that is known, it can be planned for, and once planned for, "mitigated"—a word used by hazard professionals to include an array of measures intended not to prevent natural disaster but to diminish its ill effects.

ISO's FireLine produced maps showing 97.5 percent of the area within the perimeter of the Paradise Fire of 2003 as imperiled—that is, 85.93 of 88.12 square miles. The boundaries of those most-imperiled areas were clearly shown. The case of the Cedar Fire of that year was even more dramatic: 98.3 percent of the burned area lay within fuels designated as dangerous by FireLine. These numbers gain poignancy by being read together with those that show how relatively small is the total area of the United States that ought to classified as in flame zones in general.

To put the matter in slightly different terms: the problem is manageable because the number of people affected by wildfire is still relatively small, though growing. It is manageable because that number grows in major measure because it is subsidized to grow, not because it grows naturally.

SHADES OF SCARLET

The practice of redlining entire precincts and wards earned a justifiably bad name when used by mortgage lenders for racial discrimination. But the term "redlining" might be redeemed if it were instead used to demarcate areas subject to wildfire, because all shades of red are not the same. The lining could appear in a variety of hues, differentiating areas at higher risk of fire from those at lower risk, taking account of moisture, vegetation, prevailing temperatures, and weather conditions, including frequency of ignitions by lightning. The color might graduate from the pale pink of a sky warmed by a dawning sun to the deep scarlet within a coke oven. Areas bordered in such differential redness could be depicted in the national Flame Zone Atlas, meticulously compiled, GIS-based, showing the fire-imperiled condition of settlements at the WUI.

The Flame Zone Atlas would do much to show where the problems lie, and would suggest where they need not be made worse at taxpayers' expense. The atlas would leave off those communities that did not belong in it either because they did not exist or because they were too cold, too wet, or too bare of vegetation to justify inclusion. Where settlement has actually occurred, and where a good number of people are exposed to wildfire, the areas surrounding them should receive the benefits of intensive forest fire management. If that cannot be effectual, their occupants should be told as much and offered an opportunity to withdraw. It would be better to pay for that than to pay to rebuild their houses—or to pay to bury them.

17. MANAGING BOTH SIDES OF THE INTERFACE

As Stephen Pyne has insisted for years, the presence of people defines disaster, and the avoidance of disaster "requires intensive management." "Simply calling a burn 'natural,'" he writes, "becomes a kind of ecological faith healing. Fire management done right is intrusive management. That does not mean more fussy hands, axes, and bulldozers; it means better knowledge and more targeted techniques, more wits than widgets. It means moving fire protection out of its traditional commodity-style economy and into a service-style economy."[1]

That is why a Healthy Forests and Communities Corps makes much better sense than a "Healthy Forests Initiative," which is really a timber-cutting program. With a New Deal–style idea back on the table, it makes sense to follow the learning curve back yet another generation to reexamine the contrast after the great fires of 1910 between Gifford Pinchot's fire-suppression strategy and that of Stewart Edward White. That is why White wrote of Pinchot's policy of suppression that when it was applied indiscriminately, it built "a firetrap that . . . piecemeal, but in the long run completely, . . . [defeated] the very aim of fire protection itself." Throughout the ensuing seventy years, the nation did indeed have to seek answers to his question: How could the accumulated "kindling" be gotten "rid of . . . safely?"[2]

Chad Oliver, appropriately Pinchot Professor at the Yale School of Forestry and Environmental Studies, is known to bridle at what has become, since the 1970s, an uncritical chorus of approval for White's position and derision for Pinchot's. Oliver concedes that promiscuous suppression was mistaken, but he insists that a promiscuous "Let it burn" policy would have been, and would be today, equally foolish and equally inhumane. Suppressing fires in and around settlements, he says, did "an awful lot of good. . . . A lot of towns could have burned, watersheds and water supplies could have been wrecked and the quality of wood as a usable resource would have been ruined."[3]

"The quality of wood as a usable resource" is not a major worry in the ponderosa parklands and lodgepole savannahs maintained around Sun Valley or above Canyon Road in Santa Fe. It is important, however, to the inhabitants of poor and traditional communities such as Trampas, Mora, and Truchas in New Mexico, whose residents have needed those forests for firewood and vigas (support beams) for several centuries. The nation, I submit, should have the same interest in maintaining sustainable forestry in communities such as these as it has in homesteading and agricultural husbandry. Assisting both farmers and community foresters to remain on the land is more important than subsidizing noncommunity exurban development and lumber companies.

AFTER THE SOUTH CANYON FIRE

That brings us back to chapter 2's rankings of states according to the rate at which they are receiving in-migrants and their fire exposure. Those rankings can now be brought up to date and refined to the ranking of the states *by acres occupied by people at risk in flame zones at the WUI.*

Nevada remains first among states in its rate of in-migration, though fifteenth in acres where people are imperiled by fire, because its people are highly concentrated—its urban areas lie within a vast near-emptiness. Likewise, though parts of Arizona and Nevada burn

States Requiring Firewise Action	Ranking by Pace of In-migration	Flame Zones, Ranked According to Number of Acres in Which People Are Imperiled by Wildfire
Georgia	6	2
Florida	7	5
Idaho	5	8
Washington	10	9
Colorado	3	10
Oregon	11	11
Utah	4	14
Nevada	1	15

ferociously and often, large areas of them are desert, which hardly burns at all. That returns the discussion to the outrageous infirmity of the information available to those seeking to make sound migration and fire policy.[4]

South Canyon, where the fire of 1994 killed fourteen firefighters trapped in the canyon while they were struggling to protect houses down the slope, lies in Garfield County. It is one of the most susceptible to wildfire in Colorado and also the county whose population is growing most rapidly. The killer fire of 1994 was followed by several more big blazes in the county—and by many more houses under construction and reconstruction. Since 1950, Garfield County has quadrupled its population. Amid heat, desiccation, and high summer winds, the citizens of Garfield and other fire-prone counties in the West have been busy both with construction and with firefighting. During one of those summers, the state's governor said to the press, "All of Colorado is burning." At the same time, it appeared that all of Colorado was *building*.

The Hayman Fire of 2004 did most of its damage in Douglas, Jefferson, Park, and Teller counties, whose growth in population has been as impressive as Garfield's.

County	1950	2000	Change (%)
Douglas	3,507	175,766	5011.86
Jefferson	55,687	527,056	946.46
Park	1,870	14,523	776.63
Teller	2,754	20,555	746.37

In these counties, fire itself, rather than firefighting, made the most difference in saving lives. The $40 million spent in putting out the Hayman Fire was not nearly as effective in reducing fire load as the fire itself was. The slopes of the Colorado Front Range had burned "big" on average every fifty years for a millennium, until fire suppression began in earnest after 1913. The experience thereafter was like that of the Pajarito Plateau and the Mogollon Rim: setting little fires through prescribed burns diminished the ferocity of wildfire at low elevations and near settlement. Higher up the mountainsides, the job had been done by previous fires, in 1998 and 2002.[5]

After the destruction of 132 houses, fundamental conditions on the Front Range changed little from what they had been over the preceding several thousand years. If anything, they had grown a little more dangerous, from human intrusions during recent centuries. The story is familiar enough: grazing altered the mix of fuels, followed by "mining, vegetation management, road building, urbanization, recreation, and water development," in the midst of rapid regrowth of dense, inflammable stems, as fire suppression permitted the accumulation of fire load. After fire suppression, the forest became denser, and so did the population; programs of subsidized dispersion encouraged migration into these counties to the accompaniment of the persistent marketing. If forests must be managed, so must towns.[6]

Whether or not fire suppression has caused the buildup of fuels, and whether or not prescriptive fire would help much in a particular locality, some places will be dangerously prone to burning when lightning strikes. The question is: How many people will be in those places? As firewise programs are remixed for each community and accompanied by intensive management of adjacent woodlands, the nation as a whole must surely declare that it will no longer subsidize migration into fire danger. Radeloff's group is correct: "To substantially lower the fire threat to homes in the long run . . . sprawl-limiting policies may have to be paired with fuel treatments."[7]

One of the most effective of sprawl-limiting policies would be a simple device to increase tax revenues—which would also increase individual responsibility among homeowners, and reduce deaths in wildfires—perhaps accompanied by two further simple ideas. As things stand, anyone who wants to build a house in a zone of extreme fire danger, one in which fires recur every year, can finance that home with a federally insured mortgage, and then deduct from taxable income all the interest paid on such a loan. Let us assume that a federally authenticated Flame Zone Atlas is now available. Let us further assume that Congress authorized the IRS to refuse to accept any deductions for interest on mortgage loans made to finance construction or ownership of houses constructed or bought in an acute flame zone. Perhaps it could further be declared that thereafter there would not be any federal mortgage insurance available on such a loan. And perhaps federal policy could assure that no further federal funds, and no more young firefighters, would go to rescuing the people residing in such homes. Those who wanted to go ahead could do so. At their own cost. At their own risk.

THE USES AND ABUSES OF INSURANCE

It has been assumed too long that the federal government would be the protector, rescuer, and insurer of last resort. Rutherford Platt of the University of Massachusetts at Amherst, author of the standard textbook *Land Use and Society*, writes that there has everywhere been "a tendency for property owners . . . to demand the right to build wherever they wish without public regulation limiting their freedom. But then when there is a threat from a natural hazard, they do expect federal protection." They also expect federal mortgage insurance and hazard insurance. So far, the hazards they have grown accustomed to believe the federal government will share with them have been limited to those caused by too much water—with flood insurance leading the list. It seems likely that there will soon be an outcry for federal protection in conditions in which there is too little water and too much fire. The balance of this chapter is devoted to an exposition of what a murderous idea this is.[8]

Some private insurers are easing away from providing fire insurance. Some are suggesting that they would be willing to insure but only at rates graduated upward with risk. It does not require political genius to predict that there will soon be public pressure for federal fire insurance, atop all other subsidies to migration into flame zones. It will be hard to resist, though federal fire bailouts will as surely encourage settlement in flame zones as federal flood insurance has encouraged developing floodplains.

Fire losses are growing rapidly. Politically ambitious state insurance commissioners cannot be expected to permit insurers to set rates depending upon degrees of fire exposure. This is because graduated premiums work very well when rating automobile drivers, but the riskiest members of the public hate them. Therefore state commissioners resist any extension of the principle of graded risk by the simple means of threatening to cap the rates, and permitting only downward graduation.

The result is accumulating pressure for another federal bailout. Those voters who would pay elevated *insurance premium rates* for elevated risks locally are not identical to the people who would pay the elevated *taxes* nationally. This is an ugly fact of political life, explaining why nearly all states now require undifferentiated rates on a statewide basis, and insurance losses are also spread on a statewide or nationwide basis.

As the smoke of the Hayman Fire drifted away, newspapers reported that "private property losses" amounted to somewhat more than $40 million. But these were not, of course, truly *private* property losses, because they became *public* through uniform rates: uniform rates spread out to everyone the costs of rebuilding in flame zones. The effect is similar to that which would occur if all taxpayers were assessed the cost of rebuilding through federal fire insurance. Without rates for fire insurance differentiated according to risk, as they now are differentiated for automobile insurance, every payer of a fire insurance premium shares the burdens (though not the delights) of those playing out the American dream beyond the limits of safety. Undifferentiated rates play into the tidal flow toward federal fire insurance. Should that tide reach the shore of legislation, the result would further worsen the problem: more people in fire danger. An unintended but no less probable outcome of federal fire insurance would be that it would kill people.

Ann Camp of the Yale School of Environment and Forestry has lamented the present condition in which "people with the responsibility for protecting lives and property have no authority to tell people that what they're doing in the WUI is inappropriate and that they have to stop." Yet all citizens in a democracy are ultimately the people with that responsibility, and all citizens can, with their votes, ordain what behavior is "inappropriate."[9]

CALIFORNIA PROMISES

Since the 1971 San Fernando earthquake, California has insisted that localities include earthquake as a hazard in their plans (though not yet dust storms, floods, fires, or mudslides). The state remains, however, conspicuously laggard in enforcement of this requirement, even in the face of repeated disasters. Its homeowners in mountainous or forested areas are required to maintain at least a thirty-foot fire-defensible space around their homes. In some communities there is an optional hundred-foot space requirement, but no more than the state's thirty-foot requirement is enforced unless an inspector demands it.[10]

Under the California Natural Hazard Disclosure Law of 1998, disclosure became more "enforceable and commonplace," according to Austin Troy of the University of Vermont, an expert in this arcane field:

This bill requires sellers of property to complete a Natural Hazard Disclosure Statement upon which they disclose whether the property is located in publicly mapped flood, fire and seismic hazard zones. . . . [It] consolidated and gave teeth to the previous, but largely un-enforced fire disclosure requirements. The form warns buyers that these hazards may limit their ability to develop or get insurance and that defensible space must be maintained around the property in accordance with local and state regulations.

But there is a convenient barn door left open to developers who find that all this candor dampens sales. The bill states that "where real estate agents and sellers are liable for disclosure . . . it permits that liability to be transferred to the third party contractor conducting the mapping report for a modest fee."[11]

Troy follows the horses out the barn door by noting that just as the Secretaries of the Interior and Agriculture winked at the self-designation of communities, allowing them to decide whether or not they wished to advertise themselves as dangerous to fire, California permitted each community "the option to choose their own designation, even if it meant designating no land as hazardous. The state had no authority to override these local designations even if they were egregiously misleading. This meant that many populous communities with significant amounts of hazardous land mapped either too little or no land as statutory hazard zones for political reasons."

Troy's critique is illustrated by the experience of the catastrophic Oakland Hills Fire of 1991: none of the areas burned by the fire, or even near it, was "mapped as being in Very High Fire Hazard zones, despite the fact that that fire led to the passage of the bill." Besides, "those municipalities where mapping was based on the local designation are under no obligation to comply with the state's defensible space requirements, but can choose their own homeowner requirements. The result is that many dangerous areas remain unmapped, and homebuyers in these areas may be misled by natural hazard disclosure forms claiming no fire hazard."[12]

California's FAIR (Fair Access to Insurance Requirements) Plan subsidizes migration into fire danger, offering taxpayer-financed bonuses to people who wish to obtain reduced rates on fire insurance in flame zones. It is perverse, and murderously so. FAIR forces private insurers who wish to do business in California to join in "a state-regulated association that acts as an insurer of last resort providing property insurance to homeowners who cannot obtain insurance in the private market, and offering it at generally subsidized rates."[13]

California is a huge state and hugely complicated, but it has one simplifying quality: much of it is uninhabitable. A rough estimate based upon Radeloff's and Aplet's criteria suggests that only 7 percent of California's land area is really in the WUI. That percentage is low because much of the state is either desert or mountain or, conversely, no longer wild—already paved, so to speak. But that 7 percent includes five million houses, and it suffered $2 billion in fire losses in 2003 alone. In June 2001, the State Insurance Commission made things worse by expanding the FAIR Plan brush-fire coverage to include the entire state—it had previously been available in a limited geographic area. Just as private insurers were putting some roadblocks in the path of migration into fire danger by refusing coverage, the state stepped in to wave the migrants onward into the teeth of probable disaster. "By providing coverage in areas where the private market would not, and by doing so at highly subsidized rates, the FAIR Plan significantly underprices wildfire risk in California and encourages too much new development in the most hazardous areas." Troy suggests that "one way to mute the effect of this policy on development patterns would be to limit FAIR Plan coverage to existing buildings. This would allow the insurance market's pricing of risk to steer development away from the most hazardous areas."[14]

WHY DON'T PRIVATE INSURERS FIX THE PROBLEM?

Why, then, don't the insurance and reinsurance companies just fix all this mess by letting the "market's pricing of risk . . . steer development away from the most hazardous areas"? Because they are not permitted to do so. The market is not allowed to price risk. The pricing of insurance is political. The powerful are receiving the benefits of that power in lower prices than the market, acting alone, would establish.

Once again, however, we may take comfort from manifest absurdity: something that malfunctions because of political distortions can be made functional by changing the politics. That is one of the best arguments for democracy. The gimcrack federal system of subsidies to sprawl into fire danger can be fixed by the political process. Likewise, the absurdities of political manipulation of the pricing that may be offered by private insurers can be repaired as well, by permitting premiums to be priced according to risk.

The insurance companies and reinsurance companies are not free to fix all this. They cannot do business in states that will not certify them to do so. Many states will not certify companies that will not acquiesce to distortions of premiums. Sometimes all insurance markets are closed if the aspiring entrant is unwilling to put up with distorted prices in any submarket. Sometimes the gatekeepers exclude those companies unwilling to join in subsidizing building in hazardous places by forced participation in what is called "pooled risk." This is a euphemism for compulsory sharing in a process whereby a small number of householders can assume extraordinary risk and have the cost of their insurance spread to all others—indeed, in some big pools, to all who want casualty insurance of any kind.

One insurance company executive has summarized, of necessity anonymously, the result of the federal sprawl subsidies acting together with state pooling of risk. "Society is currently funding—and actually encouraging—the perilous behavior of a small percentage of the population. These people knowingly move into hazardous areas and often do little to remediate their exposure to the hazard." They expect and receive "a disproportionate share" of tax-supported protection, rescue, and rebuilding, and of insurance protection. As a result, society as a whole subsidizes their behavior.[15]

This same executive and others in the insurance industry have assured me that it is a canard to insist, as some commentators do, that because the insurers themselves "pool" risks, they should be expected to remedy the problem on their own. This assertion confounds *pooling persons* with *pooling liability*. Pooling insured persons spreads among them all risks that may randomly strike any participant. Pooling liability forces insurers to join in paying the costs of losses to those who may have incurred special risk with those who sought to avoid those special risks. For example, pooling persons treats equally those who regularly practice firewise action with those who thumb their noses at the sky—and at their neighbors. And pooling insurers requires that all companies desiring to do business in, say, California agree to take what comes from undifferentiated acceptance of risk.

A second infirmity in the "Why don't the insurers fix it?" approach lies in the assumption that those insurers do not want risk-differentiated premiums for casualty insurance. But reinsurers do not necessarily have a stake in things the way they are. If they had a monopoly, they could spread the risks into an elevated rate base. But there is competition among them, and there is also a developing practice among reinsurance companies of bundling.

The term "bundler" does not refer to one Yankee who shares a bed with another, as the term is used in Early American history courses. Instead it denotes someone who shares with a buyer, for a fee, a bundle of assets having defined and limited qualities. One could bundle spaniels, or battleships of more than forty thousand tons, or the seeds of one species of gingko. Bundling of this sort has a long history, but it became intensely popular just after the Second World War. Many of us who were then managing small banks bundled together mortgages we wished to make for other business reasons and sold them off to investors. We did not have the resources to compete on our own with our bigger competitors, and we did not know much about the mortgage banking business. We got more money to lend by disposing of the mortgages, and we got paid for "originating."

It all sounds primitive today, after the growth of FNMA and GNMA, and after trillions of dollars in differentiated bundles have been spread into investment portfolios. (In other hands and conditions, it also gave rise to redlining and other discriminatory practices.) Now, the huge international reinsurers, of which the largest are the Swiss Reinsurance Company and the Munich Reinsurance Company, themselves bundle relatively uniform risks, distinct from bundles of other risks, and sell them off to investors. Bundling is big business. It is based upon differential rates for differential risks.

Pooling destroys the efficacy of bundling. It is indiscriminate. Its effects, as noted earlier, are sometimes murderous. And it is also not as profitable to reinsurers as a market in which risks were not pooled but, instead, broken into bundles and sold as means to provide diversification to investors. There is no desire on the part of reinsurers to deny themselves bundling profits.

Nor, however, are they eager to get on the bad side of the insurance commissioners, who control access to important markets—such as California. Therefore, as my informant was willing to say off the record, "the insurance industry should not be relied on to carry the torch for reducing aggregate exposures to wildfire." Whatever might be the interest of taxpayers in general, or of insurers, "home builders and lenders . . . may not weigh in in support." That is a fair guess. Second, while insurers "may start differential rating," they are not in a hurry to do so because "they're still writing business," a lot of it. And, third, "wildfire loss is small in comparison to overall loss from fire in America (it's about 1 percent) and catastrophe loss (wildfire represents 2 percent of catastrophe losses, tornadoes 32 percent and hurricanes 28 percent)." They have larger matters on their minds.[16]

The subject at hand, however, is wildfire, not merely because it is at hand but because it is sufficiently conspicuous to attract attention to other systematic problems. So we will stay with it, hoping that if we can improve matters with regard to wildfire, saving some lives and much money in the process, we might be able to do likewise with other hazards. As my insurance-writing friend went on to say, that improvement can begin with differentiating levels of risk in fire-prone places. Once differentiated, responses to those risks can be made known to homeowners and policymakers, given what the industry calls "face validity" and accessibility by a Flame Zone Atlas, to encourage rate setting and subsidy reduction "consistently across geographical areas . . . without gerrymandering."[17]

There is hope. The federal *flood* insurance precedent has already been heeded by private insurers, as it demonstrated how insurance could be withheld and migration into excessive hazards discouraged. Since there is not yet federal *fire* insurance to withhold, the insurance-withholding lever is not available to discourage migration into flame zones by encouraging recognition of fire hazards. The federal flood system, however, has taken steps to adjust its rate structure to "steer" migration away from floodplains, though so far only by trivial amounts. The American Planning Association has prepared model state legislation that could be given teeth by sharply cutting federal rates and by coupling those reductions to facts demonstrated in a Flame Zone Atlas. Raymond Burby of the University of North Carolina and others have urged that the federal government get tougher by requiring local hazard plans before making available any federal flood insurance. No plan, no taxpayer subsidy. Burby has "done the numbers" and concludes that "approximately $230 million" could have been saved in "private insured losses to residential property" between 1994 and 2000 had "all states . . . required comprehensive plans with hazard mitigation elements." Plans do not save money, but they do induce recognition of problems. After recognition often comes mitigation—and mitigation saves both money and lives.[18]

18. THE LEGACIES OF STEWART CHASE
AND GILBERT WHITE

During the summer of 1936 the sky across most of the United States was darkened with dust and smoke. The dust had been dirt lying between sod and caliche or sand on the High Plains, but plows had ripped off the sod, the sun had dried the dirt, and the winds had come to pick it up, intermixed with sand, and up whirled the mixture in dense, suffocating clouds. Most of the smoke had been leaves, branches, and stems of trees and brush left to dry by lumbering in the forests lying north and east of the plains. Nature spoke its piece that summer, and among the responses were two that have outlived the grim conditions of the time: those of Stewart Chase and Gilbert White. Both had listened, watched, and warned against further humiliations to the earth and the forests, lest more people suffer from what nature would do when further affronted.

The weather thereafter got better, and after 1939 the Second World War drew many farmers off the land and into the armed forces, diverting the nation to other threats. The lessons of Chase and White got little attention in the aftermath of war, when there appeared to be larger problems at hand than wildfire and dust clouds. Now, however, the Cold War is over, and attention can go back to the land, drawn there by a new body of scientific findings about global climate change. A new generation is learning to find lessons for itself in dusty or smoky skies, as well as in the photographs of Dorothea Lange, and the books of John Steinbeck, Chase, and White.

In 1936 it was possible to think that a little more rain and a little less heat would make things just dandy again. Now, as the climate of what has been a temperate zone in North America changes toward conditions conducive to dust and fire, that pleasant and irresponsible thought does not come so readily to mind. We have had nearly seven more decades to learn about the dynamics both of nature and of our own civil systems. Another science, risk assessment, owes much to two writers of 1936—Chase, in his *Rich Land, Poor Land*, and White, in the first of many papers for the *Planners Journal*.

Rich Land, Poor Land was the forerunner to Rachel Carson's *Silent Spring*; Chase was, however, more political than Carson. From his seat in President Franklin D. Roosevelt's Kitchen Cabinet, he went forth to extol the work of Hugh Hammond Bennett and his Soil Erosion Service, warning of the further degradation of the fire- and flood-prone West.

White, a geographer born in 1911, is the grand master of hazard mitigation. From the beginning of his career, he has urged that the federal government steer migration away from flood zones and to safer places. Hazard-mitigation conferences are still regularly energized by restatements of White's thesis, and sometimes by White himself. It is high time that his lessons be systematically applied to help slow the pace of the current land rush into wildfire.[1]

White has understood all along, as did Chase, that identification of dangerous places is the necessary precondition to protecting people. Degrees of danger can be graduated both by probable severity and by probable frequency. Metronome marks—time in large intervallic beats—can be overlaid upon severity gradations, in fires from manageable embarrassments around the barbeque pit to catastrophic crown fires. In musical terms these would be dynamics.

We have seen how the insurance and reinsurance companies use this kind of "scoring"—even the term has musical analogies—in nine states, and have noted also that public agencies, and the public generally, do not yet have the full benefit of the application of modern technology either to fire policy, or—to recall Chase's contribution to this discussion—to migration-steering policy. Nor do individual householders or home buyers have access to this kind of necessary information as they choose where they will accept the risk of remaining or settling. A Flame Zone Atlas would be useful in stating where wildfire is likely to strike. Once that is known, it can be planned for, and once planned for, "mitigated"—by an array of measures intended not to prevent natural disaster but to diminish its ill effects. After that comes planning—and enforcement of plans.

Without planning, mitigation becomes haphazard and wasteful; without enforcement, it is ineffectual. Though neither planning nor regulation comes easily to a nation of optimists and self-helpers, both are necessary. Self-help cannot avert disaster coming down a mountainside as a wall of flame. Regulation is the last resort when all the "selves" do not help. Blithe optimism becomes shameful when it leaves people imperiled by dangers that can be reduced by mitigation, planning, and regulation.

Who, then, should plan and regulate? State and local governments seldom plan or mitigate on their own when doing so costs money; legislatures and councils are often dominated by economic interests that seek to deny the likelihood of trouble. Though Congress is no more noble, from time to time it can act in the national interest. When it does, the federal government can offer incentives to nudge "the locals" forward. Raymond Burby has concluded that "if the benefits of plans for hazard mitigation are to be realized, federal incentives and state mandates for planning will be required." Attention alone is not enough, though giving "hazards adequate attention" does help remind people how disgusted they feel when inadequate information or niggling measures leave them to suffer needlessly, how ugly it is to pick up the debris, and how terrible it is to face the grief and bury the bodies. Only after all that—only with the tears still drying—are we likely to do better planning and bestir ourselves to act more wisely.[2]

The record is not bad. Here again is the list of states ranked by acres occupied by people at risk in flame zones:

States Requiring Firewise Action	Ranking by Pace of In-migration	Flame Zones, Ranked According to Number of Acres in Which People Are Imperiled by Wildfire
Georgia	6	2
Florida	7	5
Idaho	5	8
Washington	10	9
Colorado	3	10
Oregon	11	11
Utah	4	14
Nevada	1	15

In Idaho, North Carolina, and Oregon, hazards were required to be recognized in local plans in the 1970s, in Florida and South Carolina in the 1980s, and in Arizona, Maryland, and Nevada in the 1990s. Colorado joined the others in 2002—perhaps the deaths in South Canyon helped. "Among these . . . four [not including Arizona, Maryland, Nevada, and Colorado] have detailed prescriptions and pay serious attention to state oversight of local compliance with the laws' requirements." Oregon, in many matters a model, not only requires and monitors hazard planning, but also encourages "avoiding development in hazardous areas where risks cannot be mitigated, including the benefits of open space uses of hazardous areas."[3]

Colorado, the newcomer to the planning, regulating, and sometimes enforcing states, requires local planners to consult with the state divisions of mines, geology, and forestry (though oddly, in a state half of whose lands are in federal ownership, not with the Bureau of Land Management or the U.S. Forest Service). Wildfire is not yet, it seems, sufficiently interesting to legislatures, and human suffering from fire not yet so widespread as to induce more than nine states to take local hazard planning seriously. Only two, Georgia and Florida, actually assist localities in planning for hazards, and obviously these two hurricane-prone states are not yet thinking much about fire as a natural hazard.[4]

They should. And so should all the other states that have been receiving large numbers of new citizens. Many of the newcomers, and most of the old-timers, have reason to be apprehensive about increasing natural hazards, but have not been warned of them. That condition of unwitting acceptance of high risk was one of the consequences of the subtlety with which dispersion strategies were carried forward in the Cold War era, and of the subsequent cleverness of the dispersion-industrial complex.

THE LEGACY OF THE DISPERSIONISTS—REVISED

The panoply of subsidies devised after 1946 to disperse American cities was laid out very early in that process by Donald and Astrid Monson, in their contribution to the *Bulletin of the Atomic Scientists* noted earlier. The desired result was to accelerate "breaking up the central mass of a large city [in a] program of planned dispersal," including "broad express highways through our large cities." Defense contracts were to be allocated—and they were—away from dense old cities. Chicago, Cincinnati, Cleveland, and the struggling towns of the Rust Belt should "receive no additional defense work in order . . . [to] induce workers to transfer to less hazardous areas."[5]

The hazards to which the Monsons and the others referred were dangers from the air (from Soviet rockets), not from the ground (wildfires or floods or earthquakes). Leaving earthly considerations unconsidered, the Monsons' recommendations are quoted in the following paragraphs, confirming the prescriptions for tax-subsidized urban dispersal offered by Teller, Marshak, Klein, and the Cambridge group working on Project Charles. I have followed each of their proposals with another of my own, modestly suggesting revisions to accommodate some biology and some recent history.

- FHA mortgage and GI insurance would be granted only to
  housing built in accordance with the plan [of dispersal].

This was done. In recent years there has been some reversal of this
pattern, but it is still essentially in place. It is now time to reverse this
incentive, and to channel the granting of federal mortgage insurance
to "less hazardous places" as defined by natural, rather than political,
hazards.

- FHA public housing would be built only in accordance with the
  plan, [with priority to those] displaced from slum or other
  central city areas being cleared.

Very little "slum clearance" still goes on, but new low-income
construction can and should be subsidized in urban settings.

- Federal slum clearance loans and grants would be given only . . .
  [when] fitted into the dispersal plan—i.e., . . . reduced the
  density of an overcrowded area.

A simple reversal of this polarity would be useful—loans and
grants should come only when "fitted into" an anti-dispersal plan, so
that there is a tug away from places exposed to natural hazards.

- RFC and other government loans would be made only to
  industries locating in areas designated by the plan. . . . Defense
  contracts, materials, allocations, tax concessions and other
  inducements would be given to firms locating new plants . . .
  with special encouragement [to relocate given] to firms now
  located in areas within the central city designated for clearance.

The RFC is long gone, but defense contracts and loans could well
be made "only to industries locating in areas designated" by a better
plan—one that took account of natural hazards. Other federal, state,

and local grants, loans, and subsidies could be similarly reformed. The fast-food industry is the largest recipient of Small Business Administration loans. These loans should be conditioned by a national policy that takes account of avoiding natural hazards and reinforcing traditional communities.

- Federal aid for highway construction and other public works
  would be granted only for projects essential in carrying out the
  dispersal plan and would be stepped up in order to speed the
  rate of their completion.

Highway construction ran away with aid during and after the Cold War. Mass transit was a stepchild. If all federal and state roadbuilding were to be conditioned not by a "dispersal plan" but by a hazard-avoidance plan (which in many cases would be an anti-dispersal plan), many lives might be saved at the end of the road or tracks.

- Other aids to cities would be conditional on their implementing
  the dispersal plan by amending and enforcing zoning regulations,
  refusing building permits for new construction, . . . etc.

A simple amendment, substituting "anti-hazard" for "dispersal," would help.

- Land . . . within the central city . . . cleared . . . and not rebuilt,
  such as strips bordering on expressways . . . can serve as
  separation strips buffering off one community from another.

Once again, an amendment substituting "in flame zones" for "within the central city" would open up splendid vistas, literally and figuratively. The Land and Water Conservation Fund might be used by localities to reduce natural hazards by acquiring and setting aside pretty places that are also fire-prone as open space. Thus "separation strips buffering off one community" could be adjusted to include separating the human community "from another," the natural community.

- Such slum areas are not to be rebuilt. . . . [They] will form . . . firebreaks. . . . Slum clearance should be speeded up.

What might happen if, in this formulation, "areas repeatedly burned" were substituted for "slums" as the dangerous places to be avoided? What if, after two floods or fires, houses in flame zones were not rebuilt—as the old, dense, wooden London was not rebuilt after its Great Fire? What if the owners of houses destroyed were compensated to build where things are safer? What if the old rubble were then itself to become part of a firebreak?

One probable outcome would be saving a lot of money. Another, in all likelihood, would be saving lives. Removing the income-tax deduction for interest payments on mortgages financing disaster-inviting houses would be a grand beginning. (Income-tax deductions for interest paid on mortgages, wherever that mortgaged property may be, are implied grants to assist householders in building in flame zones.) The Taxpayers for Common Sense have rightly written that "it is better not to build houses in the first place if they are likely to face destruction in the path of wildfire." Indeed. Much better. As things stand, the income-tax interest deduction, like all such deductions, operates to shift the burden from one set of taxpayers to all the rest. It was put in place to encourage home ownership. It has acted in conjunction with FNMA and GNMA mortgage insurance to disperse home ownership without distinctions of safety. The result has been that building in unsafe locations is treated as if taking those risks were in the national taxpayers' interest.[6]

Jack Wright of the University of New Mexico at Las Cruces has suggested rolling back another federal housing subsidy that crept in even before the Cold War years, but got worse after 1950. Noting that Farmers Home Administration (FmHA) loans require that houses be built outside of cities and towns, "mandating sprawl," Wright has suggested that annual appropriations to the FmHA and its successor agencies be limited to the FmHA's original purpose of assisting family farmers who could not otherwise secure financing. The rest, now going to exurban developers, could then be returned in block grants for housing in the cities from which the bulk of the tax money came.

Wright notes "in this same vein" that county Rural Special Improvement District bonds (RSIDs) are issued with federal blessing (and in effect subvention) and now pay for roads and other infrastructure in rural subdivisions, "thus underwriting the development of land that bare-bones developers could not otherwise pull off. The buyers of the lots assume an annual payment (RSID taxes) which allows the county to pay off the debt. Investors buy these bonds and receive tax free return." What if these bonds could be issued only by counties that had firewise plans, that had accepted the American Planning Association's guidelines, and that required developers to include hazard mitigation in their plans?[7]

Federal encouragement of settling in flame zones has long been reinforced and accelerated by states and localities eager for the growth though insufficiently conscious of the hazards of growth in the wrong places. National programs such as the Interstate Highway System for decades brought these localities offers they could not refuse, including a 90 percent match to their local funds for road construction. Not every state and locality has fallen for this. Some have not only refused to be baited into following federal foolishness, but have also withheld from dangerous places subsidies to their own infrastructure and development. Maryland pursued this approach under Governor Parris N. Glendening (1994–2002) as a way to manage development better. Even those without the vigor of Maryland or, more recently, New Jersey could at least refuse further encouragement to development in dangerous places inherent in policies such as California's FAIR Plan. Other states, realizing that there are limits beyond which growth becomes dangerous, have also taken note of the delayed price to taxpayers embedded in development that thereafter requires rescue and expensive evacuations. Some states seek to manage growth by concentrating development in areas suited for it, while sustaining other areas as farmland, ranchland, parks, or forests. They could do so more efficiently and economically if they were provided with the scientific data available in a national Flame Zone Atlas.

Areas too dangerous for human habitation could be zoned to halt, if not preclude, residential or commercial development. In areas that remained risky but manageably so, local officials could use such an atlas to restrict development to that managed on firewise principles. And permits would not be issued at all if the proposed structures were not easily accessible for emergency responders. Many lives could be saved and much destruction averted by such regulatory reforms. The pain caused by wildfires will commend them in time. Meanwhile, land-conservation strategies can continue to steer development away from areas that are manifestly dangerous, which are often also beautiful, pleasant, and ebullient with natural life. These strategies include outright purchase for conservation purposes—the purchase or transfer of development rights, conservation easements, and various tax credits.

Avoiding the development of flame zones is wholly compatible with saving productive farmland, ranchland, scenic wonders, historic sites, and recreational areas. All that is urged in these pages is a modest extension of Smart Growth to include humane growth and the deliberate eschewing of growth that occasions pain—to humans and to other endangered species.

THE AMERICAN DREAM AND FREEDOM FROM FIRE

Throughout this book, I have described the problem of people migrating into dangerous areas, and thus creating a class of endangered householders. Unlike some other writers identified in these pages, I do not assert that my fellow citizens are besotted by a desire for danger. Extreme athletes we have aplenty, without looking for extreme homesteaders. Instead of being in the grip of a frenzy for self-immolation, I think our fellow citizens are trying to make prudent and economical choices, and will make them intelligently if given the necessary facts. The high cost of housing is a besetting problem for most Americans, and in their desire to find places to live that they can afford, many have flocked into fire-prone places, insufficiently warned, and indeed encouraged to accept undue peril. Manifestly, the positive side of protection from wildfire is providing alternatives to living dangerously. Good wildfire-avoidance policy is, therefore, good housing policy. Moreover, increasing the housing supply in areas that are already developed brings economic activity to these traditional, established, and relatively safe places and also meets an increasing demand for compact, walkable communities that are relatively close to jobs. Once again, Maryland has shown the way, coupling its withholding of subsidies from sprawling areas to the establishment of "Priority Funding Areas."

Local officials can follow such state initiatives by revising their zoning and building codes to allow for denser development where water, sewers, and transportation are already in place to handle growth. A good way to channel migration away from danger and away from the destruction of natural systems would be to put in place sound housing policies for lower-wage workers.

There are two essential complements to declaring some areas off limits to development. The first is the provision of attractive alternative development opportunities where there are fewer natural hazards—in nearly all cases in communities that have survived long enough to demonstrate their safety. Those communities already have much of their infrastructure built, a matter of some importance to those joining me in the taxpayer revolt against subsidized sprawl. Growth is a good thing when it is growth of opportunity for safe, pleasant, and economical housing. Growth is not a good thing when it is unsafe, unpleasant, and unnecessarily expensive in dollars, environmental costs, and human life.

As long as population increases there will be a need to house more people, and as long as there is space, more space will go to housing. Of course there are many kinds of space—adding a person to a household in Tokyo produces different results from putting someone new into a household in Topeka. But identifying endangered householders has already suggested that species other than humans have a place in the world—a theological principle that will be more fully discussed in the next chapter. For the moment, I suggest that it be stipulated that the lessons taught by fire in a charred landscape have included far too many ruins of houses previously occupied by humans. Though some forest fires do not burn out places where somebody has lived, too many do. And when a charred landscape includes previous habitations of other living things, these ruins, blackened nests and lairs, may also be seen as warnings and admonitions. From them, lessons about the location of growth can be read. From them, also, are sharper lessons forced upon us. Then, having accepted the warnings about what fire can do, and is likely to do again, the observer can take joyous account of the recurrence of life after a wildfire. The animals return. The green sprouts spring up again—or they do when space is kept for them.

Donald Chen of Smart Growth America suggests a range of devices to support respectful growth, keeping space for other species both through targeted conservation of places that are too dangerous to be developed and targeted development of safe places. These devices for channeling new migrations include outright purchase, acquisition of development rights by purchase or donation, conservation easements, and tax credits—all of them less ambitious and expensive than were the Cold War subsidies to sprawl, and all conducive to a lot of good growth.[8]

Chen has shown that good growth not only protects natural places and individual people, it also encourages the continued growth of traditional communities. As Chen has written me recently, "Our success in protecting people from fire danger depends very much on our willingness to restore and maintain the viability of our existing places—and allow[ing] them to accommodate the many millions of people that we anticipate will be needing to be housed safely." He went on to say, "I believe your taxpayer revolt is certainly about our [government's] wrong-headed encouragement of development of dangerous places. It is also about our willingness to sap the vitality out of older communities."[9]

Chen is right. It is time to lock the doors to the treasury against further raids to finance dumb growth, the kind of growth that destroys precious places, including natural communities as well as human communities, and puts lives at risk. When we stop to think about it, we know a lot about how to take better care of one another and of the other species with which we share this earth.

19. SUN DAGGERS, GRACE, LIMITS, AND THEOLOGY

The operational part of this book is done, and for some readers, perhaps, the practical part. I want now to invite a little further discussion with those who share with me an interest in the moral underpinnings of politics.

Early on, I sought to lay before you the experiences of my life that led me to write this book. Now something more is required, I think. When an author asks a reader to join in a theological inquiry, that reader should be offered an occasion to know the religious convictions that gave fervor to the author's discussion. I have put that at the end rather than at the beginning to permit an easy exit for those made uncomfortable by any discourse about religion. But when life, death, and the interactions of humans with one another and the rest of creation are at stake, there are those people—and I am one of them—who want a direct statement of the author's convictions about such matters.

I did not put this chapter earlier because I have not wanted to put a barrier across the path of those who consider religious discourse to be surplusage. Some secularists feel that working at such problems is sufficiently justified by simple humanistic principles, and do work at them, very hard. Others of us—the theologically bent—need something more than that. That does not mean that we have an easy time getting away from the transient and confusing toward what we feel to be permanent and stable. Plato did not find that search easy. Neither do we. Those of us who lack Plato's poetic gifts often turn to familiar liturgies and objects to help steady us.

It helps me from time to time to engage in the ancient practice of rapt concentration upon an icon. This requires dropping all else, turning off the cell phone and the computer, and for a sustained period looking hard at a physical object that conveys a complex meaning. For me, radiant icons, such as those in stained glass, are too dazzling and too open-ended. Steadying comes to me most readily when the icon is neither transmitting nor radiating light, but is set solidly on stone. I think of thumbprints on the cave walls in Utah, for example.

A thumbprint whorl is an affecting icon for me because, though small, it can be a hieroglyph of some very large matters: at the most basic, it can be a sign of individuality. The FBI treats it that way. A thumbprint can also assert something collective, speaking for all persons. Many ancient peoples left whorls on cave walls, and on rocks at the entrance to sacred spaces. Outside Utah, others that come to my mind are at New Grange, in Ireland, on the island of Malta, and on a butte in Chaco Canyon. Their locations were all carefully selected to be invocative—to receive shafts of sunlight, sometimes called "sun daggers." The whorls were put in places where natural intercessions were invited to cut through the insistence of humans on being noticed. The environment would thus trump the marks of humankind, making a mockery of any claims to "dominance."

These sun daggers striking across thumbprints can impart a third level of meaning. They can bring a higher trump—reassurance. A sun dagger can suggest the possibility of grace, of sudden beneficial change in what seems to be inevitable. A shaft of light across the marks we make—"his mark," "her mark"—can encourage us to believe that some of the errors and depredations of our errant species may be reversible, if we pray a lot and do our best. A sun dagger is a happier symbol than a lightning bolt.[1]

We have left our thumbprints on all parts of the earth. We have been everywhere—if we have not quite touched everything, our effects have. Having exceeded our limits, we must now deal with what we have done. There are places that are said to be unaffected by human action, but this is an illusion; every crag everywhere is warmer now than it would have been without human action, or it soon will be. The air breathed by plants and the light they photosynthesize are affected by human action. We cannot escape our relationship to them even if we do not choose to think we are part of the same intentional creation. Surely, even if God did not create all, man has fussed with all.

That last statement requires expansion to include acknowledgment of the fussing done by man's suite of attendants. We are responsible for what they do when we introduce animals and microbes to places in which they, and we, are exotic. That insight of Albert Crosby's forms the basis of any truly responsible fire-and-people policy. People do not travel alone. Crosby, like Stephen Pyne, synthesizes biology into history and anthropology; years ago, in his *Ecological Imperialism*, he provided the reasons why those who write of human interventions into forests should include in them human-caused interventions of "suites" of species, comprising humans themselves and their domestic animals, together with their parasites and hangers-on, including their courtier microbes.

Sometimes these were introduced deliberately: tamarisk, kudzu, cattle, and starlings were planted or released in North America. Sometimes it happens by mistake: snakes are carried from one island to another in the landing gear of aircraft; rats and viruses come ashore from coasting vessels; tuberculosis and syphilis germs are insinuated into trading patterns. The old order changes, yielding place to the new and often not better. Species exotic in 20,000 B.C. were no longer exotic in A.D. 900. The Norse and their livestock carried armies, indeed galaxies, of microbes. Two centuries later, in 1492, all Europe broke loose into America. In 2004, nothing is primitive. If there was an American Eden, it was gone before mastodons were brought down by exotic competitors—swarming humans—twelve millennia ago and more.[2]

True, at one time or another North America may have seemed to be an American Eden or a Virgin Land, and some portions still seem so. But it is also true that moral people living in a much-invaded and much-adjusted world have no choice but to make decisions about which among the grand "suite" of species present are to be encouraged where, and which are not. We cannot come to these decisions free of selfishness or stupidity, so we must be careful about irreversible consequences. On the other hand, we are here, surrounded and attended by our dogs, cats, and viruses. The rest of nature is saying to us, in the words of Ezekiel, that we "eat that which ye have trodden with your feet; and . . . drink that which ye have fouled with your feet."[3]

There are times when the slag heaps and brownfields and clear-cut mountainsides seem all we have to mark our passage. Were it not for the possibility of grace we would despair indeed, but there are other places where we have affected the earth beneficially. Everything we do does not make things worse. We are capable of gardening and of brownfield cleanup. Beyond these immediate achievements—close in, so to speak—we can be proud of some successes in both forestry and migration management.

And we can be proud, too, of designating wilderness. We do not make wilderness, but we can designate it, a process showing us at our most realistically diffident as we acknowledge our limits. When we designate a wilderness, we are proclaiming that even after all the messing around done by humans therein, and all the human warping and twisting of its natural processes, it remains a place still healthy enough to make it on its own. Some of us pause at the threshold of wilderness to genuflect before wonders of creation manifested with unusual clarity and freedom from confusion, feeling wilderness to be a sort of geographic Sabbath. The signboard DESIGNATED WILDER-NESS carries invisible but potent subtexts: MAMMON KEEP OUT, and CITIZENS: KEEP AN EYE ON THIS, BUT LEAVE NO TRACE.

My colleague Donald Scott of the National Park Service has recently reminded his friends of John Muir's theological reasons for urging the creation of wilderness areas. On June 23, 1869, thirty-four days before the birth of Stephen Mather, the first director of the Service, Muir wrote, "Oh, these vast, calm, measureless mountain days, inciting at once to work and rest! Days in whose light everything seems equally divine, opening a thousand windows to show us God." This sounds to me as if Muir, a tireless reader as well as a tireless walker, had been reflecting upon the work of Jonathan Edwards.

JONATHAN EDWARDS

Edwards was the first great philosopher to be born in the European colonies in the Western Hemisphere. The founder of American environmental theology—and therefore, I think, the founder-philosopher of parks and wilderness areas—was born just three years into the eighteenth century, the son and grandson of theologians. In his own ministry, Edwards was like a priest in the Roman Catholic Church, combining the offices of celebrant and rector. Truly a celebrant, he celebrated both God and the artifacts of God, inviting others into a rapturous delight in God's generous creation. Truly a rector, he was lawgiver and keeper of right courses, condemning those who defiled that creation. In his parish at Northampton, Massachusetts, and then, after exceeding the tolerance for reproof among his congregants there, as a missionary among the refugee Indians of Stockbridge, not far away, Edwards urged his humblest congregant to take an upright role in a magnificent world, and called down the wrath of heaven upon the selfish and the proud. Because he insisted that God's creation was grand, intentional, and entire, he insisted that our species must live within limits—politically and environmentally. Edwards was clear about that a century before George Perkins Marsh and Henry David Thoreau, and anticipated Muir by yet another fifty years.

There is not space in a book about wildfire and Americans for any extended discourse on the environmental ethics of Marsh, Thoreau, and Edwards, or their views on the related subject of living within political limits. Nor can there be room for more than a word or two about the views of Marsh, Thoreau, and Albert Gallatin on the specific instance of the war between the United States and Mexico. But there can be little harm in noting in passing that Edwards, Marsh, and Gallatin used much the same language in warning their fellow citizens against environmental and political bullying. This was that sin Saint Augustine had called "a proud lust for domination." Edwards, Marsh, and Thoreau used many of the same expressions in warning against both faces of imperialism. Bullying was anathema to them all. Its failure to respect other persons or animals as components of creation displayed a failure of respect for the Creator.

Gallatin's views sprang from Rousseau's Geneva, rather than Calvin's Geneva, from whence came much of Edwards's doctrine. Yet the insights Marsh gained from studying the Edwards-Calvin tradition while he was at Dartmouth College brought him easily into alliance with Gallatin—and Abraham Lincoln—in opposing the Mexican War. Edwards was unpopular because of his advocacy of Indian rights; Gallatin and Marsh were unpopular for denying an alleged inferiority of Mexicans or Indians. Just as with Edwards, at the core of their political and environmental beliefs there glowed a due regard for other people and a due regard for other species. And when Gallatin directed research and contemplation toward the ruins of Indian cities and ceremonial places revealed in archaeology, he was suggesting something even more subtle. His contemporaries might learn from the evidence of forced withdrawal what could happen when people failed to be sufficiently careful when testing what nature would tolerate.

Respect for others and humility toward nature, and nature's God, had been at the core of the doctrines of Edwards. He did not put his stress upon good works, but neither did he condone bad works. Edwards was a philosopher of living within limits, affirming the indivisibility of the created world. He included all species, including all humans—rich, poor, black, white, and red—among the wonders of creation. All were co-created, not merely as creatures but as aspects of God. The brimstone-scented side of Edwards appeared when he was delivering sermons to those who had failed to treat their fellow beings accordingly, directing his anger especially toward those who abused the Indians and those who cheated the poor.[4]

Heeding Jonathan Edwards has been made easier in the last decade by a massive effort to publish more of his legacy—twenty-seven newly edited volumes and a small library of commentaries. Despite all that labor, the myth of Edwards-the-unrelentingly-ferocious persists, because the sermons still most readily accessible are the ferocious ones, not the loving ones. He is often represented in survey courses in intellectual history only by his "Sinners in the Hands of an Angry God," calling the smug and avaricious to repent. That sermon is surely a valuable message for today, but so is Edwards's celebratory style in "Concerning the Ends for Which God Created the World" and his youthful notes on nature.

Edwards produced these marvelous works a hundred years after the beginning of the great migration of English-speaking people into New England led by clergymen migrating for religious reasons, who bore with them their Old Testament and who associated themselves with other migratory people described in the books of Genesis and Exodus. Had they been Muslim they might have given equal emphasis to the Hegira. Edwards, therefore, sprang from a tradition of accommodating other factors than price, for reasons transcending markets, when migrating, settling, and organizing communities. For religious reasons, separatists explored the backcountry of Plymouth Rock, Roger Williams founded Rhode Island, and Thomas Hooker took his flock from Cambridge to Connecticut, as Quakers found asylum in Pennsylvania, Moravians in North Carolina, Catholics in Maryland, Huguenots in Florida and South Carolina, and Jews in relatively tolerant Georgia and Rhode Island. Sorting and weighing those motivations has occupied battalions of graduate students, but even in this age of grim, crabbed, and desiccating secularism, few have concluded that religious motivation was unimportant.

Edwards had his bitter side, but primarily, I believe, because he was so serious about social ethics. His stiff sense of what was right in the ways people dealt with one another was often affronted. The records of New England before his time suggest very little land speculation or land fraud, in part because a theology of community still balanced private avarice. As that balance became destabilized, Edwards set himself against the exploiters and speculators. He stood before the prim white folk who sat in their prim white pews in their prim white churches, and expressed his abhorrence of hypocrisy. His tone affronts some today who point out (rightly enough) that he was also intent on restoring the authority of the clergy, an outcome his modern secular critics regard as deleterious. True enough, his manner suggests an insufficient respect for the ethical aspirations of members of that congregation struggling on their own. Those of us who admire him might indeed wish he had been more politic and less direct, if we were convinced that then the consequence would have been to strengthen the hands of those in his flock who were already imbued with "caring for God's creation." However that may be, there is no doubt that Edwards stood nearly alone in his insistence that nature and natives were worthy of respect for precisely the same theological reasons.

In exchanging e-mails about Edwards with some secular environmentalists, I have found that using the word "Puritan" is likely to set off a hyperlink that brings glowing to the computer screen another word: "dominion." It is often accompanied by citations of passages roughly repeated in two accounts of creation in the opening chapters of the book of Genesis: "And God said unto them, be fruitful, and multiply, and replenish the earth, and subdue it: and have dominion over the fish of the sea, and over the fowl of the air, and over every living thing that moveth upon the earth." This does not sound like the God of Jonathan Edwards, and it is not. Nor is it the God of the subsequent chapters of Genesis. Genesis has to be read slowly and carefully, as rabbinical scholars have consistently done when discerning in these dense passages a transition of immense importance for legal theory and for human conduct.

After Adam and Eve betrayed Him, God no longer offered them "dominion." That word appeared only as a part of the commission received *before* the Fall. The Founding Father and Mother were then in a state of grace. As things stood between them and their creator, they were worthy to be fully in charge of God's garden. Things changed after they ceased to be worthy and took Satan's advice. They acted as have other transgressors of limits ever since—they made a travesty of trusteeship, breaking their covenant with God. Having forfeited their conditional dominion, they were sent forth to shiver in nakedness. After the catastrophic overreaching of Adam and Eve, after the breach of their covenant, after their transgression of their limits, Law replaced Covenant. Legislation replaced reliance upon responsible innocence.

This point was not lost on the scripture-reading Social Compact theorists of the seventeenth century, who preceded the Founding Fathers, nor had it been lost on the Church Fathers. Saint Augustine observed the removal of authorized dominion from the fallen Adam and Eve in a passage memorized by many at church camp as "The Two Loves" but seldom recited at the American Enterprise Institute: "There are two loves, the one of which is holy, the other unholy; one social, the other selfish; one takes heed of the commonweal because of the heavenly society, the other reduces even the commonweal to its own ends because of a proud lust of domination; the one is subject to God; the other sets itself up as a rival to God."[5]

Ecclesiastes had issued the same warning: "That which befalleth the sons of men befalleth beasts; even one thing befalleth them: as the one dieth, so dieth the other; yea, they have all one breath; so that a man hath no preeminence above a beast: for all *is* vanity." The Puritans knew both their Ecclesiastes and their Saint Augustine, as did Thomas Jefferson, who drew the conclusion that humankind's lust of domination or preeminence, unless limited by law, could do irreparable harm, for "if one link in nature's chain might be lost, another and another might be lost, till this whole system of things should vanish by piece-meal." Somewhat later, the lawgivers of the Endangered Species Act drew the same lesson.[6]

The drafters of the Clean Air and Clean Water Acts took their text from that passage in Ezekiel quoted earlier:

Seemeth it a small thing unto you to have eaten up the good pasture, but ye must tread down with your feet the residue of your pastures? And to have drunk of the deep [clear] waters, but ye must foul the residue with your feet? And as for my flock, they eat that which ye have trodden with your feet; and they drink that which ye have fouled with your feet.

These passages, like the experience of wildfire, teach that all privileges carry obligations. It is not just that all human rights are bounded; the biblical truth is that there is no right and no power that is not inextricably braided into a system of obligations. That was true before the Fall. It remains true, as fire and flood remind us.

Jonathan Edwards has been with us for two hundred years now to lighten the dour message of Ecclesiastes with the affirmation that every living thing in creation is equally meritorious as an expression and exfoliation of God. "The beams of glory come *from* God, and are *of* God, and are, in his term, refunded back again to their original. Thus the whole is *of* God, and *in* God, and *to* God, and God is the beginning, middle and end in this affair." This was transcendentalism a century ahead of itself, anticipating environmentalism by more than another century.[7]

EDWARDS AND THE LAND

In Edwards's time, the failure of his parishioners to accept so capacious a Christianity was expressed in injuries committed against Indians, and afflictions meted out to nature. People bent upon war with the Indians—and with nature—were living out, "acting through," so to speak, estrangement. To many of them, a forest, even when emptied of "lurking savages," remained dark and dangerous. Every hemlock-shadowed stream might be a place of "be-wilderment," every cave a den of devils. Edwards was asking them to revere nature for its own value, as an emanation of the nature of God Himself. That was not a message that would make a preacher popular in New England towns whose leading men were increasingly treating land as a commodity.

Land speculators did not hire preachers to tell them that they were moneychangers in a very large temple. Like Adam and Eve after they listened to the Serpent, they were busy getting from nature what they wanted when they wanted it. They wanted no cavil from the pulpit.

To the English, "Edwards turned a face of flint, telling them he would have better success preaching to the people of Sodom." To the Indians he addressed the hope that because they came freshly to Christ, unspoiled by easy acquaintance with the Gospel, they did not bear a legacy of seventeen hundred years of avoidance and self-deception, and therefore might redeem the delinquencies of the fallen and failed Yankee "saints." Edwards assured his Indian congregation that Christ looked on them as "members of his body and flesh of his bone," and that the English were "no better than you." Humankind were one—Indians, blacks, and English—and nature and humankind were one. "God has made us with such a nature, that we cannot subsist without the help of one another. Mankind in this respect are as the members of the natural body, one cannot subsist alone, without an union with, and the help of the rest. [Therefore] . . . he who is all for himself and none for his neighbors, deserves to be cut off from the benefit of human society, and to be turned out among wild beasts, to subsist by himself as well as he can. A private niggardly spirit is more suitable for wolves and other beasts of prey, than for human beings."[8]

These words were written when the old theocratic communities in New England were shattering into classes. The rich were being assigned the best seats in the meetinghouses, displacing the most learned. Edwards was scornful of ministers or magistrates or rising men in the county who were insufficiently "forward to use their powers for the promotion of the public benefit" but were instead "governed by selfish motives, or to become great, and to advance themselves on the spoils of others." On a still-raw frontier, full of striving competition and bent on gain, he condemned those who "grind the faces of the poor, and screw their neighbors." The avaricious were themselves wild beasts "tearing one another apart . . . a prey of one another." Speculation in necessities included speculation in land, for in an agricultural society, land for farming is a necessity. Edwards heaped scorn upon sellers who "take advantage of their neighbor's poverty to extort unreasonably from him for those things that he is under a necessity of procuring for himself or family." After he had done with the land speculators he turned his disdain upon the merchants who sold seed, salt, and tools to distressed neighbors at high prices, raising "the price of provisions, even above the market."[9]

Others were unable to keep their moorings. I believe that Edwards was tortured by the land-sharking of his senior colleague in Stockbridge, Timothy Woodbridge. Woodbridge had given many years of his life to service to the Indians, ministering to the sick and the infirm as well as preaching the Gospel, but could not resist speculating in Indian lands. Shaw Livermore, mentioned earlier as a mobilizer of war production and an advocate of urban dispersion on the scale of the Marshall Plan, was an expert on this economic history, a subject intriguing to those attempting to come into closer understanding of Edwards the man as well as Edwards the pastor. A lengthy discourse on colonial economic history and the role of the clergy in that history does not, however, belong here. Edwards the man is before us. Besides, my view of the matter is probably a minority one. Nonetheless, because at my age I cannot be sure I will return to this subject in print, I am putting a page or two about Livermore, Woodbridge, Edwards, and land speculation in an appendix.

During Edwards's lifetime, land speculation in the United States depended upon obtaining from the Indians the assets to be sold. A large profit margin depended on a low acquisition cost, often achieved by force or fraud. On the other side of the transaction, the selling price could be elevated by promising the buyer an illusory safety. Sharp practice toward Indians was followed by sharp practice toward buyers.

The greatest of early theologians in America was present as the commoditization of its land got fully under way. Edwards witnessed the collapse of trusting relationships of clergy to Indians, this time simultaneously with the degeneration of the community-based organization of society among the English. The "River Gods" (an evocative term if there ever was one) as the enriched landowners and land sellers of the Connecticut River Valley became known, included many magistrates who had become land speculators. Clergymen also sought to preempt choice tracts for themselves and their friends, some by using their influence upon the Indians to extort land, which they then sold at speculative prices to the poor.

EDWARDS AND THE INDIANS

The Indians to whom Edwards ministered in Stockbridge were mostly Mohicans who had been dispossessed by his former parishioners in towns such as Enfield. As noted earlier, these "fields" were ready to be taken and planted because controlled burning by Indian farmers had cleared them. When those agriculturalists returned in war paint, they made use of fire as their most fearsome weapon, controlling it in another way, as burning tinder tied to arrows sent upon the thatched roofs of the new settlers' houses. Edwards's landscape was bloody with war, contaminated by hatred and betrayal, and ravaged by misuse. It was a challenging setting in which to preach the beauties of God's word, or of His world.[10]

The "tamed" Indians were reduced to squalor, drink, and dependence, while the "untamed" were incited to violence by both the French and the English. The French and Indians raided the British outpost at Deerfield in the winter after Edwards's birth, and there was no peace on that frontier until well after his death. And always, there was fire, not only fire used deliberately as a weapon of war, but fire as a consequence of the misuse of the land. The light, controlled burning of the Indians was replaced by disastrous slash-and-burns in the aftermath of hasty lumbering, after the stripping of hemlock bark for tannin left the trees and branches exposed and ready to burn. Larger and larger masses of inflammable material were left for the lightning or the inadvertent spark.

Edwards's home in Northampton and his parsonage at Stockbridge were both fortified, housing garrisons of soldiers as well as Edwards's family. The men of that family went out to the fields bearing arms; meanwhile, Edwards went on preaching to Indians whose relatives were told at Fort Stanwix not long after his death: "You are a subdued people." To the victors went the spoils. The doctrine set forth at Fort Stanwix prevailed, and was later put in evangelical terms by Theodore Roosevelt: "The most ultimately righteous of all wars is a war with savages. . . . It is a silly morality which would forbid a course of conquest that has turned whole continents into seats of mighty and flourishing nations . . . whether the whites won the land by treaty, by armed conquest, or, as was actually the case by a mixture of both, mattered comparatively little so long as the land was won."[11]

It did matter, of course. Easy riches were secured by bribing and defrauding Indians of land, selling it quickly to those unaware of the dangers lurking there, and moving on. Yet as those in its grip moved westward, an affronted native population and an affronted nature awaited them. From time to time, both the Indians and nature expressed their affronts with fire.

THE GOSPEL OF JONATHAN EDWARDS

The doctrine and practice of Edwards came not of fear of nature but of love—the kind of love that draws, engages, and leads to understanding. Analysis was as natural to Edwards as rapture; the two were aspects of the same reverence for a God capable of creating a world susceptible to inquiry by one of its aspects—the human mind. That was the message of his "Concerning the Ends for Which God Created the World." The joyous observer, wrote Edwards, should delight and attend to nature's "sounds, colors, and smells . . . the colors of the woods and flowers, and the smell, and the singing of birds—which 'tis probable consist in a certain proportion of the vibrations that are made in the different organs."

What a great distance was Stockbridge from Plymouth. Much had happened between the terrible December when the sick and storm-tossed Pilgrims reached their "hideous and desolate wilderness, full of wild beasts and wild men." A century of exploration and cultivation, of planting where Indians had planted, and setting in orchards, and watching livestock grow fat. Yet it was not only the happy consequences of agronomy and domestication that Edwards observed, but in nature itself "innumerable other agreeablenesses." Edwards exulted in the riotous fall colors of the Berkshires: "The fields and woods seem to rejoice, and how joyful do the birds seem to be in it. How much a resemblance is there of every grace in the fields covered with plants and flowers. . . . And each sort of rays play a distinct tune to the soul, besides those lovely mixtures that are found in nature—those beauties, how lovely, in the green of the face of the earth, in all manner of colors in flowers, the color of the skies, and lovely tinctures of the morning and evening."[12]

When these words were published in 1755, Edwards was nearing the end of his life. Despite all his disappointments, in the evening light there appeared to him "the reason why almost all men, and those that seem to be very miserable, love life: because they cannot bear to lose the sight of such a beautiful and lovely world."

The sound of the axe and the snarl of the bulldozer are absent from this scene. Nowhere in Edwards's works is there a syllable compatible with the speculators' version of the "American dream" or their transgressions of natural limits. Edwards turned the full fire-hose force of his contempt upon them, as he would have today upon the profiteers from the asphalting of America. The sinners most exposed to his anger were desecrating one side of the wildland/urban interaction. On the other side, he insisted, there was always, open to those who would seek it or destroy it, God's "beautiful and lovely world."[13]

His veneration of God's nature encouraged him to parse out its beauty: " 'Tis very probable that that wonderful suitableness of green for the grass and plants, the blue of the sky, the white of the clouds, the colors of flowers, consists in a complicated proportion that these colors make one with another, either in the magnitude of the rays, the number of vibrations that are caused in the optic nerve, or some other way."[14]

Edwards was a scientist and also an artist accustomed to singing his prayers. He was also a scholar of the Bible, of the Church in its infinite varieties, and of other religions, including those of his Indian friends, so he was well aware that he did not sing and think alone. He was—as we are—members of a silent chorus. There are the Psalms. And there are the newer psalms, some very old, some sung new every day. More than a thousand years before the Gospel of Christ reached Ireland, people were singing:

> For my shield this day I call:
> Heaven's might,
> Sun's brightness
> Moon's whiteness,
> Fire's glory,
> Lightning's swiftness,
> Wind's wildness,
> Ocean's depth,
> Earth's solidity,
> Rock's immobility.

As Jonathan Edwards walked the woods of the Berkshires, was there not a presence beside him, another singer, Saint Francis of Assisi?

> Praised be my Lord God with all creatures;
> and especially our brother the sun,
> which brings us the day and the light;
> fair is he, and shining with a very great splendor:
> O Lord, he signifies you to us!
>
> Praised be my Lord for our sister the moon,
> and for the stars,
> which God has set clear and lovely in heaven.

Praised be my Lord for our brother the wind,
    and for air and cloud, calms and all weather,
    by which you uphold in life all creatures.

Praised be my Lord for our sister water,
    which is very serviceable to us,
    and humble, and precious, and clean.

Praised be my Lord for brother fire,
    through which you give us light in the darkness;
    and he is bright, and pleasant, and very mighty,
    and strong.

Praised be my Lord for our mother the Earth,
    which sustains us and keeps us,
    and yields diverse fruits,
    and flowers of many colors, and grass.

Fire is—and was—"brother" to those who take the creation to be entire.

Like Edwards, Thomas Jefferson asserted that all creation was "made by God," and therefore worthy of respect and protection from the predatory behavior of humans after the Fall. Daniel Boorstin was wont to remind his readers, and the visitors to his house, that in Jefferson's "writing, we frequently come upon the appropriate verses of the Psalmist, 'O Lord, how manifold are thy works! In wisdom hast thou made them all: the earth is full of thy riches.'" The implication of Jefferson's and Edwards's celebration of the wonders of creation must surely be that we humans must walk humbly in our fallen state, seeking a wry, repentant wisdom. We must not dare to assume that we have enough of that wisdom to be entrusted with responsibilities as great as those of Adam and Eve. We must keep always in mind the peril of making irreversible mistakes. But we can do our best to protect the full panoply of those "riches"—which include ourselves and our neighboring species.[15]

This was the context within which Jefferson warned that "if one link in nature's chain might be lost, another and another might be lost, till this whole system of things should vanish by piece-meal." And so it may, unless men and women learn their limits. National fire and migration policy must become truly respectful of God's creation, all of it. Thus the Founders' "New Order in the Universe," given a new birth by Abraham Lincoln, might have yet another new birth in this generation.

Appendix:

Jonathan Edwards and Imperial Connecticut

There was a great enrichment opportunity in land speculation in Jonathan Edwards's time. Connecticut had made a mistake, but had been amply rewarded for repentance. It had supported Oliver Cromwell's Commonwealth, but upon the restoration of the Stuart dynasty to the British Crown, it was quick to swear fealty and exchange its old corporate charter for a royal one. Charles II, who had other things on his mind, signed a grant implying that his new friends might extend themselves all the way from Rhode Island to the Pacific—wherever that might be—as if New York did not exist, or Pennsylvania either. New York mobilized, threatening to squash Connecticut should it become too assertive, inducing the practical men of Hartford and Northampton to treat the Hudson Valley as a sort of Polish Corridor, to be skipped over while they fixed their avarice upon the fertile Wyoming Valley of Pennsylvania, west of Scranton.

Pennsylvania's Quakers had been at pains not to provoke the Indians, setting aside the Wyoming Valley from *their* considerably earlier royal grant to be a reservation for their allies the Iroquois. Notwithstanding their prior status, when Benjamin Franklin brought the Iroquois and the British colonists together at Albany in 1754 to discuss the common defense against the French, Connecticut took the occasion to attempt a stealthy seizure of the Wyoming Valley. Timothy Woodbridge and two of Edwards's kinsmen, Oliver Partridge and Elisha Williams, were assigned the task of turning the international conference into a commercial coup. By means of the wiles and rum of the corrupt Indian trader John Henry Lydius, they secured a great block of central Pennsylvania's Indian reserve. The reserve had been surveyed by Woodbridge to determine its appropriateness for missionary work. Thus they betrayed both the colonists' common search for peace and their own relationship of trust with the Mohicans and Iroquois. Woodbridge was in many ways a saint, but now he was a corrupted saint, bringing home a poisoned chalice. As a result, two overlapping colonial claims bedeviled relations between Connecticut and Pennsylvania until, in the 1780s, Connecticut traded these claims to the Continental Congress for a substantial portion of Ohio. That only occurred, however, after the Susquehanna Company of Elisha Williams and Timothy Woodbridge had been put to rest.[1]

The economist Shaw Livermore appeared early in this narrative in his role in war mobilization in the 1940s and in urban dispersion in the 1950s, and briefly in the chapter on Jonathan Edwards. In the 1960s he became the author of the classic account of the transition of yeoman and villager New England into full-tilt agricultural capitalism and land speculation. Livermore provided a detailed description of the economic context of Edwards's theology, presenting Connecticut's Susquehanna Company as "the best example" of a corporate colony hiving off a commercial enterprise "to exploit a new colony [the Wyoming project of Williams and Woodbridge]. The establishment of new towns . . . [had until then been] by a true group effort." Livermore was no naïve academic, having made a small fortune at Dun and Bradstreet, and was welcomed by mining executives as one of their own in the war years. He was, however, of an earlier generation, and subsequent environmental historians have suggested that his version of the "new towns" was somewhat romantic. Brian Donahue, for example, has interposed the correction that these new towns were "often led by a few well-off individuals. Ordinary residents of older towns got involved in these new ventures (sometimes as a reward for military service) with a couple of ends in mind—one to find land for their numerous offspring, the second to indulge in a little speculation."[2]

When the absentee speculators urged settlement on the farthest frontiers, they knew that their profits would require inducing settlers to go where they were not welcome. On the fringes of Pennsylvania, Iroquois reprisals did, in fact, ensue in the "Wyoming Valley Massacres." "It is in such an enterprise as the Susquehanna that the speculative motive is seen emerging," Livermore tells us. Perhaps only a shift in emphasis emerged, but it was an important shift. Some of those who profited from the speculation—absentee developers, in our contemporary parlance—were endangering the lives of people who had only a little earlier been part of their own congregations. Edwards took no part in these transactions. Nonetheless, they soured his friendship with the Mohawks and the other Iroquois.[3]

Edwards's old euphoria of living amid a landscape aglow with God's love, amid people all of whom were God's chosen, no longer sustained him when his Indian charges and his non-Indian parishioners were being betrayed by his closest colleagues. Edwards the rapturist became so ill from "strain, exhaustion, disappointments, and anxieties" that he "became like a skeleton" and was "unable to preach for the better part of seven months." He was living in a corrupted and corrupting creation.[4]

Notes

1. THE PLAN OF THE WORK

1. Thomas Ribe, in a personal communication by e-mail on May 31, 2005.

2. Truman's estimate of the atomic scientists' achievement appeared in a White House press release dated August 6, 1945, quoted in Dan O'Neill, *The Firecracker Boys*, New York: St. Martin's Press, 1994, p. 13; Teller on Reagan as a very good listener: June 10, 1987, quoted in *Anchorage Daily Times*, p. B-1, requoted by O'Neill, *Firecracker Boys*, p. 290; c.f. *Science* 266 (October 28, 1994): 663.

3. Here are excerpts from the Web pages of two of the atomic towns to give an idea of their sense of themselves as instant creations. Raymond, Washington: "The facility encompassed three small towns—Hanford, White Bluffs, and Richland. . . . Sheep had grazed the flat, rocky countryside, which was dotted with orchards, vineyards, and farms. As at Oak Ridge, 1,500 people were relocated in the process. Close to a half-million acres were purchased for more than $5.1 million by the spring of 1943." And Oak Ridge says of itself: "The 'Secret City' grew to a population of 75,000, was the fifth largest city in Tennessee and was not even on the map. Some 60,000 acres of valleys and ridges chosen as a major site for the now historic Manhattan Project. . . . The communities of Scarboro, New Hope, Robertsville, Elza and Wheat were chosen and given notice that their 3000 residents were to vacate their 1000 properties as they were to be required to support the war effort. The people were given a matter of weeks to remove their possessions and relocate."

4. James Schlesinger, quoted in O'Neill, *Firecracker Boys*, p. 23; "nature's oversights," ibid.

5. Teller's "drop us a card" statement was quoted in the *Anchorage Daily Times* of June 26, 1959, quoted by O'Neill, *Firecracker Boys*, p. 92.

2. "THE LAB" AND "THE LAB" EXTENDED

1. *Towering Inferno* was the title of a motion picture about skyscraper fires, not timber fires, but the fusion of the two images seemed to me arresting.

3. FROM DANGER INTO DANGER

1. "Recent Population Trends in Nonmetropolitan Cities and Villages: From the Turnaround, Through Reversal to the Rebound," published in 1997 by Glenn Fuguitt, Calvin Beale, John Fulton, and Richard Gibson of the Center for Demography and Ecology at the University of Wisconsin, *Rural Social Development* (1998): 8.

2. Calhoun, "Report of the Secretary of War (1819) to Congress, Fifteenth Congress, Second Session," H. Doc. 462, 534, quoted in D. W. Meinig, *The Shaping of America, Volume 2, Continental America, 1800–1967*, New Haven, Conn.: Yale University Press, 1993, p. 339.

3. This quotation comes from the remarkable article by Kathleen Tobin, "The Reduction of Urban Vulnerability: Revisiting 1950s American Suburbanization as Civil Defence," in *Cold War History* 2, no. 2 (January 2002): 1–32. Donald Chen brought this English publication to my attention as this text was going through its final editing. I have found it of great help, full of gems such as this one— some of which I have been able to add to this and the next two chapters. Tobin's endnotes offer a feast for scholars working in this neglected field. For NSC deliberations on dispersion in 1947 and 1950, see Tobin, "Reduction," p. 10.

4. Cherwell, as quoted by Prime Minister Menachem Begin of Israel in a speech to the Knesset, June 29, 1982.

5. I have taken these numbers from Horatio Bond, ed., *Fire and the Air War*, National Fire Protection Association, 1946, as restated on such Web sites as http://www.webster-dictionary.org/definition/Bombing%20of%20Dresden%20in%20World%20War%20II.

6. Ibid.

4. UNFORESEEN CONSEQUENCES

1. Minutes of the second meeting of the Target Committee, Los Alamos, May 10–11, 1945, U.S. National Archives, Record Group 77, Records of the Office of the Chief of Engineers, Manhattan Engineer District, TS Manhattan Project File '42–'46, folder 5D Selection of Targets, 2 Notes on Target Committee Meetings.

2. My account of the Nagasaki bombing, and these quotations, are drawn from Paul Saffo, *The Road from Trinity: Reflections on the Atom Bomb*, n.p.: Shoga Kukan Press, n.d.

3. Ibid.

4. Ibid.

5. Bond, ed., *Fire and the Air War*, p. 231.

6. Elaine Tyler May, *Homeward Bound: American Families in the Cold War Era*, New York: Basic Books, 1988, p. 169.

7. Memoranda, etc., reported by Eugene Rabinowitch in "The Only Real Defense," *Bulletin of the Atomic Scientists* (September 1951): 242.

8. J. Marshak, Edward Teller, and L. R. Klein, "Dispersal of Cities and Industries," *Bulletin of the Atomic Scientists* (April 16, 1946): 13ff. This is the text:

> In atomic war, congested cities would become deathtraps. . . . Dispersal of cities may mean the difference between extermination of one third of our population and the death of only a few million people. . . . Existence of big cities . . . present[s] a tempting target. . . . A considerable part of the protection provided by complete dispersal can thus be obtained even if people live in clusters, provided these are properly spaced . . . 'ribbon' or 'linear' cities are safer than round clusters . . . a good compromise . . . continuous ribbons . . . a mesh of squares. [They would] make for cheaper transportation and other public services than would be possible for round clusters, . . . [especially if adapted] to the terrain and to existing major communications lines . . . about 600 people and 160 houses per linear mile along a communication artery. . . . With our cities stretched out we shall have to rely more than ever on our transportation system . . . having several widely spaced highways. . . . The new dwellings should be built . . . to conform to minimum standards and thus slums are eliminated. . . . In order to live in ribbon cities we shall have to abandon many of the habits which the people of our big cities have acquired in the course of a century . . . life will depend upon fast transportation . . . in the age of the automobile . . . [we have already] built widely decentralized cities such as the modern Los Angeles. [To achieve such an outcome] a master plan of network cities and communications will have to be adopted . . . [inducing] the free and automatic flow of labor and enterprise which will follow the relocated key industries along the main communications arteries. . . . The shorter the time, the less we can rely upon the free movement of labor and the free planning of private enterprise. . . . We cannot do this without government regulations, just as restrictive or more restrictive than those of the recent war years.

9. Ibid.

10. Ibid.

11. Kaysen, often an adviser to McGeorge Bundy during my ten years working for Bundy at the Ford Foundation, gave me his recollections of Teller in personal conversation in March 2004.

12. Eisenhower Library, Abilene, Kansas, Couch, Virgil L. Papers 1951–1980, Accession A91-19, 96-4; Operation You, Your Role in Civil Defense, (cont.) fallout shelters, evacuation, women in civil; Project East River, 1952–1953 (1)–(4); 4 Project East River, 1952–1953 (5)–(9); "key men" comes from a Project East River report cited by Tobin, "Reduction," p.13. In the Truman Library, Project East River is the subject of files in Box 34 of the Gordon Gray Papers, 384.51

Project East River [civil defense]. See also, *Federal Leadership to Reduce Urban Vulnerability: Project East River,* New York: Associated Universities, 1952.

13. My references to Gray are quoted from the Web site of the Truman Library.

14. Augur quoted in Tobin, "Reduction," p. 22.

15. These quotations come from Tobin, "Reduction," pp. 18–21.

16. My quotations come from *Common Ground,* a publication of the National Park Service (Winter 2004): 4.

17. Ibid.

18. My description of tritium comes not from a scientific treatise but from McGeorge Bundy, in his *Danger and Survival,* New York: Random House, 1988, p. 205.

19. Marshak, Teller, and Klein, "Dispersal," p. 14. I spoke with Larry Klein on January 20, 2004.

20. Ibid.

21. O'Neill, *Firecracker Boys,* p. 20, citing John McPhee, *The Curve of Binding Energy,* New York: Ballantine, 1979, pp. 123ff.

22. Teller quoted in O'Neill, *Firecracker Boys,* p. 25.

23. Rabinowitch in "The Only Real Defense," p. 242.

24. Truman as quoted in the *Bulletin of the Atomic Scientists* (September 1951): 263. See also May 1948, September 1948, August–September 1950. I am indebted to the current editor, Linda Rothstein, for these citations.

25. Monson and Monson, "A Program for Urban Dispersal," in the *Bulletin of the Atomic Scientists* (September 1951): 245ff.

26. Ibid.

27. Merriam, "Cities Are Here to Stay," *Bulletin of the Atomic Scientists* (September 1951): 251ff.

28. Augustin M. Prentiss, *Civil Defense in Modern War,* New York: McGraw-Hill, 1951, pp. 13–23. I am grateful to Kathleen Tobin for this reference in her "Reduction of Urban Vulnerability." Ralph Eugene Lapp, in "Industrial Dispersion in the United States," *Bulletin of the Atomic Scientists* (September 1951). See also Ralph Eugene Lapp, *Must We Hide?* Cambridge, Mass.: Addison-Wesley, 1949, pp. 256ff.

29. Private mechanisms, etc.: Charles Abrams, quoted in Tobin, "Reduction," p. 11.

30. Lapp, "Industrial Dispersion in the United States," pp. 256ff.; Senate Committee in Tobin, "Reduction," pp. 10 and 11; Teller on his access to O'Mahoney, Edward Teller's testimony in the Oppenheimer hearings, April 28, 1954, In the Matter of J. Robert Oppenheimer, Transcript of Hearing Before Personnel Security Board, Washington, D.C., April 12, 1954, through May 6, 1954, United States Government Printing Office, Washington, D.C., 1954.

31. For Senate Bill 1385, see Tobin, "Reduction," pp. 3–4. For Eisenhower, see Lapp, "Industrial Dispersion," pp. 256ff.

32. Lapp, "Industrial Dispersion," pp. 356ff.

33. Livingston, Goodhue, "The Blight of Our Cities," *Bulletin of the Atomic Scientists* (September 1951), 260ff.

34. Personal communication from Volker Radeloff, dated February 1, 2005.

35. Livermore quoted in an interview with James R. Fuchs, in Tucson, Arizona, March 4, 1974, on the Truman Library Web site.

5. TRUMAN, EISENHOWER, AND THE ROAD GANG

1. Details of Truman's early affinity to highways appear in the Federal Highway Administration's official history, as carried on its Web site, under "Infrastructure."

2. Ibid., in the section under Truman. The primary author appears to be Richard F. Weingroff.

3. Mark H. Rose, *Interstate: Express Highway Politics, 1939–1989*, Lawrence: University Press of Kansas, 1979, pp. 38–39.

4. Jack Gorrie, "Federal Dispersion Policy Stresses Local Initiative," *Bulletin of the Atomic Scientists* (September 1951): 270.

5. William Wheaton, "Federal Action Toward a National Dispersion Policy," *Bulletin of the Atomic Scientists* (September 1951): 275.

6. Wheaton, "Federal Action," p. 275; Oak Ridge, in that city's self-description on its Web site.

7. Tennessee plans quoted in the archives of the Tennessee Emergency Management Agency, available on its Web site.

8. Eisenhower, in a memorandum dated November 3, 1919, to the Chief Motor Transport Corps, in section on Eisenhower in the Federal Highway Administration's official history, as carried on its Web site.

9. Ibid.

10. Eisenhower quoted in Richard F. Weingroff, "The Federal-Aid Highway Act of 1956: Creating the Interstate System," on the U.S. Department of Transportation, Federal Highway Administration Web site.

11. Ibid.

12. Meeting in the President's Office, Interim Report on the Interstate Highway Program, April 6, 1960, 10:35 a.m., as carried in the Federal Highway Administration's official history, on its Web site. This is the text:

    The President went on to say that the staff had also advised him that in the course of the legislation through the Congress, the point had been made that cities were to get adequate consideration on a "per person" basis in view of the taxes they paid; in fact, that they were to get more consideration since they paid much more in taxes per person and in total than persons in rural areas. The President added that this was what

the Congress had been told, and that he was given to understand that
this, together with the descriptions in the Yellow Book which they had
before them when considering the legislation, were the prime reasons
the Congress passed the Interstate Highway Act. In other words, the
Yellow Book depicting routes in cities had sold the program to the Congress. The President referred to a previous conversation with General
Bragdon. He went on to say that the matter of running Interstate routes
through the congested parts of the cities was entirely against his original concept and wishes; that he never anticipated that the program
would turn out this way. He pointed out that when the Clay Committee Report was rendered, he had studied it carefully, and that he was
certainly not aware of any concept of using the program to build up an
extensive intra-city route network as part of the program he sponsored. He added that those who had not advised him that such was being done, and those who had steered the program in such a direction,
had not followed his wishes.

[One of the terrified minions] interjected that the interstate concept
was nothing new—that it had been developed as far back as 1939. The
President stated that, while that might be so, he had not heard of it and
that his proposal for a national highway program was his own; furthermore, that there was a tremendous difference between the present
90-10 Federal sharing type of program and any that had been considered 18 or 20 years ago. In conclusion, he reiterated his disappointment
over the way the program had been developed against his wishes, and
that it had reached the point to where his hands were virtually tied. He
also observed that Public Works per se was considered one of the
biggest "grab bags" for Federal Funds, and that fact was one of the reasons he had directed an independent review to be made of the Highway Program by someone who would bring him the facts.

13. Ibid.

14. Ibid.

15. Ibid.

16. Ibid. The official history of the Federal Highway Administration, carried on its
    Web site, says blandly that "the autobahn was a rural network, without seg-
    ments into and through Germany's cities. This seemed appropriate to Eisen-
    hower, but . . . the absence of metropolitan segments [was] a flaw that made the
    autobahn a poor model for America's future. Unlike Germany, traffic volumes
    were high in America where car ownership was widespread. Congestion in
    America's cities had long been a serious complaint." Without informing the
    president until it was too late, the administrators and planners of the Adminis-
    tration, and their friends in the dispersion-industrial complex, addressed that
    "complaint . . . in their vision of the Interstate System."

17. Rose, *Interstate*, pp. 90–94.

18. Ibid., William Norlag, quoted on p. 85.

19. Rose, in his *Interstate*, does an elegant job of telling the story of these two views on pp. 15ff.

20. Ibid.

21. Barry Checkoway, "Large Builders: Federal Housing Programmes and Postwar Suburbanization," in the *International Journal of Urban and Region Research* 4, no. 1 (1980): 39.

22. Tom Lewis, *Divided Highways: Building the Interstate Highways, Transforming American Life*, New York: Viking Press, 1997, p. 88ff.

23. By 2003, Americans were obligated to payments on mortgages aggregating about $6.8 trillion, of which $2.7 trillion was upon the ledgers of the Federal National Mortgage Association (FNMA) and the Federal Home Loan Mortgage Corporation (FHLMC), or Freddie Mac. About $2 trillion was guaranteed by the Government National Mortgage Association (GNMA). That does not mean that these entities necessarily held those loans themselves—their government guarantees made the mortgages relatively risk-free investments. Thus many an individual citizen's promise to pay followed a channel from the "originators"—banks, "thrifts," and mortgage bankers—then briefly came within the control of FNMA ("Fannie Mae"), GNMA ("Ginnie Mae"), and the FHLMC for the application of a federally sponsored promise to pay if the individual did not, and proceeded into the portfolios of insurance companies, foundations, and pension funds themselves having obligations to pay. (Even foundations have obligations to pay under the Tax Reform Act.)

    The largest mortgage originators are no longer "thrifts" but banking and investment banking conglomerates such as Wells Fargo, Citibank, JPMorgan-Chase, and the Bank of America, though two very powerful competitors have recently emerged for them in two real estate–based lending institutions, Washington Mutual and Countryside Financial Services. These companies have been very profitable; they are paid fees to originate and then collect mortgage payments ("servicing") and seldom bear any risk of loss of principal, having passed that through to the federal insurers and to those pension funds buying and holding nonconforming loans.

24. A very large change in previous patterns of home ownership was required to achieve these ends. In the early 1930s, nearly all home mortgage loans were made and held within the portfolios of local banks. Repayment schedules seldom exceeded three to five years, ascending then into a final "balloon payment" of an amount seldom exceeding 50 percent of appraised value. Not surprisingly, two-thirds of Americans lived in rental housing.

    In 1934, in one of the New Deal's earliest stimuli to the construction business, the Federal Housing Administration (FHA) was created to guarantee loans made by lenders, mostly banks and savings and loan associations ("thrifts"). There was mass unemployment among construction workers. The FHA was as much a federally assisted employment program as a mortgage-making program. The 50 percent limit remained, but on the federal guarantee, not on the loan to appraisal value, and the maximum amount of federal guarantee was $2,000, not to exceed twenty years, with a maximum interest rate of 4 percent. Since 1934, the

FHA and the Department of Housing and Urban Development (HUD)—into whose Office of Housing FHA was consolidated in 1965—have insured almost thirty million home mortgages and thirty-eight thousand multifamily project mortgages representing 4.1 million apartments.

25. The National Mortgage Association of Washington had been chartered as a New Deal measure as part of the 1934 act. It was rechartered in 1938 as the Federal National Mortgage Association (FNMA), as a subsidiary of the Reconstruction Finance Corporation (RFC), to aid in the RFC's task of counteracting by fiscal stimulus the second dip of the depression cycle of the 1930s. The FNMA, too, was directed toward dispersion stimulus during the Cold War years. In 1948, it got its own congressional charter, and in 1954, the Eisenhower Administration directed the FNMA to participate in the national highway construction program to aid in the dispersion of targets. It was given increased power to do so by being converted into a business attracting both private shareholders and very high-priced managerial talent, with preferred stock held by the government and common stock held privately. Because the FNMA's definition of an acceptable loan—by size, location, and amenities—fitted suburban circumstances outside the rotting cities, the newly liberated yet still government-backed mixed-ownership agency was exceedingly effective in dispersing Americans from target cities.

During the ensuing acceleration of activity, FNMA enlarged its $2,000 limit of 1934 to a maximum in 2004 of $322,700. It blossomed from the Public Housing Administration to a federally chartered institution traded on the New York Stock Exchange, the second-largest corporation in the United States on the asset side of the ledger. In 1968, Ginnie Mae (GNMA) was removed from the rib of FNMA and made a wholly government-owned corporation within HUD. It was to serve low-to-moderate-income home buyers largely through providing a secondary market for GI (Veterans Administration) and FHA loans. In 1970, responding to complaints from savings and loan associations ("thrifts") that GNMA was being excessively responsive to the blandishments of banks and mortgage bankers, Congress chartered the Federal Home Loan Mortgage Corporation (Freddie Mac) to buy conventional mortgages from federally insured financial institutions. Freddie Mac introduced its own mortgage-backed securities program in 1971.

26. Applicants for these loans must be unable to get credit elsewhere at reasonable rates and terms. Communities with not more than 10,000 people may be eligible for water and sewer systems. "Other essential community facilities must be located in communities with not more than 20,000 in population to be eligible." This provides an important alternative source of credit for developers in exurban regions. Likewise, counties can issue Rural Special Improvement District bonds, exempt from federal income taxation, which are amortized by the buyer of lots or ranchettes. The money so borrowed may be used to cover developers' costs of roads and utilities.

6. MANAGING WILDFIRE

1. Stephen Pyne, *Tending Fire: Coping with America's Wildland Fires*, Washington, D.C.: Island Press, 2004, pp. 119–20.

2. Ibid., p. 63; *The Economist*, August 17, 2002. The quotation comes from a paper available on the Web entitled "ERI Papers in Restoration Policy," by Terry Cheng of Colorado State University and Hanna J. Cortner of Northern Arizona University, pp. 51ff.

3. I am quoting the masterful summary of the matter in "Wildfire and Poverty: An Overview of the Interactions Among Wildfires, Fire-related Programs, and Poverty in the Western States," prepared for the Center for Watershed and Community Health with a Ford Foundation grant by ECONorthwest, Eugene, Oregon, 2001, p. 7.

4. Christopher Smith, "Fed Fire Funding Burns Hole in Pockets," *The Salt Lake City Tribune*, May 12, 2004; Pyne, *Tending Fire*, p. 154. Stimulated to do so by that crisp summary of the problem in Pyne's *Los Angeles Times* Op-Ed piece, those who are serious about this problem should obtain a copy of Pyne's *Tending Fire*, and read pages 149 through 155. No one is likely to do a better job of presenting the options for fire management before the nation.

5. Pyne, Op-Ed piece, *Los Angeles Times*, October 30, 2003.

6. Smith, "Fed Fire Funding."

7. My figures come from the Center for Watershed and Community Health study, pp. 22–23.

8. Bruce Babbitt, "Making Peace with Wildland Fire," *Wildfire Magazine* 8 (1999): 12–17.

9. Thomas quoted in Kelley Andersson, *Wildland Firefighter*, on the *Wildland Firefighter* Web site.

10. Ibid.

11. Ibid.

12. Ibid.

7. SCAPEGOATING AS DISTRACTION IN 2000

1. Fire experience, quoted from Craig Allen, "Lots of Lightning and Plenty of People," in Thomas R. Vale, ed., *Fire, Native Peoples, and the Natural Landscape*, Washington, D.C.: Island Press, 2002, pp. 143ff.

2. White (1873–1946) recounted his own adventures in the Black Hills gold rush and in the Great Lakes lumber camps, and became a popular writer with his California trilogy *Gold*, *The Gray Dawn*, and *The Rose Dawn*. Stephen Pyne has dealt with the Pinchot suppression story in many books, especially his *Year of the Fires: The Story of the Great Fires of 1910*, New York: Viking, 2001. My quotation comes from a report on the subject by David Carle, in the *Los Angeles Times*, August 5, 2002. Carle is the author of another very good work on the subject, *Burning Questions: America's Fight with Nature's Fire*.

3. Cowan, personal communication with author, January 29, 2004.

4. Pyne, personal communication with author, February 18, 2005; see also his *Fire in America: A Cultural History of Wildland and Rural Fire*, Princeton, N.J.: Princeton University Press, 1982, pp. 397–99, 480–90.

5. Thomas Ribe, personal communication with author, June 4, 2005, "gleaned from reading thousands of pages of testimony from all the major players in the fire and doing interviews."

6. Ibid.

7. The term "criminal incompetence" appeared in an editorial in *The Santa Fe New Mexican* on May 12, 2000.

8. Romero, quoted in *New Mexican*, June 20, 2000. For Darling's detailed repudiation of Burick's assertions, see pp. 958ff. in the transcripts of the Schenck Report, obtainable from the library at the Bandelier National Monument; I am grateful to Thomas Ribe and to the park staff for this reference. The GAO Report is available in the library at the Bandelier National Monument, or under the Freedom of Information Act. I am grateful to Thomas Ribe and to the park staff for this reference.

9. GAO report, *New Mexican*, July 20, 2000; Ziehe, as quoted in *New Mexican*.

10. Babbitt and the Board quoted in *New Mexican*, May 27, 2000.

11. Domenici quoted ibid. The Bandelier fire had not occurred within Schenck's jurisdiction but within the Rocky Mountain region of the National Park Service.

12. Galvin in private communication with author dated March 18, 2004.

13. Galvin and Arnberger, private communications with author dated May 21, 2004, and May 26, 2005, respectively.

14. Ibid.

15. Romero and blame: *New Mexican*, June 20, 2000; further Weaver pay cuts, see David Barna statement in the *New Mexican*, May 12, 2000. Romero was appropriately sensitive to another proceeding "basically" on the same subject, for he had been among those fixing blame upon Weaver, thus limiting the scope of the inquiry. There has been some dispute as to what Romero's deputy told the park staff when they called for help, a dispute not relevant here. Romero did convey to the press, and presumably the GAO, that he had "warned" the chief of the preventive burn team not to burn. Babbitt had been quoted as denying that the Forest Service, which meant Romero, had in fact "formally expressed concerns to Bandelier about its plans to conduct a controlled burn," and several Park Service employees testified under oath in support of Weaver's contention that no such warning had been given. Once Weaver became the scapegoat, Romero protested that "we don't want to open any wounds; we need to heal right now." Nonetheless, after being pressed hard by a later inquiry, Romero reduced his charge to the assertion that "I did at one time express my concern saying that, again, we're sending mixed signals. You know we're telling the public that they cannot have campfires out there, and we're putting smoke in the air." He did not apparently assert, as Richard Burick did, that these "warnings" were for-

mal or at a "meeting" called to discuss the burn. Second Romero statement, to the Schenck board, Bean court reporter's transcript of hearings, p. 659, available in the Bandelier Monument library. I am grateful to Thomas Ribe and to the park staff for this reference.

16. The complete text of the Schenck Report, "The Cerro Grande Prescribed Fire Board of Inquiry Final Report," can be obtained on the National Park Service Web site.

17. Babbitt quoted in *New Mexican,* June 9, 2001. He went on to say: "The overall problem with the Draft is the manner in which it confines itself to deconstructing events into small slices, assessing each isolated slice by reference to isolated portions of the various written policies and guidelines, concluding in each case that cited specific policy language was not clearly violated." Weaver emerged from retirement for a moment, commenting mildly that, in the words of the *New Mexican* (which did not quote him directly), "it appeared to him that in his criticisms of the draft report, Babbitt appears to have forgotten the purpose of the report: to assess whether agency employees deserved to be disciplined." Weaver in *New Mexican,* June 9, 2001. (Galvin in personal communication to author, dated March 18, 2004.)

18. Wright's comment has been conveyed to me by several reporters. An independent investigator, Thomas Ribe of Santa Fe (who is preparing a book on this series of events), was drawn to pursue the matter by local knowledge that Schenck's board had asked many questions "about the process of writing the May 18 Board of Investigation report and any pressures they may have been under to come to predrawn conclusions." Ribe filed two requests under the Freedom of Information Act, the first on that narrow point. He was told that the documents he sought were available at Bandelier. They were not. On April 3, 2001, Ribe writes, he "was informed that the Secretary of the Interior had taken control of the Board of Inquiry documents. . . . Having heard nothing in July, . . . [he] filed suit and got access to a number of documents." He had filed a second FOA request on February 5. It was denied. He appealed. He won, but a year passed before the documents were made available to him for reading in the library at Bandelier. I can certify from my own experience that those documents are now fully available and readily useful—else this account would have been considerably more difficult to write. Ribe has subsequently informed me that the documents have been transferred to the National Archives. Ribe, personal communications with author, February 1, 2004, and May 31, 2005.

19. Biswell quoted in David Carle, in the *Los Angeles Times,* on August 5, 2002.

20. Kate Nash, in *The Albuquerque Tribune,* May 6, 2005.

8. SCAPEGOATING AND FALSE REMEDIES

1. *The Sierra Club Guide to the Natural Areas of New Mexico, Arizona, and Nevada,* San Francisco: Sierra Club, 1985.

2. "Status of the Sierra Nevada. Volume I: Assessment Summaries and Management Strategies." Sierra Nevada Ecosystem Project, Final Report to Congress. Wild-

land Resources Center Report No. 36, Davis, University of California, p. 62; "A Report to the President in Response to the Wild Fires of 2000; Managing the Effects of Wild Fire on Communities and the Environment," September 8, 2000; T. S. Woolsey, "Western Yellow Pine in Arizona and New Mexico," *USDA Forest Service Bulletin* 101 (1911), 64.

3. *Lewiston Morning Tribune*, quoted in Brant Short and Dayle C. Hardy-Short, "Physicians of the Forest," *Electronic Green Journal* 19 (December 2003), available on the Web.

4. Ibid.

5. Ibid.

6. Ibid.

7. Pernin is quoted on the Peshtigo Fire Web site.

8. Pernin, ibid.

9. Ibid.

10. Ibid.

11. Ibid.

12. Ibid.

13. Ibid.

14. Pyne, personal communication with author, February 19, 2005.

15. Ibid.

16. Some voters in the rapidly suburbanizing states of Arizona and New Mexico might think there was little for them in the experience of Wisconsin, but they would be wrong—quite aside from what the state learned about fire. Over time Wisconsin's character has changed to make it unrecognizable to the generation that took its impressions of the state from its greatest historian, Frederick Jackson Turner. It has become part of postagricultural America as well as posturban America. According to the U.S. Census Bureau's 2000 Decennial Census of Population, fifty-eight of the state's seventy-two counties had at least a portion of their populations categorized as urban. The Census Bureau roughly defines urban population as including all persons living in and around large cities over 50,000 in population, in addition to those who reside in smaller cities and villages down to 2,500 in population. The remainder of the population is considered to be rural. When Wisconsin became a state, more than 90 percent of its population was rural. In 2000, nearly 70 percent lived in cities and larger villages. In Robert La Follette's time (1855–1925), a million people were full-time farmers in Wisconsin. In 2004, that number was down to only 135,000—though so many people lived in the indeterminate non-urban/non-farming middle ground that full-time farmers constituted only 8 percent of the rural population.

17. *Arizona Daily Star*, August 10, 2003. McGee was quoted as saying, "We do the best we can with what we've got."

18. Ibid.

19. Anonymous, personal communication with author, January 25, 2005.

20. *Arizona Daily Star*, August 10, 2003; Forest Service, in "A Report to the President in Response to the Wild Fires of 2000: Managing the Effects of Wild Fire on Communities and the Environment," September 8, 2000.

21. *Arizona Daily Star*, August 10, 2003.

22. Ibid.

9. THE MENTORS: MARSH, GALLATIN, OLMSTED, AND THOREAU

1. George P. Marsh, *Man and Nature: Or, Physical Geography as Modified by Human Action*, ed. David Lowenthal, Cambridge, Mass.: Harvard University Press, 2000, paperback edition, pp. 118–19.

2. I have been led to reexamine this subject by a series of conversations with Brian Donahue of Brandeis and Steven Stoll of Yale, and reading their recent books: see Donahue, *The Great Meadow: Farmers and the Land in Colonial Concord*, New Haven, Conn.: Yale University Press, 2004; and Stoll, *Larding the Lean Earth: Soil and Society in Nineteenth-Century America*, New York: Hill and Wang, 2002. See also Richard W. Judd, *Common Lands, Common People: The Origins of Conservation in Northern New England*, Cambridge, Mass.: Harvard University Press, 1997.

3. I have told the story of the Duponts, Dom Pedro, and the merinos in *Orders from France: The Americans and the French in a Revolutionary World (1780–1820)*, Philadelphia: University of Pennsylvania Press, 1990, pp. 209ff.

4. Marsh, *Man and Nature*, p. 465.

5. The following is a footnote in the official National Park Service history of Mount Rainier National Park:

> Beginning in 1896, company officials took a keen interest in the legislation. The company's land commissioner, W. H. Phipps, advised the president, Edwin W. Winter, that it was "very desirable that the bill as reported to the House, be passed," and in another letter remarked, "I do not think the Northern Pacific ought to be prominent in advocating the passage of the bill, but the company has friends." While Phipps met with Doolittle in Tacoma, Winter placed the bill in the right "channel" in Washington, D.C., probably with a sympathetic member of the Committee on Public Lands. When Congress eventually passed the bill, one company official stated, "The company thought it achieved a great success in securing the passage of the act in question, which gives it property of large value in place of something of no value." Though this evidence is fragmentary, it seems indisputable that the Northern Pacific was involved in the legislative process contrary to what it always maintained afterward. Edwin W. Winters [*sic*] (president) to W. H. Phipps (land commissioner), October 12, 1896, Phipps to Winters [*sic*], November 7, 1896, and C. W. Bunn to W. J. Curtis, June 7, 1899, MHS, NPRC Papers, President, President's subject files, File 60 (1). See also

"An Act to Set Aside a Portion of Certain Lands in the State of Washington Now Known as the Pacific Forest Reserve, as a Public Park, to Be Known as Mount Ranier [*sic*] National Park. Approved March 2, 1899."

6. Marsh, *Man and Nature,* p. 280.

7. Brian Donahue, "Husbandry Was Once a Sacred Art: Environmental History and the Future of Conservation," unpublished paper, dated March 2005, p. 31.

8. Marsh, *Man and Nature,* p. 279, footnote—with helpful comment by David Lowenthal; see also Ralph Waldo Emerson, "History," in *Essays, First Series.*

9. For Harrison and Marsh, see *Man and Nature,* footnote 37 on page 40 of the Lowenthal edition, from which comes my second quotation, as well as footnotes on pp. 118 through 121, from which comes my first.

10. Butler and Washington: discussed at greater length in my book *Hidden Cities: The Discovery and Loss of Ancient North American Civilization,* New York: Free Press, 1994, first hardcover edition, pp. 104–5, from which my quotations of them come.

11. For an account of Minnesota at this time, written by Christopher Columbus Andrews (not Charles C. Andrews), see *Minnesota & Dacotah: In letters descriptive of a tour through the North-west, autumn of 1856–1857,* graphic html n/c MOA-UMich, or Andrews, Christopher Columbus, *Minnesota & Dacotah: In Letters Descriptive of a Tour Through the North-West, in the Autumn of 1856–1857,* graphic html n/c Libr Congress; for Thoreau, see Henry David Thoreau, *Minnesota Notebook: Notes on the Journey West; Ltrs with Horace Mann, Jr.,* ed. Walter Harding, N.D., MsWord n/c Walden.Org.

12. The expert on the use of fire in the ritual spaces of the Hopewell culture of Ohio is Robert Riordon, some of whose work on this subject I summarize in *Hidden Cities.*

13. Thoreau on fire: I have used my edition of his *Walden,* appearing as *The Annotated Walden,* ed. Philip Van Doren Stern, New York: Clarkson N. Potter, 1970, pp. 67, 178, and 224. We can be grateful to Stern for informing us that in Concord, Thoreau's neighbors pronounced that name "thorough"—accent on the first syllable. My interpretations of Thoreau's parables are not Stern's, but my own and, I confess, unconventional.

14. Paul Nadasdy, "Transcending the Debate over the Ecologically Noble Indian: Indigenous Peoples and Environmentalism," *Ethnohistory* 52, no. 2 (Spring 2005): 333–69.

15. Marsh, *Man and Nature,* p. 279, footnote. The Gallatin and Washington stories also appear at greater length in *Hidden Cities.*

16. Olmsted, quoting "*Georgia Scenes,* by the Rev. and Hon. Judge Longstreet, now President of the University of Mississippi. Harper's edition, p. 76." Frederick Law Olmsted, *A Journey in the Seaboard Slave States; With Remarks on Their Economy,* electronic edition, pp. 533–34.

17. An anonymous southerner quoted by Lewis Cecil Gray in his *History of*

Agriculture in the Southern United States to 1860, at page 913. I was amused at being lambasted by a reviewer for using this quotation drawn from one of the great classics of environmental history on the ground that it was a "New Deal–era" text—as if Gibbon were a "Pitt-era" writer or Thucydides a "Nicias-era" writer.

18. Something like this passage appeared in the midst of a longer discourse in my *Mr. Jefferson's Lost Cause: Land, Farmers, Slavery, and the Louisiana Purchase*. I hope its reappearance may induce some interested readers to glance in that earlier work's direction.

19. Thanks to the Internet, I found the text of Olmsted's "Report" simply by making use of a search engine, though others, using other engines, could not. It is also to be found in the Library of Congress.

20. Ibid.

21. Ibid.

10. CARL SCHURZ, FIRE, AND THE WISCONSIN EXAMPLE

1. My quotations about Spooner come from the entry for him in the *Dictionary of American Biography*, in the great 1946 edition published by Scribner's.

2. My source was Julian Kirby. The campaign was that of 1952. I was running for Congress.

3. The Edwin W. Winter papers are in the Minnesota Historical Society. The "czar of Russia" utterance was repeated to me by my mother, who heard it from her mother, who heard it from Winter that morning.

4. Robert J. Gough, "Richard T. Ely and the Development of the Wisconsin Cutover," *Wisconsin Magazine of History* (Autumn 1991): 11–14, 15–19.

5. "Taxable asset": quoting Robert C. Nesbitt, a forest historian, in the St. Croix Historic Resource Study, chapter 4, p. 2 of 11, available on the Web as http://www.nps.gov/sacn/hrs/hrs4.htm. See also "Status of the Sierra Nevada. Volume I: Assessment Summaries and Management Strategies," Sierra Nevada Ecosystem Project, Final Report to Congress, Wildland Resources Center Report No. 36, Davis, University of California, p. 62.

6. Folsom, quoted in Anna M. Rice, "General Christopher C. Andrews: Leading the Minnesota Forestry Revolution," 2002, available on the Web at http://www.historycooperative.org/journals/ht/36.1/rice.html.

7. Ibid.

8. Ibid.

9. Ibid.

10. Donnelley has been a hero of mine since I first rode my bicycle fifteen miles to visit the shell of his abandoned house near Hastings, Minnesota, in the late 1930s. I have written about other aspects of his political, literary, and economic contributions in three earlier books, but I had no knowledge of his having pro-

vided General Andrews with a constituency until 2005, when I came upon the forest historian Jeff Forester's just-published work on logging in northern Minnesota, *The Forest for the Trees*.

11. Jeff Forester, *The Forest for the Trees: How Humans Shaped the North Woods*, St.Paul: Minnesota Historical Society Press, 2004, pp. 22–23.

12. "A Report to the President in Response to the Wild Fires of 2000; Managing the Effects of Wild Fire on Communities and the Environment," September 8, 2000; Woolsey, "Western Yellow Pine in Arizona and New Mexico," *USDA Forest Service Bulletin* 101 (1911), 64; Eileen M. McMahon and Theodore J. Karamanski, *Time and the River: A History of the Saint Croix*, A Historic Resource Study of the Saint Croix National Scenic Riverway, Omaha, National Park Service, 2002.

13. McMahon and Karamanski, *Time and the River*.

14. Ibid.

15. Ibid.

16. Mike Dombeck, Chris Wood, and Jack Williams, *From Conquest to Conservation: Our Public Lands Legacy*, New York: Island Press, 2000, p. 20, electronic version available on the Web; Frederick Coville, "Forest Growth and Sheep Grazing in the Cascade Mountains of Oregon," U.S. Department of Agriculture, *Division of Forestry Bulletin*, 15, Washington, D.C., p. 10.

17. Ibid.

11. MIGRATION, FIRE, EROSION, AND JOHN WESLEY POWELL

1. This passage, and several in the paragraphs that follow, owe much to my book of forty years ago, *Minnesota Houses*.

2. McMahon and Karamanski, *Time and the River*.

3. As these words were being rewritten somewhat from a longer passage in my *Minnesota Houses*, published forty years ago and long out of print, I was pleased to get a call from the Minnesota Historical Society, which told me that it was republishing and revising that book into a new title, *Historic Homes of Minnesota*, to which I have contributed a new opening essay offering new opinions and a few new facts.

4. These data come from my *Minnesota Houses*.

5. The line about cottonwoods is a favorite of mine. I think it first appeared in my *Burr, Hamilton, and Jefferson: A Study in Character*.

6. Powell quoted in William deBuys, ed., *Seeing Things Whole: The Essential John Wesley Powell*, Washington, D.C.: Island Press, 2001, pp. 182ff.

7. Ibid.

12. SMOKE, DUST, AND THE LAND

1. Stephen J. Pyne, *Year of the Fires: The Story of the Great Fires of 1910*, Seattle: University of Washington Press, 2001, p. 30.

2. Ibid., pp. 20ff.

3. John Steinbeck, *The Grapes of Wrath*, New York: Library of America, 1996, pp. 223–24.

4. I am using statistics correlated by Dan Flores, in his *The Natural West: Environmental History in the Great Plains and Rocky Mountains,* Norman: University of Oklahoma Press, 2001, p. 92.

5. Thornthwaite, "Climate and Settlement in the Great Plains," *The Handbook of Agriculture*, Washington, D.C.: U.S. Department of Agriculture, 1941, p. 184. I am grateful to Douglas Helms for this reference.

6. Data from John D. Hicks, *The Populist Revolt: A History of the National Farmer's Alliance*, Minneapolis: University of Minnesota Press, 1931, p. 32.

7. Ibid. I have reused some of the material covered considerably more extensively in my *Men on a Moving Frontier* and *Rediscovering America*.

8. Thornthwaite, "Climate and Settlement in the Great Plains."

9. I cannot resist placing on record in this note a reference to a passage in a history of that period of which I am especially proud: it appears on page 491 of Robert Newman's *Owen Lattimore and the "Loss" of China*, Berkeley: University of California Press, 1992.

10. Douglas Helms, personal communication with author, June 8, 2004.

11. Douglas Helms, in "Conserving the Plains: The Soil Conservation Service in the Great Plains," *Agricultural History* 64 (Spring 1990): 58–73.

12. Helms on overgrazing, etc.: ibid., p. 3.

13. Eisenhower agricultural and conservation programs: ibid., pp. 5, 6.

14. Marq de Villiers, *Water: The Fate of Our Most Precious Resource*, Boston: Houghton Mifflin/Mariner Books, 2000, pp. 314ff.; see also Donald Worster, *Rivers of Empire: Water, Aridity, and the Growth of the American West*, New York: Pantheon, 1985, pp. 313ff.

15. See both de Villiers, *Water*, and Worster, *Rivers*.

16. Federal report cited in de Villiers, *Water*, p. 157; Reisner in *Cadillac Desert: The American West and Its Disappearing Water*, New York: Penguin, 1993, and in several personal communications while he was writing it in our country cabin.

17. Helms on Butz and replanting grassland, "Conserving the Plains," p. 8.

18. Ibid., p. 9.

13. URBANISM, DISPERSION THEORY, MIGRATION, AND FIRE DANGER

1. David Brooks, *On Paradise Drive: How We Live Now (And Always Have) in the Future Tense*, is the basic text for these views, though my quotations come from a piece in which the book was given a loyal send-off, rather than the Keilloresque send-up it deserved, by *The New York Times Magazine*.

2. Ibid.

3. Ibid., p. 183n.

4. The expression "New American Mixing Bowl" is the contribution of the demographer William Frey.

5. Quoted from Dombeck, Wood, and Williams, *From Conquest to Conservation*, p. 20, electronic version available on the Web. I am following their account.

6. The Hispanic tradition is as much Mexican as Spanish. Fifth-century Teotihuacan held nearly as many people as the Rome that fell to the Goths. These townspeople made up perhaps 80 percent of the population of the Valley of Mexico. When assaulted by Cortez a thousand years later, the next great metropolis of the valley, Tenochtitlan, held half that valley's people—the Aztec capital was many times larger than London, Rome, or Madrid.

7. For these paragraphs and for much else over the years, I am indebted to Donald Meinig of Syracuse University, the dean of American geographers. He pulled together the migration history of the United States in the three magisterial volumes of his *The Shaping of America*, from the third of which these passages are drawn. Meinig in *The Shaping of America, Volume 3, Transcontinental America, 1850–1915*, New Haven, Conn.: Yale University Press, 1998, pp. 101ff.

8. Quoted from Meinig in *The Shaping of America, Volume 2, Continental America, 1800–1967*, New Haven, Conn.: Yale University Press, 1993, p. 248; also see Richard Wade, *The Urban Frontier: Life in Early Pittsburgh, Cincinnati, Lexington, Louisville, and St. Louis* (Chicago: University of Chicago Press, 1967).

9. William H. Frey, *The New Urban Revival in the United States: Metro Renewal, Minority Growth and Suburban Dominance* (Population Studies Center Research Report No. 93-268), Ann Arbor: University of Michigan Population Studies Center, 1993, pp. 2–3.

10. Ibid.

11. Ibid.

12. Ibid., p. 741.

13. Bruegmann and Pyne, in personal communications with author, February 2005.

14. Frey, *The New Urban Revival*.

14. LONGER AND LARGER PRECEDENTS

1. Thomas Le Duc in Howard W. Ottoson, ed., *Land Use Policy in the United States*, Washington, D.C.: Beard Books, 2001, reprint, p. 22. Le Duc points out that it is not true to say that "the whole idea of conservation and public ownership is

a recent concept." Instead, "the Land Ordinance of 1785 reserved to the public an interest in minerals and . . . early in national history one finds a number of measures surprisingly modern in their recognition of the public interest."

2. My *Burr, Hamilton, and Jefferson* and *Mr. Jefferson's Lost Cause* deal with the distinctions between what the Founders said and what they did. Those differences are important, but not to the subject at hand; Thomas Jefferson to Albert Gallatin, December 24, 1807, and Jefferson in *Notes on Virginia*, Library of America edition, pp. 289ff.

3. Hamilton on primogeniture, *Report to the Society of the Cincinnati*, July 6, 1786, *Hamilton Papers*, II, pp. 335–36; Madison in John R. Brewster, "Relevance of the Jeffersonian Dream Today," in Ottoson, *Land Use Policy*, p. 95. The speculators overwhelmed Hamilton, as the planters overwhelmed Jefferson, so the Public Land Ordinance of 1796, the first to have much effect upon what actually happened on the frontier, offered only big units of 640 acres at auction, with a minimum of two dollars an acre with only twelve months' credit for half that amount. My discussion on the capacity of the southern planters to buy land lies mostly in *Architecture, Men, Women, and Money*, in chapters devoted to the Halifax Whigs of Virginia and the Hamptons of Virginia and South Carolina.

4. Please see discussion in *Mr. Jefferson's Lost Cause*, appendix, "Jefferson, Madison, Adam Smith, and the Chesapeake Cities."

5. Boorstin, *The Lost World of Thomas Jefferson*, New York: Henry Holt, 1948. Andrew R. L. Cayton quotes Jefferson on page 23 of his *The Frontier Republic: Ideology and Politics in the Ohio Country, 1780–1825*, Kent, Ohio: Kent State University Press, 1986, at p. 21. As public land policy evolved in the United States, Jefferson's advocacy of the use of the public domain to improve citizenship ripened into a kind of therapeutic doctrine in contrast with Hamilton's treating of the public estate primarily as an asset to be pieced out to reduce taxes. Though one can hear it said, and even written, that Jefferson wrote the phrase "We the People," which opens the Constitution, he was not there to write it, being fully engaged at the time in Paris, and such language did not come naturally to him.

6. Washington to Arthur Young, December 12, 1793, and December 5, 1791, quoted in Richard N. Smith, *Patriarch: George Washington and the New American Nation*, Boston: Houghton Mifflin, 1993, p. 138. Washington on yeomen and small lots quoted in Fritz Hirschfeld, *George Washington and Slavery: A Documentary Portrayal*, Columbia: University of Missouri Press, 1997, p. 76.

7. Washington, quoted ibid; Jefferson quoted in agreement in Avery O. Craven, *Soil Exhaustion as a Factor in the Agricultural History of Virginia and Maryland, 1606–1860*, Peter Smith Publisher, 1965, p. 34. This is the subject of my *Mr. Jefferson's Lost Cause*.

8. The Mariettans' story is well told in Cayton, *Frontier Republic*. This passage is a précis of my own treatment in *Mr. Jefferson's Lost Cause*.

9. Le Duc, "U.S. Land Policy to 1862," in Ottoson, *Land Use Policy*, p. 8.

10. Among the Europeans, it was customary to draw upon Roman prototypes for the architecture of these bristling nuclei. King Ferdinand and Queen Isabella

sent Columbus off to the New World from the joint monarchs' base of operations for the siege of Granada, a rectilinear armed camp, a form that could have fitted over that of many Roman fortified camps across Europe as far as the delta of the Danube. The Roman *campus martius*, slightly revised after a thousand-year interval, became the pattern for presidios marking Spanish presence in North America from St. Augustine through San Antonio to San Francisco. The French gave equivalent forms to garrison towns at Detroit, St. Louis, and New Orleans, which they called bastides. The forms were the same, though the saints' names were different. When General Washington's officers, re-formed as the order of the Cincinnati, established their outpost at Marietta, Ohio, they called it their "Campus Martius," and built it in a rectangular form with corner towers that might have been seen along the Rhine fifteen centuries earlier. A fragment of one of those towers remains in place to this day.

11. The allocation of public obligations to private persons is a sort of recurrence to feudalism, learned by the people of the United States at the colonizers' knees. There are landowners along the Vermont shore of Lake Champlain whose title deeds reach back to seigneuries granted by the King of France to soldiers who would garrison outposts against the Dutch and British. Offsetting the seigneuries, the Dutch gave blocks of land to Livingstons and Van Rensselaers whose descendants today still live where they were supposed to live in order to put up a good fight against the French. The title bestowed upon them along with the land and obligations was "patroon."

    After the Duke of York seized for the British the Dutch possessions in that region, some of the people who had been patroons became manor lords. Thereafter, along the Hudson, a small civil war and the burning of many barns were required to erase those feudal privileges and feudal obligations. By then, the recalcitrance of the manor lords had induced much migration to the West. Thus land use denied by neo-feudalism pushed, while land use invited by the Northwest Ordinance pulled.

12. Throughout its New World possessions, the Europeans made use of the medieval practice of turning freebooting captains into servants of the state by making them nobles. Hernán Cortés, having washed his hands of Indian blood, was presented with lands, obligations, and a parchment patent of nobility as Marquis of Oaxaca. See my *Mr. Jefferson's Lost Cause*.

13. When the Paxton Boys, frontier ruffians bent upon acquiring land by tomahawk title, violated assurances given to the Indians of Pennsylvania, even the generally pacific Benjamin Franklin took up his rifle to resist them. Many a later American hero did as much; one thinks especially of Sam Houston's efforts to ensure compliance with the treaties made with the Cherokees by the Republic of Texas.

14. McGillivray and Washington are major figures in my book *Mr. Jefferson's Lost Cause*, in chapters in which the Indian statehood concept is discussed at length.

15. Frederick Coville, "Forest Growth and Sheep Grazing in the Cascade Mountains of Oregon," p. 10; *Light v. U.S.* (220 U.S. 523, 55 L. Ed. 570, 32 Sup. Ct. Rep. 485) and *U.S. v. Grimaud* (220 U.S. 506, 31 S. Ct. 480, 55 L. Ed. 563).

16. There is to this day no apparent consensus on how big the Navaho reservation really is. A search of the Web produced six differing totals within the first twenty-two sites; the Navaho Nation itself probably has it right. In 2002 it testified that the reservation is "located on 26,109 square miles, or 17.1 million acres within the exterior boundaries of New Mexico, Arizona, and Utah. It is roughly the geographic size of West Virginia." Testimony of the Navajo Nation, submitted for the record of the Committee on Environment and Public Works, Subcommittee on Transportation, Infrastructure, and Nuclear Safety, Hearing on the Federal Lands Highway Program, August 8, 2002.

17. The precedent for reservation has been in place since the seventeenth century. In Massachusetts, for example, "the Trustees of Reservations" preside over a network of privately maintained areas for special environmental or historic interest beyond the reach of speculators and developers. There was no likelihood that the animal species so protected in Massachusetts would be as dangerous as Seminoles or Apaches unless they were provided for. The public saw the wisdom of restoring to public purposes areas that might otherwise have paid real estate taxes because the benefits of doing so outweighed the costs.

18. For the Neutrality Act, see my *Orders from France: The Americans and French in a Revolutionary World* and *Burr, Hamilton, and Jefferson*.

19. After the failure of the Grand Jury in Richmond, under instruction from Chief Justice John Marshall, to permit prosecution of Aaron Burr for treason in 1806, President Jefferson sought to have him prosecuted under the Neutrality Act.

15. TOWARD A HEALTHY FORESTS AND COMMUNITIES CORPS

1. The firewise program is sponsored by the National Wildfire Coordinating Group, a consortium of wildland fire organizations and federal agencies responsible for wildland fire management in the United States, including the International Association of Fire Chiefs, the National Association of State Fire Marshals, the National Association of State Foresters, the National Emergency Management Association, the National Fire Protection Association, the Forest Service, the Bureau of Indian Affairs, the Bureau of Land Management, the U.S. Fish and Wildlife Service, the National Park Service, the Federal Emergency Management Agency, and the U.S. Fire Administration. Most of the consortium's operating money comes from the Agriculture Department budget. I am quoting from its history as carried on its Web site.

2. Pyne, *Tending Fire*, p. 120, using terms similar to those in his Op-Ed piece in the *Los Angeles Times*, October 30, 2003.

3. Pyne, *Tending Fire*, p. 121.

4. These quotations are drawn from sections (not carrying page numbers) in the Forest Service report "Social and Economic Issues and Home Destruction," available on the Forest Service Web site.

5. Ibid.

6. Ibid.

7. Muller et al., "Wildfire Mitigation and Private Lands: Managing Long-Term Vulnerabilities," unpublished paper, dated August 31, 2004.

8. Christopher Smith, "Fed Fire Funding Burns Hole in Pockets," *Salt Lake Tribune,* May 12, 2004.

9. Muller et al., "Wildfire Mitigation and Private Lands."

10. Blaine, "Never Too Rich, Never Too Thin," *Forest Magazine* (Winter 2003): 16ff.

11. Ibid., citing the work of Laura McCarthy of the Forest Guild.

12. Pyne, *Tending Fire,* p. 120.

13. Jim Robbins in *The New York Times* of August 27, 2002. For TCS, see "From the Ashes: Reducing the Harmful Effects and Rising Costs of Western Wildfires," Washington, D.C.: Taxpayers for Common Sense, 2000, executive summary and pp. 4 and 5.

14. "From the Ashes," p. 7.

15. Ibid., p. 16.

16. Ibid., p. 43.

17. Ibid., p. 19.

18. Ibid., pp. 20–21.

16. TOWARD A NATIONAL FLAME ZONE ATLAS

1. Rutherford Platt, *Land Use and Society,* Washington, D.C.: Island Press, 1996, pp. 11ff. In the country as a whole, including Alaska, acres under cultivation have been constant in the 330- to 400-million-acre range, as some farms have gone derelict and become reforested, others have been chewed up by urban "sprawl," and agribusiness has acquired still others. Private timberland has also remained about constant, within a range from 340 million to 365 million acres.

2. "Reducing Wildfire Threats: Funds Should Be Targeted to the Highest Risk Areas," General Accounting Office testimony by Barry Hill, September 13, 2000," before the Task Force on Resources and the Environment, Committee on the Budget, House of Representatives. All citations to GAO testimony can be found on the GAO Web site by date and subject, or on http://www.fireplan.gov/community_papers.cfm.

3. Private communication with author from William Raichle, ISO, January 25, 2005.

4. V. C. Radeloff, R. B. Hammer, S. I. Stewart, J. S. Fried, S. S. Holcomb, and J. F. McKeefry, *The Wildland-Urban Interface in the United States: Ecological Applications,* Madison: University of Wisconsin Press, January 12, 2005, supplemented by e-mail privately on January 12, 2005; Aplet, personal communication, January 21, 2005; and Bo Wilmer and Greg Aplet, "The Community Fire Planning Zone: A GIS Analysis," Wilderness Society, April 2005, as supplemented by e-mail private communications in April 2005.

5. Noting in an e-mail on January 12, 2005, that the "communities at risk listed in the *Federal Register* are only those adjacent to federal lands," Radeloff went on to say that if one were to remove that limitation and take only the physical wildland and settlement categories it suggests, which are interface and intermix communities, it is possible to consolidate them into a single definition, and apply it to all lands, irrespective of their ownership status. The reason for this was the interest of, for example, the State and Private Forestry Division of the Forest Service, in WUI data for all land ownerships. That is why Radeloff's maps show ample WUI in Connecticut even though there are few federal lands in that state. "Especially the eastern National Forests contain many inhold-ings," writes Radeloff. That is why he is attempting "to take a closer look at this phenomenon, and assess how it affects WUI patterns."

6. At the Fort Collins, Colorado, Rocky Mountain Research Station of the Forest Service, another group of experienced fire scholars and practitioners has produced yet another way of looking at what is and is not a community at risk from wildfire. However, the Fort Collins group does not profess to provide more than a "coarse-scale assessment" as the basis for their map of "Wildland Fire Risk to Flammable Structures." That map provides "an integration of population den-sity, fuels, and weather spatial data for the conterminous United States . . . [hav-ing] looked at where the houses are (assuming three people per house), what vegetation types were likely to produce flame lengths in excess of 8 feet, and the average number of days per year when historical weather conditions had ex-ceeded thresholds and wildfires had burned structures." Rough estimates were, therefore, the best the Fort Collins project could do, guessing that each house had three inhabitants and that those hypothetical three lived there year round. That is not a census. Furthermore, while useful in comparing fire exposure in settlements in one state to that of similar settlements in other states, it does not bring the analysis down to the zip-code level, and for planning purposes it is far too general to be useful neighborhood by neighborhood, much less household by household. Nor does it rank relative risk for the composite of climate, condi-tion, and fire history. Those who have worked on the map are soldiering on with far too little encouragement from Congress or their own senior managers in the Department of Agriculture. For the Fort Collins mapping, see Kirsten M. Schmidt, James P. Menakis, Colin C. Hardy, Wendall J. Hann, and David L. Bun-nell, "Development of Coarse-scale Spatial Data for Wildland Fire and Fuel Man-agement," Gen. Tech. Rep. RMRS-GTR-87, Fort Collins, Col.: U.S. Department of Agriculture, Forest Service, Rocky Mountain Research Station, 41 p. + CD), 2002. The final map of Wildland Fire Risk to Flammable Structures is shown in appendix G of their document. Total area of the classes that have the highest risk of a wildland fire igniting flammable structures is shown in their table 10. Note also *www.landfire.gov.*

7. Wilmer and Aplet, "Community Fire Planning Zone." Having also noted that the *Federal Register* list was "not . . . comprehensive" or "accurate," Aplet's group wryly noted its understated observation that "state-level flexibility has resulted in some variance among State submissions." It then went on to use the U.S. Geological Survey national land cover data set of satellite-derived informa-tion to show where settlement actually had taken place, adding a half-mile

buffer. These areas were then overlaid upon the map of federal lands in the U.S. Geological Survey's national atlas. See "Communities at Risk from Wildfire: How Much Is on Federal Land," report of the Ecology and Economics Research Department, Wilderness Society, March 2003, no. 2. Aplet, in private communication, January 21, 2005, stated that the table shows that "nationwide, 1,883,190 acres are in the 'high' risk class (77 percent of which is non-federal), 5,034,031 acres are in the 'moderate' risk class (77 percent of which is nonfederal), and 91,329,662 acres are in the 'low' risk class (93 percent of which is non-federal). Together, these three 'highest' risk classes account for 7.86 percent of the lower 48 states."

8. Wilmer and Aplet, "Community Fire Planning Zone." See also Fort Collins study cited in note 6 above.

9. Radeloff, personal communication with author, January 13, 2004.

10. "Pinpointing Insured Losses in the Southern California Wildfires of 2003," ISO, February 2004.

17. MANAGING BOTH SIDES OF THE INTERFACE

1. Pyne, personal communication with author, January 2004, echoing passages in *Tending Fire*.

2. White trilogy (*Gold, The Gray Dawn, The Rose Dawn*); Pyne, *Year of the Fires*; Carle report, *Los Angeles Times*, August 5, 2002.

3. Oliver quoted in Marc Wortman, "How Wild Should Wildfires Be?" *Environment: Yale* (Spring 2004): 15–16.

4. And what happened to California? Jack Wright of the University of New Mexico informs us: "Regarding the Californians migrating—25% of the population gain of NM, Utah, Montana and other Western states in the 1990s was from California in-migrants." There was an outrush of "white people fleeing the crime, earthquakes, fires, mudslides, high costs, and moribund economy of the Golden State. But I should add that this process has been a two-way migration over the decades. As work dries up in the mountains (or is seen as a poorly compensating mirage) the migrants flee back to California. It has been this way since the 1920s. Montana sent tens of thousands to California, Oregon, and Washington in the '80s and received them back in the '90s. Migration of this type is like the teeth of a saw cutting up the West into subdivided parcels that ratchet up in price with each pass of the blade" (Wright, personal communication with author, January 23, 2003).

5. Ibid.

6. My quotations come from the report of the U.S. Forest Service Rocky Mountain Research Station, Missoula, Montana, released after the fire.

7. Radeloff et al., *Wildland-Urban Interface*.

8. Platt, *Land Use and Society*; quoted in *The Boston Globe*, June 30, 2002, p. A6.

9. Ann Camp quoted in Wortman, "How Wild," pp. 15–16.

10. Ibid.

11. Austin Troy writes in a personal communication with author, February 1, 2005:

> Because of the wording of the law which created these zones (AB 337, or the Bates Bill of 1992), both mapping and regulations tend to be inconsistent by jurisdiction. Some localities designated their land pursuant to the state's suggested designation Civil Code Section 51178. Localities could exempt any of their land from the State's suggested designations under Civil Code Section 51178: "A local agency may, at its discretion, exclude from the requirements of Section 51182 an area identified as a VHFHSZ by the director within the jurisdiction of the local agency, following a finding supported by substantial evidence in the record that the requirements of Section 51182 are not necessary for effective fire protection within the area." As of 1999, only 99 of 209 jurisdictions with VHFHSZs mapped by the state accepted those designations. The rest exempted themselves in one way or another.

12. Ibid.

13. Ibid. (The furious summary language is my own.)

14. Ibid.

15. Understandably anonymous communication, dated May 23, 2005. The company for which this executive works does not wish to suffer retribution from developers, insurance commissioners, home builders, or lenders.

16. Ibid.

17. Ibid.

18. Raymond J. Burby of the University of North Carolina, in a paper entitled "Have State Comprehensive Planning Mandates Reduced Insured Losses from Natural Disasters?" *Natural Hazards Review* 6, no. 2 (2005): 21.

18. THE LEGACIES OF STEWART CHASE AND GILBERT WHITE

1. Burby, "Have State Comprehensive Planning Mandates . . . ?" p. 21.

2. Ibid., p. 19. Biblical scholars take note: after Adam and Eve break the covenant, an Abraham is required.

3. Ibid., pp. 8–9.

4. Ibid., p. 10.

5. Monson and Monson, "A Program for Urban Dispersal."

6. TCS Report, "From the Ashes," p. 28.

7. Wright, personal communication with author, January 23, 2003.

8. Chen, personal communication with author, May 15, 2005.

9. Ibid.

19. SUN DAGGERS, GRACE, LIMITS, AND THEOLOGY

1. The archaeologically inclined can think of each half of my bifurcated concentric circles as looking like Poverty Point, the great three-thousand-year-old earthwork in Louisiana.

2. The term "suite" was, I believe, introduced into anthropology and history by the grand mentor of us all, Albert Crosby, *The Columbian Exchange: Biological and Cultural Consequences of 1492*, Thirtieth Anniversary Edition, Cambridge, UK: Cambridge University Press, 2003; and *Ecological Imperialism: The Biological Expansion of Europe, 900–1900*, Cambridge, UK: Cambridge University Press, 1986.

3. Ezekiel 34:18–19.

4. Thus it is infuriating to read, among the scrivenings of popular journalists of our own time, comfort being offered the selfish and proud by claims that Edwards might be an accessory to the destruction of any part of God's creation. Never!

5. I am grateful to Elisa New for this quotation, which appears on page 249 of her *The Line's Eye*, Cambridge, Mass.: Harvard University Press, 1998.

6. Ecclesiastes 3:19–22.

7. The "of God" line is from "Concerning the Ends." *The Works of Jonathan Edwards*, vol. 8, p. 530, as quoted in George M. Marsden, *Jonathan Edwards: A Life*, New Haven, Conn.: Yale University Press, 2003, at p. 463.

8. Lion G. Miles, "The Red Man Dispossessed: The Williams Family and the Alienation of Indian Land in Stockbridge, Massachusetts, 1736–1818," *New England Quarterly* 67 (1994): 46–76. Sermon on II Cor. 5:17, September 1751, quoted in Rachel Wheeler, "Friends to Your Souls: Jonathan Edwards' Indian Pastorate and the Doctrine of Original Sin," *Church History*, December 1, 2003, p. 23. I am grateful to Kenneth P. Minkema of the Edwards Papers for leading me toward these references, and to him and Harry S. Stout for the line about a face of flint and Sodom, from a joint essay on Edwards to be found on the Web.

9. Gerald McDermott, *One Holy and Happy Society: The Public Theology of Jonathan Edwards*, University Park: Penn State University Press, 1992, pp. 131, 132, 136.

10. My friend William deBuys, the best chronicler John Wesley Powell ever had, straightened out my misuse of the term "controlled burning" in this application by pointing out that "controlled burning implies control: fire lines, treatment boundaries, crews, etc.; what the Indians used was 'light fire'—igniting short-duration, low-temp fuels, which in the absence of livestock and fire suppression were abundant, and then they let the fire go its own way. . . . They did not try to direct or control it. So: nearly all controlled burning involves light fire, but a lot of man-caused, intentional light fire is not controlled." Personal communication with author, February 10, 2005.

11. Fort Stanwix Treaty language, quoted in Peter S. Onuf, *Jefferson's Empire: The Language of American Nationhood*, Charlottesville: University of Virginia Press, 2000, p. 40; Roosevelt quoted in Daniel M. Friedenberg, *Life, Liberty and the Pursuit of Land*, Buffalo: Prometheus Books, 1992, p. 298.

12. Edwards, in "Concerning the Ends," cf. William Bradford, as quoted in Sidney E. Ahlstrom, *A Religious History of the American People*, New Haven, Conn.: Yale University Press, 1974, p. 136. I have modernized the spellings.

13. Jonathan Edwards the environmentalist can be studied directly in his *Sermons and Notes* in George Marsden's biography of Edwards; and in McDermott's *One Holy and Happy Society*.

14. "Concerning the Ends for Which God Created the World" (1755) in *J. Edwards, Typological Writings*, ed. W. E. Anderson and M. I. Lowance, New Haven, Conn.: Yale University Press, 1993; C. A. Holbrook, *Jonathan Edwards, the Valley and Nature*, Lewisburg, Pa.: Bucknell University Press, 1987; Perry Miller, *Jonathan Edwards*, Greenwood Press, 1949 and *Errand into the Wilderness*, New York: Harper, 1956; H. P. Simonson, *Jonathan Edwards: Theologian of the Heart* (Eerdmans, 1974); J. E. Smith, *Jonathan Edwards: Puritan, Preacher, Philosopher*, Notre Dame, Ind.: University of Notre Dame Press, 1992.

15. See Boorstin's *The Lost World of Thomas Jefferson*.

APPENDIX: JONATHAN EDWARDS AND IMPERIAL CONNECTICUT

1. I am largely following the account in Marsden's biography of Edwards, pp. 407ff.

2. Brian Donahue, private communication with author, September, 2005. For Livermore, see Shaw Livermore, *Early American Land Companies*, New York: Octagon Press, 1968, p. 83.

3. Livermore, *Early American Land Companies*.

4. Marsden's biography of Edwards, pp. 407ff.

Acknowledgments

Where to begin, when the book at hand is the product of sixty and more years of thinking and talking and writing, and innumerable kindnesses? It is impossible to thank everybody who has helped, so the best I could do was to review my e-mails, classified according to the subject matter of the book, and to list the people whom I had occasion to thank for one significant service or another. Before becoming computerized, however, I could look about me in my study and recognize the immediate circle of helpers: Frances Kennedy, always and for everything; our daughter, Ruth Kennedy, of whom I am very proud, and who gives me joy; then, just outside the family circle, Neal Etre, who succeeded Doug Lynam. Neal did all the heavy-duty mapping and contacting and kept me reasonably sane amid computerized complexities.

Once again, my friend, editor, and publisher Thomas LeBien has been there from the beginning, understanding, endorsing, urging, and making all things printed possible. Jenna Dolan was the copy editor for the manuscript, making dozens of beneficial changes.

Beyond them, there are several score whose contributions appear in individual acknowledgments in the notes, as well as the e-mailers and e-mailees whose names follow, as they came up by category. This all seems a little bloodless, but if I didn't organize things so, the list of kindnesses received in making this work possible would be longer than the book itself. I have certainly missed some, and can only plead that in my eightieth year my memory even for kindnesses is not as strong as once it was, or should be.

In the final stages, Carol Lieb found and procured images. Alan Berger, Case Brown, Greg Aplet, and Volker Radeloff created new wonders of computerized synthesis.

Don Chen of Smart Growth America was of immense and consistent aid. Close behind him as sponsors and participants were Luther Probst and Dennis Glick of the Sonoran Institute; Ralph Grossi and Ed Thompson of the American Farmland Trust; Larry Selzer of the Conservative Fund; and Henry Carey and Laura McCarthy of the Forest Guild.

The financial help necessary to hire researchers and produce maps came from the Thaw Charitable Trust and the McCune Foundation.

In my e-mail exchanges I came upon helpful correspondence with the following:

Demographers: Ken Prewitt, Bill Frey, John Haaga, and Jack Wright.

Economists: John Geanokoplis, Carl Kaysen, Larry Klein, Austin Troy, Rich Howarth, and Peter Bernstein.

At the Santa Fe Institute: George Cowan.

Among urban planners and practitioners: Alexander von Hoffman and James DeNormandie of the Joint Center; Chris Leinberger of the Brookings Institution.

Among planner-economists: Ed Whitelaw, Ernie Niemi, Kathy Lynn, and Helen Rosenau of ECONorthwest.

Among geographers: Rutherford Platt of the University of Massachusetts, Billy Turner and Colin Polsky of Clark University, and Don Meinig of Syracuse University (one more time).

Among historians—too many to list, in the dozens—Max Page and Brian Donahue have been especially thoughtful with their suggestions.

Among archaeologists: Linda Cordell, Steve Lekson, Jon Gibson, Steve Williams, Dave Thomas, and Doug Erwin.

At Harvard: Dan Schrag, Jim McCarthy, Allen Berger, Case Brown, and David Foster.

At Yale: Ann Camp, John Geanokoplis, Chad Oliver, and Steven Stoll.

At MIT: Sam Bass Warner, Sanford Anderson, Judy Layzer, and Mike Hawley.

At the University of Wisconsin: Volker Radeloff, Mike Dombeck, and Bill Cronon.

Among fire experts: Steve Pyne and dozens of others, as cited in the text, plus weather and environmental experts, including Roger Pielke, Jr.

Among urban geographers: Bob Bruegmann, Volker Radeloff, Greg Aplet, Bill Baker, and Brian Muller.

Among master planners and architects: Cecil Steward and Richard Weinstein.

Among environmental philosophers: Andrew Light.

Among New Deal and Cold War scholars: Pete Andrews and Kathleen Tobin.

Among journalists: Cornelia Dean, Frank Clifford, and Ed Marston.

Among writers on the West: Bill deBuys, Dan Flores, Ivan Doig, Tom Ribe, and Dave Warren.

Among people in the insurance and reinsurance businesses: Dave Durbin, Walter Anderau, and Bill Raichle.

Among lawyers: Jim Gilliland and John Leshy.

Among the Firewise: Michelle Steinberg and Jim Smalley.

Among generally wise people: Stewart Brand, Danny Hillis, Paul Saffo, Patty Limerick, and Dan Kemmis.

And, on The Hill, the chances of all this having a beneficial effect have been much increased by the skill and fortitude of Janine Benner and Earl Blumenauer.

What should I say of the several hundred members of the National Park Service, the National Forest Service, and the National Biological Service who gave aid to this project as it grew over two decades?

Naming some individually would leave out others, and some careers would not, at this writing, be forwarded by association with my views. Anonymity is probably the best reward in a time when dissent is not welcome. I will thank them all when I see them—in safe places. Among those retired and immune to retribution, I thank especially: Jack Ward Thomas, Mike Dombeck, Deny Galvin, Jerry Rogers, John Reynolds, and Rob Arnberger.

And as soon as this book is published, I will think of many more, to whom I offer now the apologies of a grateful if forgetful man.

Index

Abilene (Kansas), 173–74
Abnaki Indians, 132
Academy of Achievement, 50
accelerated depreciation, 179
Adams, John, 79
Adams, John Quincy, 183
Adams-Onis Treaty (1819), 183, 184
Addis Ababa, Italian assault on, 35
Adirondacks, 112, 113, 119, 161
African-Americans: fear of, urban
    dispersion and, 28, 29, 34, 54;
    housing discrimination against, 233;
    segregation of, 165; *see also* slavery
agriculture, 16, 27–28, 149, 181, 184,
    188–90; acres under cultivation,
    304*n1*; on arid lands, 164–67,
    169–78, 248; Cold War and, 177–78;
    colonial-era, 271–72, 275;
    commercialized, 122; erosion and,
    152–53; and Founders' land policies,
    200–203; Indian, 120; labor systems
    and, 154, 197 203; preservation of
    land for, 257; reforestation of land
    used for, 143–44, 155; restrictions
    on, 156, 158, 176, 209; slash-and-
    burn, 135; subsidization of, 13, 169,
    172–74, 176–78, 210; sustainable, 27,
    124–25, 170–71, 236
Agriculture, U.S. Department of
    (USDA), 75, 79, 107, 149, 172, 178,
209, 225, 303*n1*; Division of
    Forestry, 148
Air Force, U.S., 46, 60
air quality, improvement of, 73
Alabama, 206; population growth in, 22
Alaska, 223, 224; harbor project in,
    10–11, 46; Russian control of, 206
Albuquerque (New Mexico), 14, 24,
    166, 187; Hispanics in, 185
Albuquerque Tribune, 104
Allen, Craig, 96–97, 99
allotment laws, 212
American Enterprise Institute, 269
American Farm Bureau, 178
American Forest Resource Council, 115
American Forestry Association, 145
American Institute of Architects, 47–48
American Institute of Planners, 48
American Planning Association (APA),
    247, 256
*Ancient Monuments of the Mississippi
    Valley* (Squire and Davis), 128
Andrews, Charles, 129
Andrews, General Christopher
    Columbus, 145–46, 148, 151, 221,
    298*n10*
Apaches, 105–6, 108, 126, 303*n17*
Aplet, Greg, 229, 243, 305*n7*
Appleby, Rylon, 153
aquifers, 174–77

architecture, 151, 153; Indian, 120,
    127–30, 26
Arizona, 20, 106, 131, 146, 186,
    294*n16*; hazard planning in, 251;
    Indians in, 181, 182, 211; population
    growth in, 22; wildfires in, 116, 122,
    114–16, 157 (*see also* Rodeo-Chediski
    Fire); *see also* Four Corners
Arizona (battleship), 224
Arizona Daily Star, 114
Arkansas, 62
Armed occupation legislation, 208
Armstrong, William, 96–97, 99
Army, U.S., 57, 151, 204, 208, 212;
    Cavalry, 3, 141, 198, 210; Corps of
    Engineers, 173–74; Tank Corps, 62
Arnberger, Robert, 100–101
Associated Press, 113
Atlantic City (New Jersey), 161
Atlas intercontinental ballistic missiles,
    60
atomic bomb, *see* nuclear weapons
atomic energy, 48, 51
Atomic Energy Commission (AEC), 10,
    50; Personnel Security Board, 46
Augur, Tracy, 48
Augustine, Saint, 269
Australia, 191
automobile industry, 48–49, 59, 72;
    advertising and promotional
    strategies of, 32–33, 70–71
Azilia, plan for marquisate of, 207

Babbitt, Bruce, 79, 84–86, 95, 99–102,
    292*n15*, 293*n17*
Baden, John, 221
Bandelier National Monument, 4, 5, 7,
    89–93, 96–101, 106, 182, 292*n15*,
    293*n18*
Bank of America, 289*n23*
Barronett (Wisconsin), 112
Bates Bill (1992), 307*n11*
Battle of Britain, 35
Bel Geddes, Norman, 70
Belgrade, bombing of, 35
Bennett, Hugh Hammond, 168–71, 176,
    178, 249
Benoit (Wisconsin), 112

Berlin Blockade, 60
Bible, 27, 276; Old Testament, 267; *see
    also specific books*
"big box" retailing, 48, 72, 179
Billings, Frederick, 123–25, 127
Biltmore estate (Asheville, N.C.), 133
Biswell, Harold, 103
Blaine, Mark, 219
Boeing Aircraft, 55
Boise (Idaho), 186
Bonus March, 74
Boorstin, Daniel J., 202, 277
Boulder (Colorado), 14, 15, 22, 24, 166,
    231
Bourbons, 183
Bozeman Trail, 197, 211
Bragdon, General John S., 288*n12*
Britain, 199, 206, 208, 267, 271, 273,
    279, 302*n11*; in War of 1812, 30; in
    World War II, 32, 35–36
British Broadcasting Company (BBC), 7
Broadacre City concept, 71
Brookline (Massachusetts), 133
Brooklyn Rapid Transit Company, 143
Brooks, David, 179–80
Bruegmann, Robert, 191
Budget, Bureau of the, 54
Buffalo (New York), 72
Bulletin of the Atomic Scientists, 42, 43,
    48, 49, 52, 54, 69, 70, 73, 252
bundling, 245–46
Burby, Raymond, 247, 250
Burick, Richard, 96, 98, 292*n15*
Burnham, Daniel, 51
Burr, Aaron, 303*n19*
Bush, George H. W., 7
Bush, George W., 114–16
Butler, General Richard, 128, 130
Butz, Earl, 177, 178
Byzantine Empire, 161

Caddo Indians, 164
Cahokia–American Bottom region, 131
Calhoun, John C., 30
California, 20, 137, 206, 208, 228, 245,
    246, 306*n4*; Fair Access to Insurance
    Requirements (FAIR) Plan, 243, 256;
    floods in, 15; Hispanics in, 183;

Natural Hazard Disclosure Law
  (1998), 241–42; sequoias of, 141;
  State Insurance Commission, 243;
  wildfires in, 14, 232; wildland/urban
  interface (WUI) in, 243
California, University of, School of
  Forestry, 103
Calvin, John, 266
Camden (South Carolina), 214
Camp, Ann, 241
Canada, 113, 190, 191
Canton (Mississippi), 15
Card, Ira, 153
carpet bombing, 32, 35
Carson, Rachel, 249
Carter, Jimmy, 7, 43
Catholics, 267
Catskills, 113, 119, 161
cattle, 90–91, 121, 122, 166, 170, 184
Cedar Fire (2003), 233
Census Bureau, U.S., 21, 57, 163, 185,
  294n16
Central Intelligence Agency (CIA),
  Psychological Strategy Board, 46, 47
Central Motor Freight Association, 68
Cerro Grande Fire, 5, 7–8, 84, 93–107,
  219
Chaco Canyon, 262
Chancellorsville, Battle of, 140
Chance Vought aircraft works, 55
Chariot, Project, 10, 46
Charles, Project, 45–46, 252
Charles II, King of England, 279
Chase, Stewart, 248–50
Chavez, Dennis, 60
Checkoway, Barry, 70
Chen, Donald, 259–60
Cherokee Indians, 209, 302n13
Cherwell, Lord, see Lindemann,
  Frederick, 1st Viscount Cherwell
Cheyenne Indians, 197
Chicago, 51, 161–62, 166; dispersion of
  industrial production away from,
  252; Great Fire of 1871 in, 109, 110
Chicago, University of, 50
China, 60; immigrants from, 190
Chippewa National Forest, 146
Christianity, 270

Churchill, Winston, 35
Cincinnati (Ohio), 174, 187; dispersion
  of industrial production away from,
  252
Cincinnati, Order of the, 302n10
Citibank, 289n23
city planning, 34, 186; urban dispersal
  and, 49, 52, 57, 70
civil defense, 46, 57, 62
Civilian Conservation Corps (CCC), 166,
  171, 177, 218
Civil War, 132, 133, 136–37, 140, 145,
  155, 201
Clay, Lucius, 65, 67, 288n12
Clean Air Act, 269
Clean Water Act, 269
Clear Skies Initiative, 226
Cleveland, Grover, 148
Cleveland (Ohio), 72; dispersion of
  industrial production away from, 252
climate change, see global warming
Clinton, Bill, 7
Cloquet (Minnesota), 113, 218, 222
coal mining, 199, 201
Cohen, Jack, 220
Cold War, 37, 49, 92, 188, 248, 255;
  agricultural policy of, 177–78;
  dispersion policy of, see urban
  dispersion; prestige of science
  during, 5–6
Colorado, 15, 23, 131, 174, 232, 236–38;
  Front Range of, 13, 22, 215–16, 231,
  238; hazard planning in, 251;
  Indians in, 182; migration to, 164;
  Ogallala Aquifer under, 174, 175;
  population growth in, 22; wheat
  production in, 177–78; wildfires in,
  see Hayman Fire; South Canyon Fire;
  wildland/urban interface (WUI) in,
  230; see also Four Corners
Colorado, University of, 216
Colorado Cattlemen's Association, 178
Colorado Springs, 215–16
Columbian Exposition (1893), 51
Columbia University, 46
Columbus, Christopher, 301n10
"Communities at Risk," 227; data
  banks of, 228–29

Commerce, U.S. Department of, 55
common law, 216
commons, 184, 218; grazing, 209
community forestry, 126, 171, 236
Comstock (Wisconsin), 112
Concord (Massachusetts), 128, 130
Confederate States of America, 151
Congested Areas Urgency Committee, 61
Congestion Mitigation and Air Quality
    Program (CMAQ), 73
Congress, U.S., 4, 79, 81, 83, 84, 107,
    139, 221, 226, 239, 250; Cerro
    Grande Fire investigated by, 98; farm
    subsidies and, 169, 178, 210; forest
    reserves approved by, 146; Founders
    and, 202, 204, 209; lobbying in, 28,
    147, 148; National Parks created by,
    124, 137, 295n5; places of national
    significance designated by, 224;
    public lands and, 125, 149, 206,
    217–18; thermonuclear research
    laboratories established by, 50;
    urban dispersion programs funded
    by, 64, 66, 68, 71, 74, 287n12,
    290n25
Connecticut, 161; colonial, 267,
    279–81; relocation of industrial
    production out of, 55; wildland/
    urban interface (WUI) in, 230
Constitution, U.S., 205
Continental Congress, 280
controlled burns, 5, 308n10; by
    Indians, 90, 91, 173, 273; see also
    prescriptive burning
Cooke, Jay, 123, 124
Coolidge, Calvin, 165
Cornell University, 46
Coronado, Francisco de, 182
Coronado National Forest, 114–15
"corridopolis" areas, 188
Cortéz, Hernán, 300n6, 302n12
cost-benefit analysis, 211–12
Couch, Virgil L., 46
Countryside Financial Services, 289n23
Coventry, bombing of, 35, 36
Cowan, George, 89–90
Cowles Commission for Research in
    Economics, 50–51

Craig, Larry, 81, 82, 217–18, 223
Crawford, Thomas, 136
Crazy Horse, 211
Creative Act (1891), 148–49
Creek Indians, 209
Cromwell, Oliver, 279
Crooked Ryan Gulch Fire (2000), 222
crop insurance, federal, 172, 176, 178
Crosby, Albert, 263, 308n2
Cuban Missile Crisis, 92
Custer, General George Armstrong, 211

Dakotas, see North Dakota; South
    Dakota
Dakota Sioux, 129
Dallas (Texas), 185
dam building, 173, 174, 195
Dartmouth College, 120, 266
Davis, Edwin H., 128
Davis, Jefferson, 151
Death and Life of Great American
    Cities, The (Jacobs), 74
De Bow, James, 135
deBuys, William, 308n10
Deerfield (Massachusetts), 273
Defense Department, U.S., 56–57, 229
Defense Mobilization, Office of, 48, 52
Delaware, 122
Democratic Party, 59–60, 64, 74, 79
demographic analysis, 57
Denver, 24, 166, 215
Deschutes National Forest, 38
Desert Land Act (1877), 145, 158
Detroit, 187, 206
De Voto, Bernard, 176
Discourse on the Aborigines of the Valley
    of the Ohio (Harrison), 127
Discovery Channel, 7
dispersion-industrial complex, 6,
    11–12, 34, 58, 69–70, 173, 195–96,
    206, 252; fire-industrial complex
    and, 83, 221; highway subsidies and,
    61, 66, 67; lobbying by, 12; see also
    urban dispersion
Doctor Huguet (Donnelley), 146
Dombeck, Mike, 85, 184
Dome Fire, 4
Domenici, Pete, 94–95, 97, 99

Donahue, Brian, 126, 280
Donnelley, Ignatius, 119, 146–48, 297*n10*
Dresden, firebombing of, 32, 33, 36
droughts, 161–62, 164–66, 169, 172, 176, 177
Dun and Bradstreet, 280
du Pont de Nemours family, 122
dust, 87, 138, 153, 159–72, 178, 180, 210, 222, 248–49; water resources and, 174, 176, 177
Dutch colonies, 302*n11*

earthworks, 128–29
East River, Project, 46, 48
Ecclesiastes, book of, 269, 270
Ecological Imperialism (Pyne), 263
Economic Cooperation Administration, 57
Economist, The, 80
ECO-Northwest, 81
ecosystems, fuel types in, 231–32
education, provision of public lands for, 199, 200
Edwards, Jonathan, 16, 47, 58, 133, 180, 265–68, 270–77, 279–81, 308*n4*; Marsh influenced by, 120–21, 125, 132, 265, 266
Eglin Air Force Base, 208
Einstein, Albert, 8
Eisenhower, Dwight D., 7, 35, 54, 56, 60, 168; farm policy of, 171–74, 176–77; highway construction program of, 62, 64–67, 71, 72*n*, 288*nn12, 16*, 290*n25*; military career of, 31, 62–64
Eisenhower Library, 46
Emancipation Proclamation (1863), 136
Emerson, Ralph Waldo, 128, 130
Endangered Species Act (1973), 107–108, 154, 269
Enfield (Massachusetts), 273
environmental activists, scapegoating of, 107–108, 116
Environmental Impact Statements, 47
Environmental Protection Agency (EPA), 139
Erie Canal, 153–54

erosion, 152–53, 178; lumbering and, 152; overgrazing and, 122; plantation system and, 135; of watersheds, 150; wind, *see* dust
Estes Park (Colorado), 231
Ethnohistory, 131
Evans, Walker, 169
Exodus, book of, 267
exotics, invasive, 263
Ezekial, book of, 27, 264, 269–70

Fallen Timbers, Battle of, 212
Farm Bill (1985), 171, 178
Farmer, Silas, 154
Farmers Home Administration (FmHA), 75–76, 255–56
Farmers Union, 172
farming, *see* agriculture
Federal Bureau of Investigation (FBI), 262
Federal Civil Defense Administration, 46
Federal Emergency Management Agency (FEMA), 104, 303*n1*
Federal Highway Act (1956), 64, 66–68, 71
Federal Highway Administration, 287*n12*, 288*n16*
Federal Home Loan Mortgage Corporation (FHLMC; Freddie Mac), 75, 289*n23*, 290*n25*
Federal Housing Administration (FHA), 53, 56, 73, 253, 289*n24*, 290*n25*
Federalist Papers, 202
Federal National Mortgage Association (FNMA; Fannie Mae), 75, 245, 255, 289*n23*, 290*n25*
Federal Register, 226–27
Federal Reserve Board, 60
Federal Wildland Fire Policy (1995), 79, 95
Ferdinand V, King of Castile, 301*n10*
Fire Administration, U.S., 303*n1*
firebombing, 30–37, 43, 92
firebreaks: highways as, 35, 56; in Los Alamos, 4; slum clearance and, 54
firewise measures, 5, 214–17, 239, 256, 245

fire load, 23, 91, 93, 99, 156, 230;
global warming and, 18;
identification of, 228; lumbering
and, 4, 87, 106–107, 218–20;
reduction of, 5, 83, 90, 92, 97, 115,
147, 214–17, 219, 222, 223, 229, 238
(*see also* prescriptive burning)
fire protection districts, 144; *see also*
flame zones
Fire Sciences Laboratory, 220
fire suppression, 83, 91, 93, 94, 219,
238; costs of, 103, 217, 220, 221;
Pinchot's strategy of, 88–89, 165,
235–36
First Transcontinental Motor Convoy,
62
Fish and Wildlife Service, U.S., 224,
303*n1*
Fisher, Carl, 48–49, 56
Flagstaff (Arizona), 113, 186
flame zones, 73, 84, 144, 172, 180, 190,
191, 251; atlas of, 223–34, 239, 247,
250, 257; costs of rebuilding in, 241,
255; development in, 103, 254–57;
migration into, 19, 22–24, 34, 68,
155, 163, 196, 236–39, 243;
reservation of, 208, 210, 212
flood zones, 13–15, 73, 174, 180, 210,
222, 255; erosion in, 152–53;
migration into, 19, 69, 196, 247, 249
Florida, 20, 184, 208, 230; colonial,
267; hazard planning in, 251, 252;
Hispanics in, 183; prescribed
burning in, 216
Folsom, William H. C., 144, 151
Ford, Gerald, 139
Ford Foundation, 42, 45, 81
Forest Crop Law (Wisconsin, 1927),
143–44
Forest Magazine, 219
Forest Reserve Act (1891), 148
Forest Service, U.S., 184, 215–16, 221,
223, 225, 226, 251, 303*n1*;
environmentalist lawsuits against
lumbering on land of, 107, 108; fire
suppression policy of, 88–89, 91;
founding of, 149, 165; Los Alamos
and, 3–5, 93, 95, 96, 98, 101, 292*n15*;
nuclear weapons program funding
of, 92; on lumbering and increase in
fire risk and severity, 106–107, 116,
119, 146–47, 220; outsourcing
thinning proposed for, 115; Rocky
Mountain Research Station of, 305*n6*;
and South Canyon Fire, 84, 85; State
and Private Forestry Division of,
305*n5*; *see also specific national forests*
Forest Stewards Guild, 115, 222
Forest Trust, 115, 222
forestry, sustainable, 116, 124, 126–27,
143–44, 150, 171, 236, 264
Founding Fathers, 269, 278; Indians
and, 209, 212; public land policy of,
198–205, 207; *see also* Jefferson,
Thomas; Washington, George
Four Corners region, 131, 182
France, 60, 70, 191, 206, 212, 273,
302*n11*; urban dispersion in, 71;
watershed protection in, 127; in
World War I, 59; in World War II, 64
Francis of Assisi, Saint, 276–77
Franconia (Minnesota), 151–52
Franklin, Benjamin, 180, 279, 302*n13*
Frey, William, 185, 190–91
From Conquest to Conservation
(Dombeck, Wood, and Williams),
184
Futurama exhibit, 70
futurists, 70–71

Galena (Illinois), 153
Gallatin, Albert, 119, 127-28, 130–33,
139, 200–201, 265–66
Galvin, Denis, 100–101
Garibaldi, Giuseppe, 138, 140
Geddes, Peter, 221
General Accounting Office (GAO), 95,
97, 98, 100, 221, 226; *see also*
Government Accountability Office
General Land Office, 156
General Motors, 70
Genesis, book of, 267–69
Genêt, Edmond-Charles-Édouard, 212
Geographic Names Information System,
227
geographical engineering, 51

George III, King of England, 189, 199, 208

Georgia, 20, 134–35, 165, 205, 206; colonial, 207, 267; fire risk in, 227, 230; hazard planning in, 251; prescribed burning in, 216

Germany, 35, 36, 40; atomic bomb research in, 39; autobahn in, 31, 63–64, 288n16; bombing of cities in, 32–33, 36, 42; immigrants from, 139, 140, 151–54, 189; revolution of 1848 in, 139–40, 151; silviculture in, 126–27

Gettysburg, Battle of, 140; cemetery on site of, 224

GI Bill of Rights, 53, 73, 74, 253, 290n25

GIS (geographic information system), 228, 234

Glacier National Park, 124, 231

Glenwood Springs (Colorado), 79, 86

Glickman, Dan, 79, 84

globalization, 190

Global Positioning Systems (GPS), 233, 234

global warming, 15, 18, 19, 23, 80, 103, 230, 248, 249

Goodrich, George, 145

Gorrie, Jack, 61

Government Accountability Office (GAO), 220, 226, 292n15; see also General Accounting Office

Government National Mortgage Association (GNMA; Ginnie Mae), 75, 245, 255, 289n23

Grand Canyon, 124, 155; fire on north rim of, 100–101

Grant, Ulysses S., 136

Grantsburg (Wisconsin), 109

Grapes of Wrath, The (Steinbeck), 166, 169

Gray, Gordon, 46, 47

grazing, 158, 238; excessive, see overgrazing; restrictions on, 156, 209–10

Great American Desert, 164, 174, 178

Great Chicago Fire, 109, 110

Great Colorado and the Semi-Civilization of New Mexico, The (Gallatin), 127

Great Depression, 20, 60, 74

Great Fires of 1803–1804, 121, 124

Great Northern Railroad, 124

Great Peshtigo Fire, 109–11

Great Plains, droughts in, 169, 172; see also dust

Great Plains Agricultural Council, 172

Great Smoky Mountains National Park, 224

Greeks, ancient, 132

Green Mountain National Forest, 150

Gruen, Victor, 48

Guernica (Spain), 35

Guide to Historic America (Kennedy), 7

Hague Convention, 35

Hamburg, bombing of, 36

Hamilton, Alexander, 201, 202, 301nn3, 5

Hampton, Wade, II, 151

Hanford National Laboratory, 3, 9–10, 283n3

Hapsburgs, 183

Hardy, Porter, Jr., 55, 69

Harrison, Benjamin, 148

Harrison, William Henry, 127–30

Harvard University, 10, 45, 46, 61

Harvey Girls, 124

Hastings (Minnesota), 152

Hayes, Rutherford B., 140, 141, 148, 209

Hayman Fire (2004), 215–16, 218, 219, 237–38, 240

hazard planning, 241–42, 247, 250–52

Healthy Forests and Communities Corps (HFCC), proposal for, 217, 235

Healthy Forests initiative (2002), 80, 114, 226, 235

Hearst newspapers, 64

Helms, Douglas, 169, 178

Highlands Ranch (Colorado), 75

highways, 13, 32–33, 44, 188, 238; development of roadside culture along, 48–49, 196; intra-urban, as firebreaks, 35, 56; military use of, 31, 35, 62–65, 288n16; subsidies for, 14, 29, 33, 52–53, 59–62, 64–73, 155, 179, 185, 195, 200, 254, 256

Highway Trust Fund, 71
Himmler, Heinrich, 36
Hinckley (Minnesota), 111, 112, 145, 222
Hiroshima, atomic bombing of, 37, 40, 41, 43, 51
Hispanics, 3, 158, 181–85, 300n6
Hitler, Adolf, 35, 36
Homestead Act (1862), 145, 148, 158, 203, 205
homesteading, 141, 143, 144, 147, 149, 236; on arid lands, 164; scattered, 184
Homeward Bound (May), 42
Hooker, Thomas, 267
Hoover, Herbert, 74, 173
Hoover Dam, 173, 174
Hopi Indians, 157
House of Representatives, U.S., 55, 156, 295n5
housing: good growth policies for, 258–59; subsidized, 68, 253 (see also mortgages, federally insured)
Housing Act (1949), 61
Housing and Home Finance Agency, 61
Housing and Urban Development (HUD), U.S. Department of, 290n24
Houston, Sam, 302n13
Houston (Texas), 15; Hispanics in, 185
Huguenots, 267
Hull, Jane, 106, 107, 115
Humphrey, Hubert, 139
hurricanes, 13, 19, 210, 252
husbandry, 121–22, 126, 132, 149, 236; forest, 126, 171
hydrogen bomb, 9, 49–50, 60

Ickes, Harold, 139
Idaho, 231–32; hazard planning in, 251; population growth in, 22; wildfires in, 222; wildland/urban interface (WUI) in, 230
Illinois, 162; migration to, 153, 154
Illinois, University of, 70
immigrants, 189–90; German, 139, 140, 151–54, 189; Hispanic, 182–85
imperialism, 266
income tax shelters, 179

Independence Hall, 224
Independent Review Board, 99
Indiana, 154, 158, 183
Indian Affairs, Bureau of, 303n1
Indianapolis, 48, 76
Indian Linguistic Families of America North of Mexico (Gallatin), 128
Indians, 126, 130–32, 153, 181–85, 207–209, 302nn12, 13; architecture of, 120, 127–30; controlled burns used by, 90, 91, 173, 273; Edwards and, 265–67, 270–76, 279–81; opening to settlement of lands of, 154, 155, 186, 187, 198, 202, 204, 210–12; puebloan, 90, 157, 158, 181–82, 184; wildfires blamed on, 156; see also specific tribes
Indian Vocabulary (Butler), 128
industrial production; dispersion of, 42, 55–56, 61, 252, 253; public land policies and, 200
insurance, 239–40, 249; crop, 172, 176, 178; fire, 15, 240–41, 243–47; flood, 13, 15, 247; mortgage, 13, 14, 18, 29, 69, 73–75, 155, 179, 185, 195, 239, 253
Interagency Fire Investigation Team, 95–96
intercontinental ballistic missiles, 60
Intergovernmental Relations, Commission on, 48
Interior, U.S. Department of, 79, 103, 107, 147, 224, 226
Intermodal Surface Transportation Efficiency Act (ISTEA, 1991), 72–73
Internal Revenue Service (IRS), 239
International Association of Fire Chiefs, 303n1
Interstate (Rose), 67
Interstate Highway System, 64, 66–67, 71, 256, 288nn12, 16
invasive exotic organisms, 263
Iowa, 23, 158, 184; population growth in, 22
Ireland, 262, 276
Iroquois, 279–81
irrigation, 175, 176
Isabella I, Queen of Castile, 301n10

ISO, 228, 232; FireLine, 233
Italy, 35, 40, 138, 140

Jackson, Andrew, 184
Jacobs, Jane, 74
James II, King of England (previously Duke of York), 302*n11*
Japan, 35; atomic bombing of, 9, 17, 32, 37, 40–42, 92
Jefferson, Thomas, 79, 122, 183, 202, 277–78, 301*nn3, 5*, 303*n19*; Gallatin and, 127, 139, 200–201; interest in Indians of, 129–31; restrictions on land use supported by, 203, 269
Jersey City (New Jersey), 161
Jews, 267
Jim Crow segregation, 165
Jodl, General Alfred, 40
Johns Hopkins University, 46
Johnson, Lyndon B., 68, 84
Joint Fire Science Program (1998), 80
JPMorgan Chase, 289*n23*

Kansas, 162, 165; migration to, 164; Ogallala Aquifer under, 174; population growth in, 22
Katrina, Hurricane, 13–15
Kaysen, Carl, 45, 49
Keillor, Garrison, 179
Kennedy, John F., 9, 127
Kentucky, 153, 161, 198, 204, 212
Kinkel, Gottfried, 139–40
Klein, Lawrence R., 42–43, 45, 46, 49–51, 53, 64, 252, 285*n8*
Korean War, 60
Kyl, John, 106, 107, 115

labor systems, land use and, 154, 197
La Follette, Philip, 171
La Follette, Robert M., 138, 139, 142–44, 150, 171, 294*n16*
La Mesa Fire, 4
Land and Water Conservation Fund, 199, 254
land grants: for higher education, 200; to railroads, 124, 164, 187; Spanish and Mexican, 184

Land Management, Bureau of, 85, 224, 229, 251, 303*n1*
LandScan data, 57
Land Use and Society (Platt), 239
Land Use Policy in the United States (Ottoson), 198
Lange, Dorothea, 169, 249
Lapp, Ralph, 54–56
Las Vegas, 95
Lawrence, Ernest Orlando, 57
Lawrence Livermore Laboratory, 45–46, 50, 57
Le Corbusier, 71
Lemmon, Mount, 114–15
Lewiston Morning Tribune, 107
Lexington (Kentucky), 187
lightning, 23, 88, 122, 156, 158, 239; drought and, 161
Lincoln, Abraham, 133, 138–40, 180, 278; on "cultivation" versus "locomotion," 27, 125, 163, 217; Mexican War opposed by, 266; land policies of, 136–37, 205
Lincoln Highway Association, 49, 56
Lindemann, Frederick, 1st Viscount Cherwell, 35–36
Little Crow, 129
Livermore, Shaw, 57–58, 272, 280–81
Livermore Laboratory, *see* Lawrence Livermore Laboratory
livestock, overgrazing by, *see* overgrazing
Livingston, Goodhue, Jr., 56
Livingston family, 302*n11*
lobbying, 12, 13, 142, 174, 218; by lumber industry, 221; by railroads, 12; by urban dispersion interests, 12, 28, 66, 196
logging, *see* lumbering
London: bombing of, 35, 36; Great Fire of, 255
Long, Stephen, 155, 164, 174, 178
"Long March" of Navaho Indians, 211
Los Alamos National Laboratory, 3–4, 9–11, 62, 88–89, 91, 92, 206; development of nuclear weapons at, 3, 10, 39–40, 49; fires threatening, 4–5, 7, 18, 84, 89–90, 93–105, 216

Los Angeles, 24, 219; decentralization of, 44, 45; Hispanics in, 185
Lost World of Thomas Jefferson, The (Boorstin), 202
Louisiana, 154; slaves in, 135
Louisiana Purchase Agreement, 197
Lowdermilk, Walter C., 170
Luftwaffe, 35
lumbering, 105, 108, 143, 144–45, 151, 190, 230–32, 235; acres of private timberland, 304n1; of giant sequoias, 141; Healthy Forests Initiative and, 80; husbandry in, 126; illicit, of state lands, 145–47; lawsuits to prevent, 107–108; nineteenth-century migration and, 151–53, 155; subsidies for, 115–16, 221, 236; wildfires fueled by debris from, 4, 87, 106–107, 109–13, 116, 119, 122, 145–46, 155, 218–22
Lydius, John Henry, 281

Mackay, James, 85
Madison, James, 30, 127, 202
Maine, 155; Indians of, 132; wildfires in, 109, 112, 113, 161, 174
malls, see shopping centers
Malpais lava beds, 23
Malta, 262
Mandans, 164
Manhattan Project, 8–10, 39–41, 46, 93, 283n3
Man and Nature (Marsh), 123, 126, 136
Manora (New York), 112
Marengo (Wisconsin), 112
Mariposa Grove, sequoias of, 133, 136, 137, 141, 231
Marnach, Nicholas, 153
Marne, Battle of the, 59
Marsh, George Perkins, 119–20, 133, 134, 142, 157; appointed ambassador to Italy, 138–40; childhood fire experience of, 122–23; death of, 158; Edwards's influence on, 120–21, 125, 132, 265, 266; husbandry and, 125–27, 170; Indian use of fire studied by, 127–28, 130–32;

Mexican War opposed by, 149, 266; reforestation encouraged by, 124, 143
Marsh-Billings-Rockefeller Mansion and National Park, 121, 123, 124, 134
Marshak, Jacob, 42, 43, 45, 46, 50–51, 53, 252, 285n8
Marshall, John, 303n19
Marshall Plan, 272
Maryland, 256; colonial, 267; hazard planning in, 251; Priority Funding Areas in, 258
Mason (Wisconsin), 112
Massachusetts, 23, 128, 198, 133; colonial, 265–77; population growth in, 22; watershed protection in, 150; wildfires in, 112, 130; wildland/urban interface (WUI) in, 230
Massachusetts, University of, at Amherst, 239
Massachusetts Institute of Technology (MIT), 45, 46
Mather, Stephen, 264
Maui, 23
May, Elaine Tyler, 42
McCarthy, Eugene, 7
McCarthy, Joseph R., 168
McGee, John, 114–15
McGillivray, Alexander, 209
McKellar, Kenneth, 61–62
McKinley, William, 142
Meinig, Donald, 187
Memphis (Tennessee), 62
merino mania, 122
Merriam, Robert E., 54
Mexico, 182–84, 300n6; war with, 149, 266
Miami (Florida), 185
Michaux, André, 212
Michigan, 154; wildfires in, 109, 111, 122, 139, 162
Michigan, University of, 58
migration, 13, 20, 137, 138, 145, 197, 199–200, 250, 278; changing patterns of, 190–91; of early humans, 160; into flame zones, 19, 22–24, 228, 230, 236–39, 243; into

flood zones, 19, 69, 196, 247, 249; group, 187; of Hispanics, 182–85; land grants and, 124, 125; management of, 257–60; pre-Columbian, 157; seeding for, 206–208; slave-based economy and, 134, 203–205; to upper Midwest, 151–55; weather and, 163–68; *see also* settlement; urban dispersion
military-industrial complex, 67, 173–74
Milwaukee Railway, 113
Milwaukee Sentinel, 142
mining, 149, 201, 211, 238; on public lands, 199
Minnesota, 145–46, 150–55, 171, 174, 221; German immigrants in, 139, 151–54, 189; Indian reservations in, 209; lumbering in, 145, 151–52; Thoreau in, 128–29; wildfires in, 109, 111–12, 129, 138, 139, 141, 162
Mission Creek (Minnesota), 112
Mississippi, 62, 68, 165; slaves in, 135
Missouri, 62; road construction in, 59
"mitigation" of natural disasters, 233, 247, 249–50; *see also* fire load, reduction of
Mogollon Rim, 105–106, 114, 115, 122, 238
Mohawk Indians, 281
Mohican Indians, 273, 280
Monson, Donald and Astrid, 52–54, 56, 252
Montana, 22, 221, 306n4; goldfields of, 211; railroads in, 124; wheat production in, 177; wildfires in, 222
Moose Lake (Minnesota), 113
Mora (New Mexico), 236
Moravians, 267
Mormons, 181, 186
Morrill Act, 133, 148, 200, 205
mortgages, federally insured, 13, 14, 18, 29, 69, 73–75, 155, 179, 185, 195, 239, 253, 255–56
Mount Rainier National Park, 295n5
Muir, John, 264
Muller, Brian, 216

Munich Reinsurance Company, 246
Muslims, 267
Must We Hide (Lapp), 54
Myles Standish State Forest (Massachusetts), 230

Nadasdy, Paul, 131
Nagasaki, atomic bombing of, 37, 40–41, 43, 51
Nanking, Japanese assault on, 35
National Academy of Sciences, 149
National Association of Foresters, 216
National Association of State Fire Marshals, 303n1
National Association of State Foresters, 303n1
National Broadcasting Company (NBC), 7
National Civil Service Reform League, 149
National Emergency Management Association, 303n1
National Fire Center, 21
National Fire Plan (2000), 80
National Fire Protection Association, 41, 303n1
National Forestry Commission, 149
National Geographic Society, 140–41
National Interagency Fire Center, 222
National Mortgage Association, 290n25
National Municipal League, 47
National Museum of American History, 7
National Park Service, 84, 115, 123, 133–34, 141, 220, 223, 224, 264, 303n1; fire suppression practices of, 91; prescriptive fires set by, 3, 92–94, 100, 102, 103; scapegoating for Cerro Grande Fire of, 7, 8, 94–96, 99–100, 292n15; and wildcatting timber from public lands, 145
National Security Council, 32, 55
National Security Resources Board (NSRB), 46, 52, 61
National System of Interstate and Defense Highways, *see* Interstate Highway System

National Transportation Safety Board, 82

National Weather Service, 95

National Wildfire Coordinating Group, 303*n1*

National Wildlife/Urban Interface Fire Program, 214

Native Americans, *see* Indians

Natural Resources Conservation Service, 169; *see also* Soil Erosion Service

nature blindness, 5–6

Navaho Indians, 211, 212, 303*n16*

Nebraska, 162, 165, 169, 185, 201, 211; migration to, 164; Ogallala Aquifer under, 174; population growth in, 22; roads in, 62–63

"Negro problem," 29, 54

Neutrality Act (1795), 213, 303*n19*

Nevada, 14, 20, 236–37; hazard planning in, 251; population growth in, 22, 236

New Deal, 74, 166, 173, 218, 235; agriculture and forestry policies of, 171, 178; highway construction and, 60, 61; housing construction and, 60, 289*n24*, 290*n25*; soil conservation measures of, 138

New England, 23, 125, 181, 189, 198, 280; colonial, 58, 121, 267–68, 270, 271; lumbering in, 151–52; merino mania in, 122; migration from, 153–54; relocation of industrial production out of, 55; sustainable husbandry in, 126; warming in, 230; watershed protection in, 150; wildfires in, 113, 119

New Grange (Ireland), 262

New Jersey, 112–13, 161, 256

New Mexico, 14, 20, 23, 104, 131, 236, 294*n16*; community forestry in, 126; Dust Bowl and, 138; Hispanics in, 3, 183–85; Indians in, 181, 182; population growth in, 22, 306*n4*; wildfires in, 104, 161 (*see also* Cerro Grande Fire); *see also* Four Corners

New Mexico, University of, at Las Cruces, 255–56, 306*n4*

New Orleans, 15, 206

New Urbanism, 181, 190

New York City, 10, 67–68, 161; Central Park, 133; Hispanics in, 185

New York State, 153–54; colonial, 206, 279; wildfires in, 112, 113, 160, 161

New York Stock Exchange, 290*n25*

New York Times, 142, 220

New York World's Fair (1939), 70

Nixon, Richard M., 7, 139, 177

Nobel Prize, 42, 45, 57

Norlag, William, 68

Norse explorers, 263

North Carolina, 133; colonial, 267; hazard planning in, 251

North Carolina, University of, 46, 247

North Dakota, 165; Indian reservations in, 211; migration to, 164

Northampton (Massachusetts), 265, 274

"nuisance," doctrine of, 216

Northern Pacific Railroad, 123–24, 143, 295*n5*

Northwest Forest Plan, 80

Northwest Ordinance, 134, 153, 154, 184, 187, 197, 200, 203–207, 302*n11*

Norton, Gale, 102–103, 107–108

nuclear weapons, 33, 42, 47, 50, 52, 57, 64, 67, 92; detonation of, at Hiroshima and Nagasaki, 37, 40, 41, 43, 51; development of, 8–9, 39–40, 62; Soviet, 37, 43, 49–50, 60

Oakland/Berkeley Tunnel Fire, 14

Oakland Hills Fire (1991), 242

Oak Ridge National Laboratory, 3, 9–10, 57, 61–62, 283*n3*

Ogallala Aquifer, 174–75, 177

Oglethorpe, General James, 207

Ogunquit (Maine), 112

Ohio, 153, 185, 204, 207, 280

oil industry, 72

Oklahoma, 162, 169; Ogallala Aquifer under, 174

Oliver, Chad, 236

Olmsted, Frederick Law, 119, 132–37

Omaha Railroad, 143

O'Mahoney, Joseph, 55, 69

Oppenheimer, J. Robert, 8, 39, 40, 46, 50
Oregon, 306n4; hazard planning in, 251; wildfire danger in, 38
Orion Project, 51
Ottoson, Howard W., 198
outsourcing, 80–82; to lumber companies, 115
overgrazing, 90–91, 105, 121–23, 166, 169, 170, 171; prevention of, 149

Pajarito Plateau, 88, 182, 206, 238; ecology of, 90–91; wildfires on, 90, 122 (see also Cerro Grande Fire)
Panic of 1837, 174
Panic of 1873, 123
Paradise Fire (2003), 233
Partridge, Oliver, 280
Partridge (Minnesota), 112
Paxton Boys, 302n13
Pearl Harbor (Hawaii), 224
Pendleton, Edmund, 202
Pennsylvania, 187, 198, 302n13; colonial, 267, 279–81
Pennsylvania, University of, 46; Wharton School, 42, 43
Pensacola (Florida), 187
Pernin, Peter, 109
Peshtigo (Wisconsin), 109–11, 218
Phillips (Wisconsin), 112
Phipps, W. H., 295n5
Phoenix (Arizona), 185; Hispanics in, 185
Picasso, Pablo, 35
Piedmont area, 23
Pike, Zebulon, 155, 164, 174
Pilgrims, 189
Pilsen, bombing of, 39
Pinchot, Gifford, 88–89, 165, 235–36
Pittsburgh, 72; Treaty of, 209
Planners Journal, 249
plantation system, 133–35, 165, 203, 204
Plato, 262
Platt, Rutherford, 239–40
Plow That Broke the Plains, The (documentary film), 169
Plymouth (Massachusetts), 112, 230, 275
Pokegama (Minnesota), 111, 112

Poland, 36, 64
Polk, James K., 149
pooling of risk, 245, 246
Populism, 146, 165
Powell, John Wesley, 119, 128, 155–58, 160, 173, 174, 176, 181, 184, 308n10
precious metals, mining of, 199, 201, 211
Prentiss, General Augustin M., 54–55
prescriptive burning, 81, 91–92, 95, 106, 215–16, 218, 238; breakouts of, 89, 93–94, 98–101
Prest-O-Lite headlight company, 48
Production Management, Office of, Plant Site Board, 54
Profiles in Courage (Kennedy), 127
progressivism, 47, 138–40, 146, 150, 165, 170–71
Protestantism, evangelical, 132
Psalms, 276, 277
Public Broadcasting Service (PBS), 7
public health, 200, 209
Public Housing Act (1934), 74, 75
Public Housing Administration, 290n25
Public Land Ordinances (1785 and 1796), 199–200, 301nn1, 3
Public Roads, Bureau of, 66, 71
public works programs, 60
public-private partnerships, 124
Pueblo Revolt, 3
pueblos, 90, 157, 158, 181–82, 184
Pulitzer Prize, 127
Puritans, 269
Pyne, Stephen, 80–82, 93, 112–13, 161, 191, 215, 219–20, 235, 263

Quakers, 267, 279

Rabinowitch, Eugene, 52
Radeloff, Volker, 229, 232, 239, 243, 305n5
Raichle, William, 228
railroads, 90, 123–24, 143, 165; land grants to, 124, 164, 187; lumbering and, 109; markets extended by, 122; national parks and, 124, 126; suburban, 188

Rainier, Mount, 124
ranchettes, 184
ranching, *see* agriculture
Reagan, Ronald, 7, 9
Reconstruction Finance Corporation
    (RFC), 53, 253, 290*n*25
redlining, 233–34
reforestation, 124, 138, 143–44, 146, 155
reinsurance, 245–46, 249
Reisner, Marc, 175
Reno, 24
Republican Party, 7, 59, 64, 74, 79, 81,
    171–73; Liberals in, 140, 148
reservation policies, 208–13
Resources of the South (De Bow), 135
Revolutionary War, 128, 134, 139, 201,
    204, 209
Rhode Island, colonial, 267, 279
ribbon cities, 44, 45
Ribe, Thomas, 93–94, 293*n18*
Rich Land, Poor Land (White), 249
ridgetop-to-ridgetop burning, 218
risk assessment, 249–50
Rita, Hurricane, 13
Road Gang, 67, 68, 76
roads, *see* highways
Robbins, Jim, 220
Rochester, University of, 46
Rockefeller family, 121, 123–25, 134
Rocky Mountain National Park, 231
Rocky Mountains, 113, 221
Rodeo-Chediski Fire, 105–108, 219
Rogers, George, 10
Rogers, Walter, 61, 69
Romanov dynasty, 206
Romans, ancient, 206, 301*n10*
Romer, Roy, 85
Romero, John, 96, 98, 101, 292*n15*
Roosevelt, Franklin D., 8, 9, 60, 61,
    249
Roosevelt, Theodore, 88, 142, 149, 274
Rose, Mark, 67
Rothermel model of fire behavior, 92,
    93
Rotterdam, bombing of, 35
Rousseau, Jean-Jacques, 132, 266
Rural Special Improvement District
    (RSID) bonds, 256, 290*n26*

Russia, 143, 206; communist, *see* Soviet
    Union; immigrants from, 190
Russian Revolution, 35
Rust Belt, 21, 252

St. Louis (Missouri), 187, 206
St. Paul (Minnesota), 173, 187
Salt Lake City, 186
Salt Lake Tribune, 81, 82, 217
Samuelson, Paul, 45, 49
San Diego, 219
Sandstone (Minnesota), 111, 112
San Fernando earthquake (1971), 241
Sangre de Cristo Mountains (New
    Mexico), 161
Santa Fe National Forest, 92, 93, 97
Santa Fe New Mexican, 96, 99
Santa Fe (New Mexico), 14, 15, 24, 113,
    236
Santa Fe Railroad, 124
Santa Fe River watershed, 23
Santee Sioux, 129
satellite imaging, 228, 229, 232, 233
scapegoating, 7–8, 114, 164; for Cerro
    Grande Fire, 7, 94–103; of Indians,
    156; for Rodeo-Chediski Fire, 106–108,
    116; for South Canyon Fire, 85–86
Schenck, William, 99–103, 293*n18*
Schlesinger, James, 10
Schrechlichkeit, 35
Schurz, Carl, 113, 119, 125, 138–41,
    144, 156, 158, 209, 221; civil service
    reforms of, 148, 149; in German
    revolution of 1848, 139–40;
    immigration to America of, 140, 151,
    154; progressivism of, 150, 170;
    wildcat lumbering prosecuted by,
    145, 147
Scott, Donald, 264
Seattle (Washington), 55
seeding policy, 206–208
Seminole Indians, 208, 212, 303*n17*
Senate, U.S., 68, 99, 140, 142, 169;
    Appropriations Committee, 61;
    Armed Services Committee, 55;
    Public Lands Committee, 170, 295*n5*;
    Public Works Committee, 60
sequoias, 133, 136, 137, 141

settlement, 154, 155, 161, 202–204;
    expanding limits of, 159; hostility of
    Indians to, 186, 187, 198, 210–12;
    restrictions on, 156–57, 200, 206,
    208–13; scattering to isolated
    farmsteads of, 184; *see also* migration
Seven Cities of Cibola, 182
Shawnee Indians, 161
sheep, 90, 91, 121, 124, 149, 184;
    merino, 122
Sheridan, General Philip, 141
Sherman, General William Tecumseh,
    136
Shiloh, Battle of, 155
shopping centers, development of, 48,
    49
Shoshone National Forest, 148
Sicilians, ancient, 132
Sierra Nevada Project, 221
Silent Spring (Carson), 249
silviculture, 126–27
Sioux Indians, 129, 197, 210–12
Skelmorlie, Robert Montgomery, Laird
    of, 207
Skoda armament works, 39
slash-and-burn agriculture, 135
slavery, 133–37, 153, 154, 197, 199, 201,
    203–205
slum clearance, 44, 45, 47, 48, 53, 54,
    66, 68, 73, 253, 255
Small Business Administration (SBA),
    254
smart growth, 186, 257–60
Smart Growth America, 259
Smith, Al, 139
Smith, Joseph, 186
Smithsonian Institution, 7
Smokey the Bear, 89, 91
Social Compact theorists, 269
soil conservation, 138
Soil Erosion Service, 166, 169–72, 177,
    178, 249
South, antebellum, 133–36, 153, 154,
    199, 201, 204
South Canyon Fire, 79, 84–86, 102, 105,
    237, 251
South Carolina, 205, 207; hazard
    planning in, 251; colonial, 267

South Dakota, 165; migration to, 164;
    Indian reservations in, 211; wheat
    production in, 177
Southern Regional Demographic
    Group, 57
South Fork Nemote #4 Fire (2000), 222
South Sea bubble, 207
Southwest Ordinance (1790), 134
Soviet Union: agricultural policy of,
    177; fear of nuclear attacks by, 31,
    43, 49–50, 60, 61, 92, 252; in World
    War II, 36, 37, 39, 64
Spain, 183, 184, 191, 300*n6*; American
    colonies of, 90, 105, 206, 207, 212;
    Civil War in, 35; war with, 149
Spooner, John Coit, 142–44, 150
spot fires, 110
sprawl, 70, 191; apologists for, 180;
    limitations on, 239, 256, 258;
    subsidies for, 244, 255, 259; *see also*
    urban dispersion
Spring Fire, 95
Squire, Ephraim G, 128
Standish, Claudia, 96–97, 99
Stanford Research Institute, 47
Stanton, Robert, 102
Steffens, Lincoln, 142
Steinbeck, John, 162, 169, 170, 195,
    249
Stennis, John, 68
Stern, Philip Van Doren, 296*n13*
stewardship contracting, 115–16, 218
Stillwater Lumberman, 145
Stockbridge (Massachusetts), 265, 272,
    274, 275
Stuarts, 279
subsidies, government, 6, 12, 15, 19,
    98, 218, 233; farm, 13, 169, 172–74,
    176–78, 210; for flame zone
    developers, 103, 243, 244;
    homesteading, 184; for lumber
    industry, 115–16, 221, 236;
    migration policy and, 125,
    154–55, 228; for reforestation, 144;
    taxpayers' revolt against, 24; for
    urban dispersion, 13, 17–18, 28, 29,
    33–34, 45, 52–53, 56, 61–62, 64–76,
    179, 185, 190, 195–97, 238, 252–56;

subsidies, government *(continued)*
    withdrawal of, 210–11; *see also*
    insurance, federal
suburbanization, 29, 31, 68, 70;
    housing subsidies and, 74; *see also*
    sprawl; urban dispersion
Suez Canal, 11
Sunbelt, 176, 185
sun daggers, 262
Sunset Crater (Arizona), 157
Sunset Magazine, 89
Supreme Court, U.S., 209–10
Susquehanna Company, 280, 281
sustainability, 121, 126; of agriculture,
    27, 124, 125, 170; of forestry, 116,
    124, 126–27, 143–44, 150, 236; *see
    also* husbandry
Swiss Reinsurance Company, 246
Switzerland, 132
Symington, Stuart, 55
Syracuse University, 187

tariffs, 13
Taxpayers for Common Sense (TCS),
    216–18, 220–22, 255
taxpayer revolts, 6, 24, 82–83; against
    sprawl, 258–60
Tax Reform Act, 289n23
Taylor, John, 186
Taylor's Falls (Minnesota), 151, 152
Teller, Edward, 8–11, 16, 38, 49–50, 58,
    67, 180; Alaskan harbor proposal
    of, 10–11, 46; hydrogen bomb
    developed by, 9, 49; Livermore and,
    57–58; urban dispersion advocated
    by, 11, 42–45, 50–53, 55–56, 60, 64,
    66, 68–70, 186, 252, 285n8
Tending Fire (Pyne), 219–20
Tennessee, 62
Teotihuacan, 300n6
Texas, 154, 201, 206; Dust Bowl and,
    138; Hispanics in, 183; migration to,
    174; Ogallala Aquifer under, 174;
    relocation of industrial production
    to, 55, 61; Republic of, 302n13;
    trucking industry in, 68
theology, environmental, 120,
    261–78

thinning, 219, 220, 230; outsourcing of,
    115; *see also* fire load, reduction of
Thomas, Jack Ward, 84–87
Thompson, Virgil, 169
Thoreau, Henry David, 119–20,
    128–30, 132, 156, 265, 296n13
Thornthwaite, C. Warren, 164–66
thumbprints, ancient, 262
Timber Culture Act (1873), 145,
    148–49, 158
Timber Cutting Act (1878), 148
timbering, *see* lumbering
Tobin, James, 45, 49
Tocqueville, Alexis de, 54
Toledo (Ohio), 174
Tom, Mount, 121, 122
town planning, *see* city planning
Train, Russell, 139
Trampas (New Mexico), 236
transportation, 32, 51; intermodal,
    subsidies for, 72–73; *see also*
    highways; railroads
Transportation Equity Act for the
    Twenty-first Century (TEA-21,
    1998), 73
Treasury Department, U.S., 60
Trinity Site (White Sands Proving
    Ground), 40
Troy, Austin, 241–43, 307n11
Truchas (New Mexico), 236
trucking industry, 68
Truman, Harry S., 9, 40, 48, 52, 56,
    59–62, 64
Tucson, 24
Tulip bubble, 207
Turner, Frederick Jackson, 21, 181,
    183, 294n16
Twain, Mark, 156

Union Pacific Railroad, 211
United States Geological Survey
    (USGS), 227, 228, 305n7
urban dispersion, 6, 15, 20, 28–30,
    42–57, 64–76, 179–81, 189–91,
    259; highway construction and,
    49, 53, 64–73, 254; housing and,
    18, 29, 45, 53, 69, 73–75, 190,
    290n25; industrial dispersion and,

42, 55–56; national defense rationale for, 30–35, 42–43, 45–47, 56–57, 69–70; slum clearance and, 45, 47, 48, 53, 54, 73; states experiencing population growth due to, 21–22; subsidization of, 13, 17–18, 28, 29, 33–34, 45, 52–53, 56, 61–62, 64–76, 179, 185, 190, 195–97, 238, 252–56; Teller and, 11, 42–45, 50–53, 55–56, 60, 64, 66, 68–70, 186, 252, 285n8; versus traditional settlement patterns, 181–87; *see also* dispersion-industrial complex

Urban Frontier, The (Wade), 187

urbanism, 181–91; and "corridopolis," 188; of Hispanics, 182–85; of Indians, 181–82; of Mormons, 186

Utah, 131, 262; Indians in, 182; population growth in, 22, 306n4; roads in, 63; *see also* Four Corners

Vandenberg Air Force Base, 208

Vanderbilt estate (Biltmore, North Carolina), 133

Van Rensselaer family, 302n11

Varley, John, 141

VE Day, 40

Vermont, 120–23; villages in, 189

Vermont, University of, 241

Veterans Administration, 75, 290n25

villages, traditional, 44, 189; Hispanic, 184; Indian, 181–82; New England, 181, 189

Villard, Henry, 124

Virginia, 153, 187, 202; colonial, 208

Vista, Project, 46

Viveash Fire, 95

volcanic eruptions, 157

Wade, Karen, 103

Wade, Richard, 187

Wagner, Robert F., 67–68

War of 1812, 30

War Production Board, 57

Warsaw, bombing of, 35, 36

Washington, D. C.; burning of, in War of 1812, 30; construction of Capitol dome in, 136

Washington, George, 120, 128–31, 139, 203–204, 207–209, 212, 302n10

Washington Mutual, 289n23

Washington State, 306n4; wildfires in, 112; wildland/urban interface (WUI) in, 230, 232

water resources, 173–77, 238

watershed protection, 127, 150

Watertown (Wisconsin), 144

Wayne, General Anthony, 212

weather, 163–68, 175; *see also* droughts; lightning

Weaver, Roy, 92, 96, 99–102, 292n15, 293n17

Webb, Walter Prescott, 176

Weeks, John, 150

Weeks Act (1911), 150

Welch, Joseph, 168

Wells Fargo, 289n23

West, Chris, 115

Western Wisconsin Railway, 143

wetlands, preservation of, 178

Wheaton, William L. C., 61

Whig Party, 123

White, Gilbert, 248, 249

White, Stewart Edward, 89, 103, 235–36

"white flight," 29

White House Conference on Housing, 74

White Mountain Apaches, 105–106, 108, 126

White Mountain National Forest, 150

White Sands Proving Ground, 40

Wichita (Kansas), 55

wilderness, designation of, 264–65

Wilderness Society, 229

wildfire-industrial complex, 80–83, 103, 218, 221

wildland/urban interface (WUI) areas, 93, 229–30, 234, 236, 241, 243, 305n5

Williams, Elisha, 280

Williams, Jack, 184

Williams, Roger, 267

Wilson, James, 170

Wilson, Woodrow, 59, 60, 69

Winter, Edwin W., 123, 124, 142, 143, 295n5

Wisconsin, 138–45, 150, 221, 294*n16*;
    Forest Commission, 145; German-
    Americans in, 139; homesteading in,
    144; Indian reservations in, 209;
    lumbering in, 151; migration to,
    154–55; wildfires in, 109–13, 122,
    138, 139, 141, 145, 162
Wisconsin, University of, 28, 229
Wood, Christopher, 184
Woodbridge, Timothy, 272, 280
Woodstock (Vermont), 120–25
Woolsey, T. S., 107
World War I, 35, 59, 165, 177
World War II, 17, 49, 54, 61, 248;
    bombing of cities during, 30–37, 43,
    92; development of atomic weapons
    during, 8–9, 39–40; economics of
    mobilization during, 51; target
    dispersion during, 31, 54, 63–64
Worster, Donald, 174
Wright, Frank Lloyd, 71
Wright, Jack, 255, 306*n4*

Wright, John, 103
Wyoming: Ogallala Aquifer under, 174;
    population growth in, 22; roads
    in, 63

Yacolt (Washington), 112
Yale University, 46; School of Forestry
    and Environmental Studies, 236, 241
Yellow Book, 66, 288*n12*
Yellowstone National Park, 124, 141,
    148, 219, 224, 231
York, Herbert, 57
Yosemite, 133, 136, 137, 141; fire-prone
    area around, 231
Young, Arthur, 203
Young, Brigham, 186
Yount, Harry, 141, 155

Ziehe, Anne-Kathryn, 98
zoning regulations, 53, 254, 258;
    firewise, 216, 257
Zybach, Frank, 175